Little Journeys to the
Homes
of Great Philosophers
by
Elbert Hubbard

Little Journeys To the
Homes of the Great, Volume 8

SOCRATES

I do not think it possible for a better man to be injured by a worse.... To a good man nothing is evil, neither while living nor when dead, nor are his concerns neglected by the gods.

—*The* *Republic*

SOCRATES

It was four hundred seventy years before Christ that Socrates was born. He never wrote a book, never made a formal address, held no public office, wrote no letters, yet his words have come down to us sharp, vivid and crystalline. His face, form and features are to us familiar—his goggle eyes, bald head, snub nose and bow-legs! The habit of his life—his goings and comings, his arguments and wrangles, his infinite leisure, his sublime patience, his perfect faith—all these things are plain, lifting the man out of the commonplace and setting him apart.

The "Memorabilia" of Xenophon and the "Dialogues" of Plato give us Boswellian pictures of the man.

Knowing the man, we know what he would do; and knowing what he did, we know the man.

Socrates was the son of Sophroniscus, a stonecutter, and his wife Phænarete. In boyhood he used to carry dinner to his father, and sitting by, he heard the men, in their free and easy way, discuss the plans of Pericles. These workmen didn't know the plans—they were only privates in the ranks, but they exercised their prerogatives to criticize, and while working to assist, did right royally disparage and condemn. Like sailors who love their ship, and grumble at grub and grog, yet on shore will allow no word of disparagement to be said, so did these Athenians love their city, and still condemn its rulers—they exercised the laborer's right to damn the man who gives him work.

Little did the workmen guess—little did his father guess—that this pug-nosed boy, making pictures in the sand with his big toe, would also leave his footprints on the sands of time, and a name that would rival that of Phidias and Pericles!

Socrates was a product of the Greek renaissance. Great men come in groups, like comets sent from afar. Athens was seething with thought and feeling: Pericles was giving his annual oration—worth thousands of weekly sermons—and planning his dream in marble; Phidias was cutting away the needless portions of the white stone of Pentelicus and liberating wondrous forms of beauty; Sophocles was revealing the possibilities of the stage; Æschylus was pointing out the way as a playwright; and the passion for physical beauty was everywhere an adjunct of religion.

Prenatal influences, it seems, played their part in shaping the destiny of Socrates. His mother followed the profession of Sairy Gamp, and made her home with a score of families, as she was needed. The trained nurse is often untrained, and is a regular encyclopedia of esoteric family facts. She wipes her mouth on her apron and is at home in every room of the domicile from parlor to pantry. Then as now she knew the trials and troubles of her clients, and all domestic underground happenings requiring adjustment she looked after as she was "disposed."

Evidently Phænarete was possessed of considerable personality, for we hear of her being called to Mythæia on a professional errand shortly before the birth of Socrates; and in a month after his birth, a similar call came from another direction, and the bald little philosopher was again taken along—from which we assume, following in the footsteps of Conan Doyle, that Socrates was no bottle-baby. The world should be grateful to Phænarete that she did not honor the Sairy Gamp precedents and observe the Platonic maxim, "Sandal-makers usually go barefoot": she gave her customers an object-lesson in well-doing as well as teaching them by precept. None of her clients did so well as she—even though her professional duties were so exacting that domesticity to her was merely incidental.

It was only another case of the amateur distancing the professional.

From babyhood we lose sight of Socrates until we find him working at his father's trade as a sculptor. Certainly he had a goodly degree of skill, for the "Graces" which he carved were fair and beautiful and admired by many. This was enough: he just wanted to reveal what he could do; and then to show that to have no ambition was his highest ambition, he threw down his tools and took off his apron for good. He was then thirty-five years old. Art is a jealous mistress, and demands that "thou shalt have no other gods before me." Socrates did not concentrate on art. His mind went roaming the world of philosophy, and for his imagination the universe was hardly large enough.

I said that he deliberately threw down his tools; but possibly this was by request, for he had acquired a habit of engaging in much wordy argument and letting the work slide. He went out upon the streets to talk, and in the guise of a learner he got in close touch with all the wise men of Athens by stopping them and asking questions. In physique he was immensely strong—hard work had developed his muscles, plain fare had made him oblivious of the fact that he had a stomach, and as for nerves, he had none to speak of.

Socrates did not marry until he was about forty. His wife was scarcely twenty. Of his courtship we know nothing, but sure it is Socrates did not go and sue for the lady's hand in the conventional way, nor seek to gain the consent of her parents by proving his worldly prospects. His apparel was costly as his purse could buy, not gaudy nor expressed in fancy. It consisted of the one suit that he wore, for we hear of his repairing beyond the walls to bathe in the stream, and of his washing his clothing, hanging it on the bushes and waiting for it to dry before going back to the city. As for shoes, he had one pair, and since he never once wore them, going barefoot Summer and Winter, it is presumed that they lasted well. One can not imagine Socrates in an opera-hat—in fact, he wore no hat, and he was bald. I record the fact so as to confound those zealous ones who badger the bald as a business, who have recipes concealed on their persons, and who assure us that baldness has its rise in headgear.

Socrates belonged to the leisure class. His motto was, "Know Thyself." He considered himself of much more importance than any statue he could make, and to get acquainted with himself as being much more desirable than to know physical phenomena. His plan of knowing himself was to ask everybody questions, and in their answers he would get a true reflection of his own mind. His intellect would reply to theirs, and if his questions dissolved their answers into nothingness, the supremacy of his own being would be apparent; and if they proved his folly he was equally grateful—if he was a fool, his desire was to know it. So sincere was Socrates in this wish to know himself that never did he show the slightest impatience nor resentment when the argument was turned upon him.

He looked upon his mind as a second party, and sat off and watched it work. Should it become confused or angered, it would be proof of its insufficiency and littleness. If Socrates ever came to know himself, he knew this fact: as an economic unit he was an absolute failure; but as a gadfly, stinging men into thinking for themselves, he was a success. A specialist is a deformity contrived by Nature to get the work done. Socrates was a thought-specialist, and the laziest man who ever lived in a strenuous age. The desire of his life was to live without desire—which is essentially the thought of Nirvana. He had the power never to exercise his power except in knowing himself.

He accepted every fact, circumstance and experience of life, and counted it gain. Life to him was a precious privilege, and what were regarded as unpleasant experiences were as much a part of life as the pleasant ones. He who succeeds in evading unpleasant experiences cheats himself out of so much life. You know yourself by watching yourself to see what you do when you are thwarted, crossed, contradicted, or deprived of certain things supposed to be desirable. If you always get the desirable things, how do you know what you would do if you didn't have them? You exchange so much life for the thing, that's all, and thus do we see Socrates anticipating Emerson's Essay on Compensation.

Everything is bought with a price—all things are of equal value—no one can cheat you, for to be cheated is a not undesirable experience, and in the act, if you are really filled with the thought, "Know Thyself," you get the compensation by increase in mental growth.

However, to deliberately go in search of experience, Socrates said, would be a mistake, because then you would so multiply impressions that none would be of any avail and your life would be burned out. To clutch life by the throat and demand that it shall stand

and deliver is to place yourself so out of harmony with your environment that you will get nothing.

Above all things, we must be calm, self-centered, never anxious, and be always ready to accept whatever the gods may send. The world will come to us if we only wait. It will be seen that Socrates is at once the oldest and most modern of thinkers. He was the first to express the New Thought. A thought, to Socrates, was more of a reality than a block of marble—a moral principle was just as persistent as a chemical agent.

The silken-robed and perfumed Sophist was sport and game for Socrates. For him Socrates recognized no closed season. If Socrates ever came near losing his temper, it was in dealing with this Edmund Russell of Athens. Grant Allen used to say, "The spores of everything are everywhere, and a certain condition breeds a certain microbe." A period of prosperity always warms into life this social paragon, who lives in a darkened room hung with maroon drapery where incense is burned and a turbaned Hindu carries your card to the master, who faces the sun and exploits a prie-dieu when the wind blows east. Athens had these men of refined elegance, Rome evolved them, London has had her day, New York knows them, and Chicago—I trust I will not be contradicted when I say that Chicago understands her business! And so we find these folks who cultivate a pellucid passivity, a phthisicky whisper, a supercilious smirk, and who win our mystified admiration and give us gooseflesh by imparting a taupe tinge of mystery to all their acts and words, thus proving to the assembled guests that they are the Quality and Wisdom will die with them.

This lingo of meaningless words and high-born phrases always set Socrates by the ears, and when he could corner a Sophist, he would very shortly prick his pretty toy balloon, until at last the tribe fled him as a pestilence. Socrates stood for sanity. The Sophist represented moonshine gone to seed, and these things, proportioned ill, drive men transverse.

Extremes equalize themselves: the pendulum swings as far this way as it does that. The saponaceous Sophist who renounced the world and yet lived wholly in a world of sense, making vacuity pass legal tender for spirituality, and the priest who, mystified with a mumble of words, evolved a Diogenes who lived in a tub, wore regally a robe of rags, and once went into the temple, and cracking a louse on the altar-rail, said solemnly, "Thus does Diogenes sacrifice to all the gods at once!" are but two sides of the same shield.

In Socrates was a little jollity and much wisdom pickled in the scorn of Fortune; but the Sophists inwardly bowed down and worshiped the fickle dame on idolatrous knees. Socrates won immortality because he did not want it, and the Sophists secured oblivion because they deserved it.

We hear of Socrates going to Aspasia, and holding long conversations with her "to sharpen his mind." Aspasia did not go out in society much: she and Pericles lived very simply. It is worth while to remember that the most intellectual woman of her age was democratic enough to be on friendly terms with the barefoot philosopher who went about regally wrapped in a table-spread. Socrates did not realize the flight of time when making calls—he went early and stayed late. Possibly prenatal influences caused him often to call before breakfast and remain until after supper.

Just imagine Pericles, Aspasia and Socrates sitting at table—with Walter Savage Landor behind the arras making notes! Doubtless Socrates and Mrs. Pericles did most of the talking, while the First Citizen of Athens listened and smiled indulgently now and then as his mind wandered to construction contracts and walking delegates. Pericles, the builder of a city—Pericles, first among practical men since time began, and Socrates, who jostles history for first place among those who have done nothing but talk—imagine these two eating melons together, while Aspasia, gentle and kind, talks of spirit being more than matter and love being greater than the Parthenon!

Socrates is usually spoken of as regarding women with slight favor, but I have noticed that your genus woman-hater holds the balance true by really being a woman-lover. If a man is enough interested in women to hate them, note this: he is only searching for the right woman, the woman who compares favorably with the ideal woman in his own mind. He measures every woman by this standard, just as Ruskin compared all modern painters with Turner and discarded them with fitting adjectives as they receded from what he regarded as the perfect type. If Ruskin had not been much interested in painters, would he have written scathing criticisms about them?

In several instances we hear of Socrates reminding his followers that they are "weak as women," and he was the first to say "woman is an undeveloped man." But Socrates was a great admirer of human beauty, whether physical or spiritual, and his abrupt way of stopping beautiful women on the streets and bluntly telling them they were beautiful, doubtless often confirmed their suspicions. And thus far he was pleasing, but when he went on to ask questions so as to ascertain whether their mental estate compared with their physical, why, that was slightly different. It is good to hear him say, "There is no sex in intellect," and also, "I have long held the opinion that the female sex is nothing inferior to ours, save only in strength of body and possibly in steadiness of judgment." And Xenophon quotes him thus: "It is more delightful to hear the virtue of a good woman described than if the painter Zeuxis were to show me the portrait of the fairest woman in the world."

Perhaps Thackeray is right when he says, "The men who appreciate woman most are those who have felt the sharpness of her claws." That is to say, things show up best on the darkest background. If so, let us give Xantippe due credit. She tested the temper of the sage by railing on him and deluging him with Socratic propositions, not waiting for the answers; she often broke in with a broom upon his introspective efforts to know himself; if this were not enough, she dashed buckets of scrubbing-water over him; presents that were sent him by admiring friends she used as targets for her mop and wit; if he invited friends with faith plus to dine, she upset the table, dishes and all, before them—not much to their loss; she occasionally elbowed her way through a crowd where her husband was entertaining the listeners upon the divine harmonies, and would tear off his robe and lead him home by the ear. But these things never ruffled Socrates—he might roll his eyes in comic protest at the audiences as he was being led away captive, but no resentment was shown. He had the strength of a Hercules, but he was a far better non-resistant than Tolstoy, because he took his medicine with a wink, while Fate is obliged to hold the nose of the author of "Anna Karenina," who never sees the comedy of an inward struggle and an outward compliance, any more than does the benedict, safely entrenched under the bed, who shouts out, "I defy thee, I defy thee!" as did Mephisto when Goethe thrust him into Tophet.

The popular belief is that Xantippe, the wife of Socrates, was a shrew, and had she lived in New England in Cotton Mather's time would have been a candidate for the ducking-stool. Socrates said he married her for discipline. A man in East Aurora, however, has recently made it plain to himself that Xantippe was possessed of a great and acute intellect. She knew herself, and she knew her liege as he never did—he was too close to his subject to get the perspective. She knew that under right conditions his name would live as one of the world's great teachers, and so she set herself to supply the conditions. She deliberately sacrificed herself and put her character in a wrong light before the world in order that she might benefit the world. Most women have a goodly grain of ambition for themselves, and if their husbands have genius, their business is not to prove it, but to show that they themselves are not wholly commonplace.

Not so Xantippe—she was quite willing to be misunderstood that her husband might live.

What the world calls a happy marriage is not wholly good—ease is bought with a price. Suppose Xantippe and Socrates had settled down and lived in a cottage with a vine growing over the portico, and two rows of hollyhocks leading from the front gate to the door; a pathway of coal-ashes lined off with broken crockery, and inside the house all sweet, clean and tidy; Socrates earning six drachmas a day carving marble, with double pay for overtime, and he handing the pay-envelope over to her each Saturday night, keeping out just enough for tobacco, and she putting a tidy sum in the Ægean Savings-Bank every month— why, what then?

Well, that would have been an end of Socrates. Xantippe was big enough to know this and so she supplied the domestic cantharides and drove him out upon the streets—he grew to care very little for her, not much for the children, nothing for his home. She drove him out into the world of thought, instead of allowing him to settle down and be content with her society.

I once knew a sculptor—another sculptor—an elemental bit of nature, original and, better still, aboriginal. He used to sleep out under the stars so as to wake up in the night and see the march of the Milky Way, and watch the Pleiades disappear over the brink of the western horizon. He wore a flannel shirt, thick-soled shoes, and overalls, no hat, and his hair was thick and coarse as a horse's mane. This man had talent, and he had sublime conceptions, great dreams, and splendid aspirations. His soul was struggling to find expression. "Leave him alone," I said. "He needs time to ripen. He is a Michelangelo in embryo!"

Did he ripen? Not he. He married a Wellesley girl of good family. She, too, had ideas about art—she painted china-buttons for shirtwaists, embroidered chasubles and sang "The Rosary" in a raucous Quinsigamond voice. The big barbarian became respectable, and the last time I saw him he wore a Tuxedo and was passing out platitudes and raspberry-shrub at a lawn-party. The Wellesley girl had tamed her bear—they were very happy, he assured me, and she was preparing a course of lectures for him which he was to give at Mrs. Jack Gardner's. A Xantippe might have saved him.

A captious friend once suggested to Socrates this: "If you prize the female nature so highly, how does it happen that you do not instruct Xantippe?"—a rather indelicate proposition to put to a married man. And Socrates, quite unruffled, replied: "My friend, if one wants to learn horsemanship, does he choose a tame horse or one with mettle and a hard mouth? I wish to converse with all sorts of people, and I believe that nothing can disturb me after I grow accustomed to the tongue of Xantippe."

Again we hear of his suggesting that his wife's scolding tongue may have been only the buzzing of his own waspish thoughts, and if he did not call forth these qualities in her they would not otherwise have appeared. And so, beholding her impatience and unseemliness, he would realize the folly of an ill temper and thus learn by antithesis to curb his own. Old Doctor Johnson used to have a regular menagerie of wrangling, jangling, quibbling, dissatisfied pensioners in his household; and so far as we know he never learned the truth that all pensioners are dissatisfied. "If I can stand things at home, I can stand things anywhere," he once said to Boswell, as much as to say, "If I can stand things at home, I can stand even you." Goldsmith referred to Boswell as a cur; Garrick said he thought he was a bur. Socrates had a similar satellite by the name of Cheropho, a dark, dirty, weazened, and awfully serious little man of the tribe of Buttinsky, who sat breathlessly trying to catch the pearls that fell from the ample mouth of the philosopher. Aristophanes referred to Cheropho as "Socrates' bat," a play-off on Minerva and her bird of night, the owl. There were quite a number of these "bats," and they seemed to labor under the same hallucination that catches the lady students of the Pundit Vivakenanda H. Darmapala: they think that wisdom is to be imparted by word of mouth, and that by listening hard and making notes one can become very wise. Socrates said again and again, "Character is a matter of growth and all I hope to do is to make you think for yourselves."

That chilly exclusiveness which regards a man's house as his castle, his home, the one sacred spot, and all outside as the cold and cruel world, was not the ideal of Socrates. His family was his circle of friends, and these were of all classes and conditions, from the First Citizen to beggars on the street.

He made no charge for his teaching, took up no collections, and never inaugurated a Correspondence School. America has produced one man who has been called a reincarnation of Socrates; that man was Bronson Alcott, who peddled clocks and forgot the flight of time whenever any one would listen to him expound the unities. Alcott once ran his wheelbarrow into a neighbor's garden and was proceeding to load his motor-car with cabbages, beets and potatoes. Glancing up, the philosopher saw the owner of the garden looking at him steadfastly over the wall. "Don't look at me that way," called Alcott with a touch of un-Socratic acerbity, "don't look at me that way—I need these things more than you!" and went on with the annexation.

The idea that all good things are for use and belong to all who need them was a favorite maxim of Socrates. The furniture in his house never exceeded the exemption clause. Once we find him saying that Xantippe complained because he did not buy her a stewpan, but since there was nothing to put in it, he thought her protests ill-founded.

The climate of Athens is about like that of Southern California—one does not need to bank food and fuel against the coming of Winter. Life can be adjusted to its simplest forms. From his fortieth to his fiftieth year, Socrates worked every other Thursday; then he retired from active life, and Xantippe took in plain sewing.

Socrates was surely not a good provider, but if he had provided more for his family, he would have provided less for the world. The wealthy Crito would have turned his pockets inside out for Socrates, but Socrates had all he wished, and explained that as it was he had to dance at home in order to keep down the adipose. Aristides, who was objectionable because he so shaped his conduct that he was called "The Just" and got himself ostracized, was one of his dear friends. Antisthenes, the original Cynic, used to walk six miles and back every day to hear Socrates talk. The Cynic was a rich man, but so captivated was he with the preaching of Socrates that he adopted the life of simplicity and dressed in rags and boycotted both the barber and the bath. On one occasion Socrates looked sharply at a rent in the cloak of his friend and said, "Ah, Antisthenes, through that hole in your cloak I see your vanity!"

Xenophon sat at the feet of Socrates for a score of years, and then wrote his recollections of him as a vindication of his character. Euclid of Megara was nearly eighty when he came to Socrates as a pupil, trying to get rid of his ill-temper and habit of ironical reply. Cebes and Simmias left their native country and became Greek citizens for his sake. Charmides, the pampered son of wealthy parents, learned pedagogics by being shown that, in households where there were many servants, the children got cheated out of their rightful education because others did all the work, and to deprive a child of the privilege of being useful was to rob him of so much life. Æschines, the ambitious son of a sausage-maker, was advised by Socrates to borrow money of himself on long time without interest, by reducing his wants. So pleased was the recipient with this advice, that he went to publishing Socratic dialogues as a business and had the felicity to fail with tidy liabilities.

But the two men who loom largest in the life of Socrates are Alcibiades and Plato—characters very much unlike.

Alcibiades was twenty-one years old when we find him first. He was considered the handsomest young man in Athens. He was aristocratic, proud, insolent, and needlessly rich. He had a passion for gambling, horse-racing, dog-fighting, and indulged in the churchly habit of doing that which he ought not and leaving undone that which he should have done. He was worse than that degenerate scion of a proud ancestry, who a-kneiping went with his lady friends in the Cincinnati fountain, after the opera, on a wager. He whipped a man who admitted he did not have a copy of the "Iliad" in his house; publicly destroyed the record of a charge against one of his friends; and when his wife applied for a divorce, he burst into the courtroom and vacated proceedings by carrying the lady off by force. At banquets he would raise a disturbance, and while he was being forcibly ejected from one door, his servants would sneak in at another and steal the silverware, which he would give away as charity. He also indulged in the Mark Antony trick of rushing into houses at night and pulling good folks out of bed by the heels, and then running away before they were barely awake.

His introduction to Socrates came in an attempt to break up a Socratic prayer-meeting. Socrates succeeded in getting the roysterer to listen long enough to turn the laugh on him and show all concerned that the life of a rowdy was the life of a fool. Alcibiades had expected Socrates to lose his temper, but it was Alcibiades who gave way, and blurted out that he could not hope to beat his antagonist talking, but he would like to wrestle with him.

Legend has it that Socrates gave the insolent young man a shock by instantly accepting his challenge. In the bout that followed, the philosopher, built like a gorilla, got a half-Nelson on his man, who was a little the worse for wine, and threw him so hard, jumping on his prostrate form with his knees, that the aristocratic hoodlum was laid up for a moon.

Ever after Alcibiades had a thorough respect for Socrates. They became fast friends, and whenever the old man talked in the Agora, Alcibiades was on hand to keep order.

When war came with Sparta and her allies in the Peloponnesus they enlisted, Socrates going as corporal and Alcibiades as captain. They occupied the same tent during the entire campaign. Socrates proved a fearless soldier, and walked the winter ice in bare feet, often pulling his belt one hole tighter in lieu of breakfast, to show the complaining soldiers that endurance was the thing that won battles. At the battle of Delium, when there was a rout, Xenophon says Socrates walked off the field leisurely, arm in arm with the general, explaining the nature of harmony.

Through the influence of Socrates, the lawless Alcibiades was tamed and became almost a model citizen, although his head was hardly large enough for a philosopher.

"Say what you will, you'll find it all in Plato," said Emerson. If Socrates had done nothing else but give bent to the mind of Plato, he would deserve the gratitude of the centuries. Plato is the mine to which all thinkers turn for treasure. When they first met, Plato was twenty and Socrates sixty, and for ten years, to the day of Socrates' death, they were together almost constantly. Plato died aged eighty-one, and for fifty years he had lived but to record the dialogues of Socrates. It was curiosity that first attracted this fine youth to the old man—Socrates was so uncouth that he was amusing. Plato was interested in politics, and like most Athenian youths, was intent on having a good time. However, he was no rowdy, like Alcibiades: he was suave, gracious, and elegant in all of his acts. He had been taught by the Sophists and the desire of his life was to seem, rather than to be. By very gentle stages, Plato began to perceive that to make an impression on society was not worth working for—the thing to do was to be yourself, and yourself at your best. And we can give no better answer to the problem of life than Plato gives in the words of Socrates: "It is better to be than to seem. To live honestly and deal justly is the meat of the whole matter."

Plato was not a disciple—he was big enough not to ape the manners and eccentricities of his Master—he saw beneath the rough husk and beyond the grotesque outside the great controlling purpose in the life of Socrates. He would be himself—and himself at his best—and he would seek to satisfy the Voice within, rather than to try to please the populace. Plato still wore his purple cloak, and the elegance and grace of his manner were not thrown aside.

Wouldn't it have been worth our while to travel miles to see these friends: the one old, bald, short, fat, squint-eyed, barefoot; and the other with all the poise of aristocratic youth—tall, courtly and handsome, wearing his robe with easy, regal grace! And so they have walked and talked adown the centuries, side by side, the most perfect example that can be named of that fine affection which often exists between teacher and scholar.

Plato's "Republic," especially, gives us an insight into a very great and lofty character. From his tower of speculation, Plato scanned the future, and saw that the ideal of education was to have it continue through life, for none but the life of growth and development ever satisfies. And love itself turns to ashes of roses if not used to help the soul in her upward flight. It was Plato who first said, "There is no profit where no pleasure's ta'en." He further perceived that in the life of education, the sexes must move hand in hand; and he also saw that, while religions are many and seemingly diverse, goodness and kindness are forever one.

His faith in the immortality of the soul was firm, but whether we are to live in another world or not, he said there is no higher wisdom than to live here and now—live our highest and best—cultivate the receptive mind and the hospitable heart, "partaking of all good things in moderation."

It takes these two to make the whole. There is no virtue in poverty—no merit in rags—the uncouth qualities in Socrates were not a recommendation. Yet he was himself. But Plato made good, in his own character, all that Socrates lacked. Some one has said that Fitzgerald's Omar is two-thirds Fitzgerald and one-third Omar. In his books, Plato modestly puts his wisest maxims into the mouth of his master, and just how much Plato and how much Socrates there is in the "Dialogues," we will never know until we get beyond the River Styx.

Socrates was deeply attached to Athens, and he finally became the best known figure in the city. He criticized in his own frank, fearless way all the doings of the times—nothing escaped him. He was a self-appointed investigating committee in all affairs of state, society and religion. Hypocrisy, pretense, affectation and ignorance trembled at his approach. He was feared, despised and loved. But those who loved him were as one in a hundred. He became a public nuisance. The charge against him was just plain heresy—he had spoken disrespectfully of the gods and through his teaching he had defiled the youth of Athens. Ample warning had been given to him, and opportunity to run away was provided, but he stuck like a leech, asking the cost of banquets and making suggestions about all public affairs.

He was arrested, bailed by Plato and Crito, and tried before a jury of five hundred citizens. Socrates insisted on managing his own case. A rhetorician prepared an address of explanation, and the culprit was given to understand that if he read this speech to his judges and said nothing else, it would be considered as an apology and he would be freed—the intent of the trial being more to teach the old man a lesson in minding his own business than to injure him.

But Socrates replied to his well-meaning friend, "Think you I have not spent my whole life in preparing for this one thing?" And he handed back the smoothly polished manuscript with a smile. Montaigne says, "Should a suppliant voice have been heard out of the mouth of Socrates now; should that lofty virtue strike sail in the very height of its glory, and his rich and powerful nature be committed to flowing rhetoric as a defense? Never!"

Socrates cross-questioned his accusers in the true Socratic style and showed that he had never spoken disrespectfully of the gods: he had only spoken disrespectfully of their absurd conception of the gods. And here is a thought which is well to consider even yet: The so-called "infidel" is often a man of great gentleness of spirit, and his disbelief is not in God, but in some little man's definition of God—a distinction the little man, being without humor, can never see.

When Socrates had confounded his accusers, this time not giving them the satisfaction of the last word, he launched out on a general criticism of the city, and told where its rulers were gravely at fault. Being cautioned to bridle his tongue, he replied, "When your generals at Potidæa and Amphipolis and Delium assigned my place in the battle I remained there, did my work, and faced the peril, and think you that when Deity has assigned me my duty at this pass in life I should, through fear of death, evade it, and shirk my post?"

This man appeared at other times, to some, as an idle loafer, but now he arose to a sublime height. He repeated with emphasis all he had ever said against their foolish superstitions, and arraigned the waste and futility of the idle rich. The power of the man was revealed as never before, and those who had intended to let him go with a fine, now thought it best to dispose of him. The safety of the state was endangered by such an agitator—the question of religion is really not what has sent the martyrs to the stake—it is the politician, not the priest, who fears the heretic.

By a small majority, Socrates was found guilty and sentenced to death. Let Plato tell of that last hour—he has done it once for all:

When he had done speaking, Crito said, "And have you any commands for us, Socrates—anything to say about your children, or any other matter in which we can serve you?"

"Nothing particular," he said; "only, as I have always told you, I would have you to look to your own conduct; that is a service which you may always be doing to me and mine as well as to yourselves."...

"We will do our best," said Crito. "But in what way would you have us bury you?"

"In any way that you like; only you must get hold of me, and take care that I do not walk away from you." Then he turned to us, and added with a smile: "I can not make Crito believe that I am the same Socrates who has been talking and conducting the argument; he fancies that I am the other Socrates whom he will soon see, a dead body—and he asks, 'How shall he bury me?' And though I have spoken many words in the endeavor to show that when I have drunk the poison I shall leave you and go to the joys of the blessed—these words of mine, with which I comforted you and myself, have had, as I perceive, no effect upon Crito. And therefore I want you to be surety for me now, as he was surety for me at the trial: but let the promise be of another sort; for he was my surety to the judges that I would remain, but you must be my surety to him that I shall not remain, but go away and depart; and then he will suffer less at my death, and not be grieved when he sees my body being burned. I would not have him sorrow at my hard lot, or say at the burial,'Thus we lay out Socrates,' or, 'Thus we follow him to the grave or bury him'; for false words are not only evil in themselves, but they infect the soul with evil. Be of good cheer then, my dear Crito, and say that you are burying my body only, and do with that as is usual, and as you think best."

When he had spoken these words, he arose and went into the bath-chamber with Crito, who bid us wait; and we waited, talking and thinking of the subject of discourse, and also of the greatness of our sorrow; he was like a father of whom we were being bereaved, and we were about to pass the rest of our lives as orphans. When he had taken his bath, his children were brought to him—and the women of his family also came, and he talked to them and gave them a few directions in the presence of Crito; and he then dismissed them and returned to us.

Now the hour of sunset was near. When he came out, he sat down with us again after his bath, but not much was said. Soon the jailer, who was the servant, entered and stood by him, saying: "To you, Socrates, whom I know to be the noblest and gentlest and best of all who ever came to this place, I will not impute the angry feelings of other men, who rage and swear at me when, in obedience to the authorities, I bid them drink the poison—indeed I am sure that you will not be angry with me; for others, as you are aware, and not I, are the guilty cause. And so fare you well, and try to bear lightly what must needs be; you know my errand." Then bursting into tears, he turned away, and went out.

Socrates looked at him and said, "I return your good wishes, and will do as you bid." Then turning to us, he said: "How charming the man is! Since I have been in prison, he has always been coming to see me, and at times, he would talk to me, and was as good as could be to me, and now see how generously he sorrows for me. But we must do as he says, Crito; let the cup be brought."

"Not yet," said Crito; "the sun is still upon the hill-tops, and many a one has taken the draft late, and after the announcement has been made to him, he has eaten and drunk and indulged in sensual delights; do not hasten then—there is still time."

Socrates said: "Yes, Crito, and they of whom you speak are right in doing thus, but I do not think that I should gain anything by drinking the poison a little later; I should be sparing and saving a life which is already gone: I could only laugh at myself for this. Please then to do as I say, and not to refuse me."

Crito, when he heard this, made a sign to the servant; and the servant went in, and remained for some time, and then returned with the jailer carrying the cup of poison. Socrates said, "You, my good friend, who are experienced in these matters, shall give me directions how I am to proceed." The man answered, "You have only to walk about until your legs are heavy, and then to lie down, and the poison will act." At the same time, he handed the cup to Socrates, who, in the easiest and gentlest manner, without the least fear or change of color or feature, looking at the man with his eyes, Echecrates, as his manner was, took the cup and said: "What do you say about making the libation out of this cup to any god? May I, or not?" The man answered, "We only prepare, Socrates, just so much as we deem enough." "I understand," he said. "Yet I may and must pray to the gods to prosper my journey from this to that other world—may this, then, which is my prayer, be granted to me!" Then holding the cup to his lips, quite readily and cheerfully, he drank off the poison. And hitherto most of us had been able to control our sorrow; but now we saw him drinking, and saw, too, that he had finished the draft, we could no longer forbear, and in spite of myself, my own tears were flowing fast; so that I covered my face and wept over myself, for certainly I was not weeping over him, but at the thought of my own calamity in having lost such a companion. Nor was I the first, for Crito, when he found himself unable to restrain his tears, had got up and moved away, and I followed; and at that moment, Apollodorus, who had been weeping all the time, broke out into a loud cry, which made cowards of us all. Socrates alone retained his calmness. "What is this strange outcry?" he said, "I sent away the women mainly in order that they might not offend in this way, for I have heard that a man should die in peace. Be quiet, then, and have patience." When we heard that, we were ashamed, and refrained our tears; and he walked about until, as he said, his legs began to fail, and then he lay on his back, according to directions, and the man who gave him the poison, now and then looked at his feet and legs; and after a while, he pressed his foot hard and asked him if he could feel; and he said, "No"; and then his leg, and so upwards and upwards, and showed us that he was cold and stiff. And he felt them himself, and said, "When the poison reaches the heart, that will be the end." He was beginning to grow cold, when he uncovered his face, for he had covered himself up, and said (they were his last words), "Crito, I owe a cock to Asclepius; will you remember to pay the debt?"

"The debt shall be paid," said Crito. "Is there anything else?" There was no answer to this question; but in a minute or two, a movement was heard, and the attendants uncovered him; his eyes were set, and Crito closed his eyes and mouth.

Such was the end, Echecrates, of our friend, whom I may truly call the wisest, the justest, and best of all the men whom I have ever known.

SENECA

If we wish to be just judges of all things, let us first persuade ourselves of this: that there is not one of us without fault; no man is found who can acquit himself; and he who calls himself innocent does so with reference to a witness, and not to his conscience.

—*Letters* *of* *Seneca*

SENECA

True Americans and patriotic, who live in York State, often refer you to the life of Red Jacket as proof that "Seneca" is an Iroquois Indian word. The Indians, however, whom we call the Senecas never called themselves thus until they took to strong water and became civilized. Before that they were the Tsonnundawaonas. The Dutch traders, intent on pelts and pelf, called them the Sinnekaas, meaning the valiant or the beautiful. Then came that fateful day when the Reverend Peleg Spooner, the discoverer of the Erie Canal, journeyed to Niagara Falls, and having influence with the authorities at Washington, gave to towns along the way these names: Troy, Rome, Ithaca, Syracuse, Ilion, Manlius, Homer, Corfu, Palmyra, Utica, Delhi, Memphis and Marathon. He really exhausted Grote's "History of Greece" and Gibbon's "Rome," revealing a most depressing lack of humor. This classic flavor of the map of New York is as surprising to English tourists as was the discovery to Hendrik Hudson when, on sailing up the North River, he found on nearing Albany that the river bore the same name as himself.

In the eighteenth chapter of the Acts of the Apostles we read of Paul being brought before Gallio, Proconsul of Achaia. And the accusers, clutching the bald and bow-legged bachelor by the collar, bawl out to the Judge, "This fellow persuadeth men to worship God contrary to law!"

And the little man is about to make reply, when Gallio says, with a touch of impatience: "If indeed it were a matter of wrong or of wicked villainy, O ye Jews, reason would that I should bear with you: but if they are questions about words and names and your own law, look to it yourselves; I am not minded to be a judge of these matters!" And the account concludes, "And he drove them from the judgment-seat."

That is to say, he gave Saint Paul a "nolle pros." Had Gallio wished to be severe, he might have put the quietus on Christianity for all time, for Saint Paul had all there was of it stowed in his valiant head and heart.

Gallio was the elder brother of Seneca; his right name was Annæus Seneca, but he changed it to Junius Gallio, in honor of a patron who had especially befriended him in youth.

Gallio seems to have been a man of good, sturdy commonsense—he could distinguish between right living and a mumble of words, man-made rules, laws such as heresy, blasphemy, Sabbath-breaking and marrying one's deceased wife's sister. The Moqui Indians believe that if any one is allowed to have a photograph taken of himself he will dry up in a month and blow away. Moreover, lists of names are not wanting with memoranda of times and places. In America there are yet people who hotly argue as to what mode of baptism is correct; who talk earnestly about the "saved" and the "lost"; and who will tell you of the "heathen" and those who are "without the pale." They seem to think that the promise, "Seek and ye shall find, knock and it shall be opened unto you," applies only to the Caucasian race.

In the earlier translations of Seneca there were printed various letters that were supposed to have passed between Saint Paul and Seneca. Later editors have dropped them out for lack of authenticity. But the fact that Saint Paul met Seneca's brother face to face, as well as the fact that the brother was willing to discuss right living, but had no time to waste on the Gemara and theological quibbles, is undisputed.

It was the proud boast of Augustus that he found Rome a place of brick and left it a city of marble. Commercial prosperity buys the leisure upon which letters flourish. We flout the businessman, but without him there would be no poets. Poets write for the people who have time to read. And out of the surplus that is left after securing food, we buy books. Augustus built his marble city, and he also made Vergil, Horace, Ovid and Livy possible.

Augustus reigned forty-four years, and it was in the twenty-seventh year of his reign that there was born in Bethlehem of Judæa a Babe who was to revolutionize the calendar. The Dean of Ely subtly puts forth the suggestive thought that if it had not been for Augustus we might never have heard of Jesus. It was Augustus who made Jerusalem a Roman Province; and it was the economic and political policy of Augustus that evolved the Scribes and Pharisees; and ill-gotten gains made the hypocrites and publicans possible; then comes Pontius Pilate with his receding chin.

Jesus was seventeen years old when Augustus died—Augustus never heard of him, and the Roman's unprophetic mind sent no searchlight into the future, neither did his eyes behold the Star in the East.

We are all making and shaping history, and how much, none of us knows, any more than did Augustus.

Julius Cæsar had no son to take his place, so he named his nephew, Augustus, his heir. Augustus was succeeded by Tiberius, his adopted child. Caligula, successor of Tiberius, was the son of the great Roman General, Germanicus. Caligula revealed his good sense by drinking life to its lees in a reign of four years, dying without heirs—Nature refusing to transmit either infamy or genius. Claudius, an uncle of Caligula, accepted the vacant place, as it seemed to him there was no one else could fill it so well. Claudius had the felicity to be married four times, and left several sons, but Fate had it that he should be followed by Nero, his stepson, who called himself "Cæsar," yet in whose veins there leaped not a single Cæsarean corpuscle.

The guardian and tutor of Nero was Lucius Seneca, the greatest, best and wisest man of his time, a fact I here state in order to show the vanity of pedagogics. Harking back once more to Augustus, let it be known that but for him Seneca would probably have never left his mark upon this bank and shoal of time. Seneca was a Spaniard, born in Cordova, a Roman Province, that was made so by Augustus, under whose kindly and placating influence all citizens of Hispania became Roman citizens—just as, when California was admitted to the Union, every man in the State was declared a naturalized citizen of the United States, the act being performed for political purposes, based on the precedents of Augustus, and never done before nor since in America.

Seneca was four years old when his father's family moved from Cordova to Rome; this was three years before the birth of Christ. Years pass, but the human heart is forever the same. The elder Seneca, Marcus Seneca, had ambitions—he was a great man in Cordova: he could memorize a list of two thousand words. These words had no relationship one to another, and Marcus Seneca could not put words together so as to make good sense, but his name was "Loisette": he had a scheme of mnemonics that he imparted for a consideration. He was also a teacher of elocution, and had compiled a yearbook of the sayings of Horace, which secured him a knighthood. Augustus paid his colonists pretty compliments, very much as England gives out brevets to Strathcona and other worthy Canadians, who raise troops of horse to fight England's battles in South Africa when duty calls.

Marcus Seneca made haste to move to Rome when Augustus let down the bars Rome was the center of the art-world, the home of letters, and all that made for beauty and excellence. There were three boys and a girl in the Seneca family.

The elder boy, Annæus, was to become Gallio, the Roman governor, and have his name mentioned in the most widely circulated book the world has ever known; the second boy was Lucius, the subject of this sketch; the younger boy, Mela, was to become the father of Lucan, the poet.

The sister of Seneca became the wife of the Roman Governor of Egypt. It was at a time when the scheming rapacity of women was so much in evidence that the Senate debated whether it should not forbid its representatives abroad to be accompanied by their wives. France has seen such times—England and America have glanced that way. Women, like men, often do not know that the big prizes gravitate where they belong; instead, they set traps for them, lie in wait and consider prevarication and duplicity better than truth. When women use their beauty, their wit and their pink persons in politics, trouble lies low around the corner. But this sister of Seneca was never seen in public unless it was at her husband's side; she asked no favors, and presents sent to her personally by provincials were politely returned. The province praised her, and perhaps what was better, didn't know her, and begged the Emperor to send them more of such excellent and virtuous women—from which we infer that virtue consists in minding one's own business.

In making up a list of great mothers, do not leave out Helvia, mother of three sons and a daughter who made their mark upon the times. It is no small thing to be a great mother!

Women of intellect were not much appreciated then, but Seneca dedicated his "Consolations," his best book, to his mother. The very mintage of his mind was for her, and again and again he tells of her insight, her gentle wit, and her appreciation of all that was beautiful and best in the world of thought. In a letter addressed to her when he was past forty, he says, "You never stained your face with walnut-juice nor rouge; you never wore gowns cut conspicuously low; your ornaments were a loveliness of mind and person that time could not tarnish."

But the father had the knighthood, and he called his family to witness it at odd times and sundry.

In Rome, Marcus Seneca made head as he never did in Cordova. There he was only Marcus Micawber: but here his memory feats won him the distinction that genius deserves. There is a grave question whether a verbal memory does not go with a very mediocre intellect, but Marcus said this argument was put out by a man with no memory worth mentioning.

Rome was at her ripest flower—the petals were soon to loosen and flutter to the ground, but nobody thought so—they never do. Everywhere the Roman legions were victorious, and commerce sailed the seas in prosperous ships. Power manifests itself in conspicuous waste, and the habit grows until conspicuous waste imagines itself power. Conditions in Rome had evolved our old friend, the Sophist, the man who lived but to turn an epigram, to soulfully contemplate a lily, to sigh mysteriously, and cultivate the far-away look. These men were elocutionists who gesticulated in curves, and let the thought follow the attitude. They were not content to be themselves, but chased the airy, fairy fabric of a fancy and called it life.

The pretense and folly of Roman society made the Sophists possible—like all sects they ministered to a certain cast of mind. Over against the Sophists there were the Stoics, the purest, noblest and sanest of all ancient cults, corresponding very closely to our Quakers, before Worth and Wanamaker threw them a hawse and took them in tow. It is a tide of feeling produces a sect, not a belief: primitive Christianity was a revulsion from Phariseeism, and a William Penn and a wan Ann Lee form the antithesis of an o'ervaulting, fantastic and soulless ritual.

The father of Seneca hung upon the favor of the Sophists: he taught them mnemonics, rhetoric and elocution, and the fact that he was a courtly Spaniard was in his favor—we dote on a foreign accent and relish the thing that comes from afar.

Marcus Seneca was getting rich. He never perceived the absurdity of a life of make-believe; but his son, Lucius Seneca, heir to his mother's discerning mind, when nineteen years old forswore the Sophists, and sided with the unpopular Stoics, much to the chagrin of the father.

Seneca—let us call him so after this—wore the simple white robe of the Stoics, without ornament or jewelry. He drank no wine, and ate no meat. Vegetarianism comes in waves, and it is interesting to see that in an essay on the subject, Seneca plagiarizes every argument put forth by Colonel Ernest Crosby, even to mentioning a butcher as an "executioner," his goods as "dead corpses," and the customers as "cannibals."

This kind of talk did not help the family peace, and the father spoke of disowning the son, if he did not cease affronting the Best Society.

Soon after, the Emperor Tiberius issued an edict banishing all "strange sects who fasted on feast-days, and otherwise displeased the gods." This was a suggestion for the benefit of the Crosbyites. It is with a feeling of downright disappointment that we find Seneca shortly appearing in an embroidered robe, and making a speech wherein the moderate use of wine is recommended, also the flesh of animals for those who think they need it.

This, doubtless, is the same speech we, too, would have made had we been there; but we want our hero to be strong, and defy even an Emperor, if he comes between the man and his right to eat what he wishes and wear what he listeth, and we blame him for not doing the things we never do. But Seneca was getting on in the world—he had become a lawyer, and his Sophist training was proving its worth. Henry Ward Beecher, in reply to a young man who asked him if he advised the study of elocution, said, "Elocution is all right, but you will have to forget it all before you become an orator." Seneca was shedding his elocution, and losing himself in his work. A successful lawsuit had brought him before the public as a strong advocate. He was able to think on his feet. His voice was low, musical and effective, and the word, "dulcis," was applied to him as it was to his brother, Gallio. Possibly there was something in ol' Marcus Micawber's pedagogic schemes, after all!

In moderating his Stoic philosophy, Seneca gives us the key to his character: the man wanted to be gentle and kind; he wished to affront neither his father nor society; so he compromised—he would please and placate. Ease and luxury appealed to him, and yet his cool intellect stood off, and reviewing the proceeding pronounced it base. He succumbed to the strongest attraction, and attempted the feat of riding two horses at once.

From his twentieth year, Seneca dallied with the epigram, found solace in a sentence, and got a sweet, subtle joy by taking a thought captive. Lucullus tells us of the fine intoxication of oratory, but neither opium nor oratory imparts a finer thrill than successfully to drive a flock of clauses, and round up an idea, roping it in careless grace, with what my lord Hamlet calls words, words, words.

The early Christian Fathers spoke of him as "our Seneca." His writings abound in the purest philosophy—often seemingly paraphrasing Saint Paul—and every argument for directness of speech, simplicity, manliness and moderation is put forth. His writings became the rage in Rome: at feasts he read his essays on the Ideal Life, just as the disciples of Tolstoy often travel by the gorge road, and give banquets in honor of the man who no longer attends one; or princely paid preachers glorify the Man who said to His apostles, "Take neither scrip nor purse."

Seneca was a combination of Delsarte and Emerson. He was as popular as Henry Irving, and as wise as Thomas Brackett Reed. His writings were in demand; when he spoke in public, crowds hung upon his words, and the families of the great and powerful sent him their sons, hoping he would impart the secret of success. The world takes a man at the estimate he puts upon himself. Seneca knew enough to hold himself high. Honors came his way, and the wealth he acquired is tokened in those five hundred tables, inlaid with ivory, to which at times he invited his friends to feast. As a lawyer, he took his pick of cases, and rarely appeared, except on appeal, before the Emperor. The poise of his manner, the surety of his argument, the gentle grace of his diction, caused him to be likened to Julius Cæsar.

And this led straight to exile, and finally—death. To mediocrity, genius is unforgivable.

There are various statements to the effect that Claudius was a mental defective, a sort of town fool, patronized by the nobles for their sport and jest. We are also told that he was made Emperor by the Pretorian Guards, in a spirit of rollicking bravado. Men too much abused must have some merit, or why should the pack bay so loudly? Possibly it is true that, in the youth of Claudius, his mother used to declare, when she wanted a strong comparison, "He is as big a fool as my son, Claudius." But then the mother of Wellington used exactly the same expression; and Byron's mother had a way of referring to the son who was to rescue her from oblivion, and send her name down the corridors of time, as "that lame brat."

Claudius was a brother of the great Germanicus, and was therefore an uncle of Caligula. Caligula was the worst ruler that Rome ever had; and he was a brother of Agrippina, mother of Nero. This precious pair had a most noble and generous father, and their gentle mother was a fit mate for the great Germanicus—these things are here inserted for the edification of folks who take stock in that pleasant fallacy, the Law of Heredity, and who gleefully chase the genealogical anise-seed trail.

Caligula happily passed out without an heir, and Claudius, next of kin, put himself in the way of the Pretorian Guard, and was declared Emperor.

He was then fifty years old, a grass-widower—twice over—and on the lookout for a wife. He was neither wise nor great, nor was he very bad; he was kind—after dinner—and generous when rightly approached. Canon Farrar likened Claudius to King James the First, who gave us our English Bible. His comparison is worth quoting, not alone for the truth it contains, but because it is an involuntary paraphrase of the faultless literary style of the Roman rhetors. Says Canon Farrar: "Both were learned, and both were eminently unwise. Both were authors, and both were pedants. Both delegated their highest powers to worthless favorites, and both enriched these favorites with such foolish liberality that they remained poor themselves. Both of them, though of naturally good dispositions, were misled by selfishness into acts of cruelty; and both of them, though laborious in the discharge of duty, succeeded only in rendering royalty ridiculous. King James kept Sir Walter Raleigh, the brightest intellect of his time, in prison; and Claudius sent Seneca, the greatest man in his kingdom, into exile."

New-made kings sweep clean. The impulses of Claudius were right and just, a truthful statement I here make in pleasant compliment to a brother author. The man was absent-minded, had much faith in others, and moved in the line of least resistance. Like most students and authors, he was decidedly littery. He secured a divorce from one wife because she cleaned up his room in his absence so that he could never find anything; and the other wife got a divorce from him because he refused to go out evenings and scintillate in society—but this was before he was made Emperor.

God knows, people had their troubles then as now. To take this man who loved his slippers and easy-chair, and who was happy with a roll of papyrus, and plunge him into a seething pot of politics, not to mention matrimony, was refined cruelty.

The matchmakers were busy, and soon Claudius was married to Messalina, the handsomest summer-girl in Rome.

For a short time he bore up bravely, and was filled with the wish to benefit and bless. One of his first acts was to recall Julia and Agrippina from exile, they having been sent away in a fit of jealous anger by their brother, the infamous Caligula.

Julia was beautiful and intellectual, and she had a high regard for Seneca.

Agrippina was beautiful and infamous, and pretended that she loved Claudius.

Both men were undone. Seneca's friendship for Julia, as far as we know, was of a kind that did honor to both, but they made a too conspicuous pair of intellects. The fear and jealousy of Claudius was aroused by his young and beautiful wife, who showed him that Seneca, the courtly, was plotting for the throne, and in this ambition Julia was a party. A charge of undue intimacy with Julia, the beloved niece and ward of the Emperor, was brought against Seneca, and he was exiled to Corsica. Imagine Edmund Burke sent to Saint Helena, or John Hay to the Dry Tortugas, and you get the idea.

The sensitive nature of Seneca did not bear up under exile as we would have wished. Unlike Victor Hugo at Guernsey, he was alone, and surrounded by savages. Yet even Victor Hugo lifted up his voice in bitter complaint. Seneca failed to anticipate that, in spite of the barrenness of Corsica, it would some day produce a man who would jostle his Roman Cæsar for first place on history's page.

At Corsica, Seneca produced some of his loftiest and best literature. Exile and imprisonment are such favorable conditions for letters, having done so much for authorship, that the wonder is the expedient has fallen into practical disuse. Banishment gave Seneca an opportunity to put into execution some of the ideas he had so long expressed concerning the simple life, and certain it is that the experience was not without its benefits, and at times the grim humor of it all came to him.

Read the history of Greek ostracism, and one can almost imagine that it was devised by the man's friends—a sort of heroic treatment prescribed by a great spiritual physician. Personality repels as well as attracts: the people grow tired of hearing Aristides called the Just—he is exiled. For a few days there is a glad relief; then his friends begin to chant his praises—he is missed. People tell of all the noble, generous things he would do if he were only here.

If he were only here!

Petitions are circulated for his return.

The law's delay ensues, and this but increases desire. Hate for the man has turned to pity, and pity turns to love, as starch turns to gluten.

The man comes back, and is greeted with boughs and bays, with love and laurel. His homecoming is that of a conquering hero. If the Supreme Court were to issue an injunction requiring all husbands to separate themselves by at least a hundred miles from their wives, for several months in every year, it would cut down divorces ninety-five per cent, add greatly to domestic peace, render race-suicide impossible, and generally liberate millions of love vibrations that would otherwise lie dormant.

As an example of female depravity, Valeria Messalina was sister in crime to Jezebel, Bernice, Drusilla, Salome and Herodias.

Damned by a dower of beauty, with men at her feet whenever she so ordered, her ambition knew no limit. This type of dictatorial womanhood starts out by making conquests of individual men, but the conquests of pretty women are rarely genuine. Women hold no monopoly on duplicity, and there is a deep vein of hypocrisy in men that prompts their playing a part, and letting the woman use them. When the time is ripe, they toss her away as they do any other plaything, as Omar suggests the potter tosses the luckless pots to hell.

When Julia and Agrippina were recalled, the act was done without consulting Messalina; and we can imagine her rage when these two women, as beautiful as herself, came back without her permission. Messalina had never found favor in the eyes of Seneca—he treated her with patronizing patience, as though she were a spoilt child.

Now that Julia was back, Messalina hatched the plot that struck them both. Messalina insisted that the wealth of Seneca should be confiscated. Claudius at this rebelled.

History is replete with instances of great men ruled by their barbers and coachmen. Claudius left the affairs of state to Narcissus, his private secretary; Polybius, his literary helper; and Pallas, his accountant. These men were all of lowly birth, and had all risen in the ranks from menial positions, and one of them at least had been sold as a slave, and afterward purchased his freedom. Then there was Felix, the ex-slave, another protege of Claudius, who trembled when Paul of Tarsus told him a little wholesome truth. These men were all immensely rich, and once, when Claudius complained of poverty, a bystander said, "You should go into partnership with a couple of your freedmen, and then your finances would be all right." The fact that Narcissus, Pallas and Polybius constituted the real government is nothing against them, any more than it is to the discredit of certain Irish refugees that they manage the municipal machinery of New York City—it merely proves the impotence of the men who have allowed the power to slip from their grasp, and ride as passengers when they should be at the throttle.

Messalina managed her husband by alternate cajolings and threats. He was proud of her saucy beauty, and it was pleasing to an old man's vanity to think that other people thought she loved him. She bore him two sons—by name, Brittanicus and Germanicus. A local wit of the day said, "It was kind of Messalina to present her husband with these boys, otherwise he would never have had any claim on them."

But the lines were tightening around Messalina, and she herself was drawing the cords. She had put favorites in high places, banished enemies, and ordered the execution of certain people she did not like. Narcissus and Pallas gave her her own way, because they knew Claudius must find her out for himself. They let her believe that she was the real power behind the throne. Her ambitions grew—she herself would be ruler—she gave it out that Claudius was insane. Finally she decided that the time was right for a "coup de grace." Claudius was absent from Rome, and Messalina wedded at high noon with young Silius, her lover. She was led to believe that the army would back her up, and proclaim her son, Brittanicus, Emperor, in which case, she herself and Silius would be the actual rulers. The wedding festivities were at their height, when the cry went up that Claudius had returned, and was approaching to demand vengeance. Narcissus, the wily, took up the shout, and panic-stricken, Messalina fled for safety in one way and Silius in another.

Narcissus followed the woman, adding to her drunken fright by telling her that Claudius was close behind, and suggested that she kill herself before the wronged man should appear. A dagger was handed her, and she stabbed herself ineffectually in hysteric haste. The kind secretary then, with one plunge of his sword, completed the work so well begun.

A truthful account of Messalina's death was told to Claudius while he was at dinner. He finished the meal without saying a word, gave a present to the messenger, and went about his business, asking no questions, and never again mentioned the matter.

The fact is worthy of note that the name of Messalina is never once mentioned by Seneca. He pitied her vileness and villainy so much he could not hate her. He saw, with prophetic vision, what her end would be; and when her passing occurred, he was too great and lofty in spirit to manifest satisfaction.

Scarcely had the funeral of Messalina occurred, when there was a pretty scramble among the eligible to see who should solace the stricken widower. Among other matrimonial candidates was Agrippina, a beautiful widow, twenty-nine in June, rich in her own right, and with only a small encumbrance in the way of a ten-year-old boy, Nero by name.

Agrippina was a niece of Claudius, and such marriages were considered unnatural; but Agrippina had subtly shown that, the deceased Emperor being her brother, she already had a sort of claim on the throne, and her marriage with Claudius would strengthen the State. Then she marshaled her charms past Claudius, in a phalanx and back, and so they were married. There was much pomp and ceremony at the wedding, and the high priest pronounced the magic words—I trust I use the right expression.

Very soon after her marriage, Agrippina recalled Seneca from exile. It was the infamous Messalina who had disgraced him and sent him away, and for Agrippina, the sister of Julia, to bring him back, was regarded as a certificate of innocence, and a great diplomatic move for Agrippina.

When Seneca returned, the whole city went out to meet him. It is not at all likely that Seneca had a suspicion of the true character of Agrippina, any more than Claudius—which sort of tends to show the futility of philosophy.

How could Seneca read her true character when it had not really been formed? No one knows what he will do until he gets a good chance. It is unkind condition that keeps most of us where we belong.

And even while the honeymoon—or should we say the harvest-moon?—was at full, Seneca was made the legal guardian and tutor of Nero, the son of the Empress, and became a member of the royal household. This was done in gratitude, and to make amends, if possible, for the wrong of banishment inflicted upon the man by scandalously linking his name with that of the sister of the woman who was now First Lady of the Land.

Seneca was then forty-nine years of age. He had fifteen years of life yet before him, and was to gain much valuable experience, and get an insight into a side of existence he had not yet known.

Agrippina was born in Cologne, which was called, in her honor, Colonia Agrippina, and now has been shortened to its present form. Whenever you buy cologne, remember where the word came from.

Agrippina, from her very girlhood, had a thirst for adventure, and her aim was high. When fourteen, she married Domitius, a Roman noble, thirty years her senior. He was as worthless a rogue as ever wore out his physical capacity for sin in middle life, and filled his dying days with crimes that were only mental. He knew himself so well that when Nero was born he declared that the issue of such a marriage could only breed a being who would ruin the State—a monster with his father's vices and his mother's insatiable ambition.

Agrippina was woman enough to hate this man with an utter detestation; but he was rich, and so she endured him for ten years, and then assisted Nature in making him food for worms.

The intensity of Agrippina's nature might have been used for happy ends if the stream of her life had not been so early dammed and polluted. She loved her child with a clutching, feverish affection, and declared that he would some day rule Rome. This was not really such a far-away dream, when we remember that her brother was then Emperor and childless. Her thought was more for her child than for herself, and her expectation was that he would succeed Caligula. The persistency with which she told this ambition for her boy is both beautiful and pathetic. Every mother sees her own life projected in her child, and within certain bounds this is right and well.

Glimpses of kindness and right intent are shown when Agrippina recalled Seneca, and when she became the mother of the motherless children of Claudius. She publicly adopted these children, and for a time gave them every attention and advantage that was bestowed upon her own son. Gibbon says for one woman to mother another woman's children is a diplomatic card often played, but Gibbon sometimes quibbles.

Gradually the fierce desire of Agrippina's heart began to manifest itself. She plotted and arranged that Nero should marry Octavia, the daughter of Claudius. Octavia was seven years older than Nero, but the sooner the marriage could be brought about, the better—it would give her a double hold on the throne. To this end suitors for the hand of Octavia were disgraced by false charges, and sent off into exile, and the same fate came to at least three young women who stood in the way.

But the one real obstacle was Claudius himself—he was sixty, and might be so absurd as to live to be eighty. Locusta, a famous professional chemist, was employed, and the deed was done by Agrippina serving the deadly dish herself. The servants carried Claudius off to bed, thinking he was merely drunk, but he was to wake no more.

Burrus, the blunt and honest old soldier, Captain of the Pretorian Guard, sided with Agrippina; Brittanicus, the son of Claudius, was kept out of the way, and Nero was proclaimed Emperor.

Here Seneca seems to have shown his good influence, and sent home a desire in the heart of Agrippina to serve her people with moderation and justice. She had attained her ends: her son, a youth of fifteen, was Emperor, and his guardian, the great and gentle Seneca, the man of her own choosing, was the actual ruler. She was the sister of one Emperor, wife of another, and now mother of a third—surely this was glory enough to satisfy one woman's ambition!

Then there came to Rome the famed Quinquennium Neronis, when, for five years, peace and plenty smiled. It is a trite saying that men who can not manage their own finances can look after those of a nation, but Seneca was a businessman who proved his ability to manage his own private affairs and also succeeded in managing the exchequer of a kingdom. During his reign, gladiatorial contests were relieved of their savage brutality, work was given to many, education became popular, and people said, "The Age of Augustus has returned."

But the greatest men are not the greatest teachers. Seneca's policy with his pupil, Nero, was one of concession.

A close study of the youth of Nero reveals the same traits that outcrop in one-half the students at Harvard—traits ill-becoming to grown-up men, but not at all alarming in youth. Nero was self-willed and occasionally had tantrums—but a tantrum is only a little whirl-wind of misdirected energy. A tantrum is life plus—it is better far than stagnation, and usually works up into useful life, and sometimes into great art. We have some verses written by Nero in his seventeenth year that show a good Class B sophomoric touch. He danced, played in the theatricals, raced horses, fought dogs, twanged the harp, and exploited various other musical instruments. He wasn't nearly so bad as Alcibiades, but his mother lavished on him her maudlin love, and allowed the fallacy to grow in his mind concerning the divinity that doth hedge a king. In fact, when he asked his mother about his real father, she hid the truth that his father was a rogue—perhaps to shield herself, for it is only a very great person who can tell the truth—and led him to believe his paternal parent was a god, and his birth miraculous. Now, let such an idea get into the head of the average freshman and what will be the result? A woman can tell a full-grown man that he is the greatest thing that ever happened, and it does no special harm, for the man knows better than to go out on the street and proclaim it; but you tell a boy of eighteen such pleasing fallacies, and then have fawning courtiers back them up, and at the same time give the youth free access to the strong box, and it surely would be a miracle if he is not doubly damned, and quickly, too. Agrippina would not allow the blunt old Burrus to discipline her boy, and Seneca's plan was one of concession—he loved peace. He hated to thwart the boy, because he knew that it would arouse the ire of the mother, whose love had run away with her commonsense. Love is beautiful—soft, yielding, gentle love—but the common law of England upholds wife-beating as being justifiable and desirable on certain occasions.

The real trouble was, the dam was out for Agrippina and Nero—there was no restraint for either. There was no one to teach them that the liberty of one man ends where the right of another begins. No more frightful condition for any man or woman can ever occur than this: to take away all responsibility.

When Socrates put the chesty Alcibiades three points down, and jumped on his stomach with his knees, the youth had a month in bed, and after he got around again he possessed a most wholesome regard for his teacher. If Burrus and Seneca had applied Brockway methods to Agrippina and her saucy son, as they easily might, it would have made Rome howl with delight, and saved the State as well as the individuals.

Julius Cæsar, like Lincoln, let everybody do as they wished, up to a certain point. But all realized that somewhere behind that dulcet voice and the gentle manner was a heart of flint and nerves of steel. No woman ever made Julius Cæsar dance to syncopated time, nor did a youth of eighteen ever successfully order him to take part in amateur theatricals on penalty. Julius Cæsar and Seneca were both scholars, both were gentlemen and gentle men: their mental attitude was much the same, but one had a will of adamant, and the other moved in the line of least resistance.

Gradually, Nero evolved a petulance and impatience toward his mother and his tutor, all of which was quite a natural consequence of his education. Every endeavor to restrain him was met with imprecations and curses. About then would have been a good time to apply heroic treatment, instead of halting fear and worshipful acquiescence.

The raw stock for making a Nero is in every school, and given the conditions, a tyrant-culture would be easy to evolve. The endeavor to make Nero wed Octavia caused a revulsion to occur in his heart toward her and her brother Brittanicus. He feared that these two might combine and wrest from him the throne.

Locusta, the specialist, was again sent for and Brittanicus was gathered to his fathers.

Soon after, Nero fell into a deep infatuation for Poppæ Sabina, wife of Otho, the most beautiful woman in Rome. Sabina refused to accept his advances so long as he was tied to his mother's apron-strings—I use the exact phrase of Tacitus, so I trust no exceptions will be taken to the expression. Nero came to believe that the tagging, nagging, mushy love of his mother was standing in the way of his advancement. He had come to know that Agrippina had caused the death of Claudius, and when she accused him of poisoning Brittanicus, he said, "I learned the trick from my dear mother!" and honors were even.

He knew the crafty quality of his mother's mind and grew to fear her. And fear and hate are one. To secure Sabina he must sacrifice Agrippina.

He would be free.

To poison her would not do—she was an expert in preventives.

So Nero, regardless of expense, bargained with Anicetus, admiral of the fleet, to construct a ship so that, when certain bolts were withdrawn, the craft would sink and tell no tale. This was a bit of daring deviltry never before devised, and by turn, Nero chuckled in glee and had cold sweats of fear as he congratulated himself on his astuteness.

The boat was built and Agrippina was enticed on board. The night of the excursion was calm, but the conspirators, fearing the chance might never come again, let go the canopy, loaded with lead, which was over the queen. It fell with a crash; and at the same time the bolts were withdrawn and the waters rushed in. Several of the servants in attendance were killed by the fall of the awning, but Agrippina and Aceronia, a lady of quality, escaped from the debris only slightly hurt. Aceronia, believing the ship was about to sink, called for help, saying, "I am Agrippina." She erred slightly in her diplomacy, for she was at once struck on the head with an oar and killed. This gave Agrippina a clew to the situation and she was silent. By a strange perversity, the royal scuttling patent would not work and the boat stubbornly refused to sink.

Agrippina got safely ashore and sent word to her son that there had been a terrible accident, but she was safe—the intent of her letter being to let him know that she understood the matter perfectly, and while she could not admire the job, it was so bungling, yet she would forgive him if he would not try it again.

In wild consternation, Nero sent for Burrus and Seneca. This was their first knowledge of the affair. They refused to act in either way, but Burrus intimated that Anicetus was the guilty party and should be held responsible.

"For not completing the task?" said Nero.

"Yes," said the blunt old soldier, and retired.

Anicetus was notified that the blame of the whole conspiracy was on him. A big crime, well carried out, is its own excuse for being; but failure, like unto genius, is unforgivable.

Anicetus was in disgrace, but only temporarily, for he towed the obstinate, telltale galley into deep water and sank her at dead of night. Then with a few faithful followers he surrounded the villa where Agrippina was resting, scattered her guard and confronted her with drawn sword.

Years before, a soothsayer had told her that her son would be Emperor and that he would kill her. Her answer was, "Let them slay me, if he but reign."

Now she saw that death was nigh. She did not try to escape, nor did she plead for mercy, but cried, "Plunge your sword through my womb, for it bore Nero."

And Anicetus, with one blow, struck her dead.

Nero returned to Naples to mourn his loss. From there he sent forth a lengthy message to the Senate, recounting the accidental shipwreck, and telling how Agrippina had plotted against his life, recounting her crimes in deprecatory, sophistical phrase. The document wound up by telling how she had tried to secure the throne for a paramour, and the truth coming to some o'erzealous friends of the State, they had arisen and taken her life. In Rome there was a strong feeling that Nero should not be allowed to return, but this message of explanation and promise, written by Seneca, downed the opposition.

The Senate accepted the report, and Nero, at twenty-two, found himself master of the world.

Yet what booted it when he was not master of himself!

From this time on, the career of Seneca was one of contumely, suffering and disgrace. This was to endure for six years, when kindly death was then to set him free.

The mutual, guilty knowledge of a great crime breeds loathing and contempt. History contains many such instances where the subject had knowledge of the sovereign's sins, and the sovereign found no rest until the man who knew was beneath the sod.

Seneca knew Nero as only his Maker knew him.

After the first spasm of exultation in being allowed to return to Rome, a jealous dread of Seneca came over the guilty monarch.

Seneca hoped against hope that, now that Nero's wild oats were sown and the crop destroyed, all would be well. The past should be buried and remembrance of it sunk deep in oblivion.

But Nero feared Seneca might expose his worthlessness and the philosopher himself take the reins. In this Nero did not know his man: Seneca's love was literary—political power to him was transient and not worth while.

It became known that the apology to the Senate was the work of Seneca, and Nero, who wanted the world to think that all his speeches and addresses were his own, got it firmly fixed in his head he would not be happy until Seneca was out of the way. Sabina said he was no longer a boy, and should not be tagged and dictated to by his old teacher.

Seneca, seeing what was coming, offered to give his entire property to the State and retire. Nero would not have it so—he feared Seneca would retire only to come back with an army. A cordon of spies was put around Seneca's house—he was practically a prisoner. Attempts were made to poison him, but he ate only fruit, and bread made by his wife, Paulina, and drank no water except from running streams.

Finally a charge of conspiracy was fastened upon him, and Nero ordered him to die by his own hand. His wife was determined to go with him, and one stroke severed the veins of both.

The beautiful Sabina realized her hopes—she divorced her husband, and married the Emperor of Rome. She died from a sudden kick given her by the booted foot of her liege.

Three years after the death of Seneca, Nero passed hence by the same route, killing himself to escape the fury of the Pretorian Guard. And so ended the Julian line, none of whom, except the first, was a Julian.

From the death of Augustus on to the time of Nero there was for Rome a steady tide of disintegration. The Emperor was the head of the Church, and he usually encouraged the idea that he was something different from common men—that his mission was from On High and that he should be worshiped. Gibbon, making a free translation from Seneca, says, "Religion was regarded by the common people as true, by the philosophers as false, and by the rulers as useful." And Saint Augustine, using the same smoothly polished style, says, in reference to a Roman Senator, "He worshiped what he blamed, he did what he refuted, he adored that with which he found fault." The sentence is Seneca's, and when he wrote it he doubtless had himself in mind, for in spite of his Stoic philosophy the life of luxury lured him, and although he sang the praises of poverty he charged a goodly sum for so doing, and the nobles who listened to him doubtless found a vicarious atonement by applauding him as he played to the gallery gods of their self-esteem, like rich ladies who go a-slumming mix in with the poor on an equality, and then hasten home to dress for dinner.

Seneca was one of the purest and loftiest intellects the world has ever known. Canon Farrar calls him "A Seeker after God," and has printed parallel passages from Saint Paul and Seneca which, for many, seem to show that the men were in communication with each other. Every ethical maxim of Christianity was expressed by this "noble pagan," and his influence was always directed toward that which he thought was right. His mistakes were all in the line of infirmities of the will. Voltaire calls him, "The father of all those who wear shovel hats," and in another place refers to him as an "amateur ascetic," but in this the author of the Philosophical Dictionary pays Seneca the indirect compliment of regarding him as a Christian. Renan says, "Seneca shines out like a great white star through a rift of clouds on a night of darkness." The wonder is not that Seneca at times lapsed from his high estate and manifested his Sophist training, but that to the day of his death he saw the truth with unblinking eyes and held the Ideal firmly in his heart.

ARISTOTLE

Happiness itself is sufficient excuse. Beautiful things are right and true; so beautiful actions are those pleasing to the gods. Wise men have an inward sense of what is beautiful, and the highest wisdom is to trust this intuition and be guided by it. The answer to the last appeal of what is right lies within a man's own breast. Trust thyself.
—*Ethics* *of* *Aristotle*

ARISTOTLE

The Sublime Porte recently issued a request to the American Bible Society, asking that references to Macedonia be omitted from all Bibles circulated in Turkey or Turkish provinces. The argument of His Sublimity is that the Macedonian cry, "Come over and help us!" puts him and his people in a bad light. He ends his most courteous petition by saying, "The land that produced a Philip, an Alexander the Great and an Aristotle, and that today has citizens who are the equal of these, needs nothing from our dear brothers, the Americans, but to be let alone."

As to the statement that Macedonia today has citizens who are the equals of Philip, Alexander and Aristotle, the proposition, probably, is based on the confession of the citizens themselves, and therefore may be truth. Great men are only great comparatively. It is the stupidity of the many that allows one man to bestride the narrow world like a Colossus. In the time of Alexander and Aristotle there wasn't so much competition as now, so perhaps what we take to be lack of humor on the part of the Sublime Porte may have a basis in fact.

Aristotle was born Three Hundred Eighty-four B.C., at the village of Stagira in the mountains of Macedonia. King Amyntas used to live at Stagira several months in the year and hunt the wild hogs that fed on the acorns which grew in the gorges and valleys. Mountain climbing and hunting was dangerous sport, and it was well to have a surgeon attached to the royal party, so the father of Aristotle served in that capacity. No doubt, though, but the whole outfit was decidedly barbaric, even including the doctor's little son "Aristo," who refused to be left behind. The child's mother had died years before, and boys without mothers are apt to manage their fathers. And so Aristo was allowed to trot along by his father's side, carrying a formidable bow, which he himself had made, with a quiver of arrows at his back.

Those were great times when the King came to Stagira!

When the King went back to the capital everybody received presents, and the good doctor, by some chance, was treated best of all, and little Aristo came in for the finest bow that ever was, all tipped with silver and eagle-feathers. But the bow did not bring good luck, for soon after, the boy's father was caught in an avalanche of sliding stone and crushed to death.

Aristo was taken in charge by Proxenus, a near kinsman. The lad was so active at climbing, so full of life and energy and good spirits, that when the King came the next year to Stagira, he asked for Aristo. With the King was his son Philip, a lad about the age of Aristo, but not so tall nor so active. The boys became fast friends, and once when a stranger saw them together he complimented the King on his fine, intelligent boys, and the King had to explain, "The other boy is mine—but I wish they both were."

Aristo knew where the wild boars fed in gulches, and where the stunted oaks grew close and thick. Higher up in the mountains there were bears, which occasionally came down and made the wild pigs scamper. You could always tell when the bears were around, for then the little pigs would run out into the open. The bears had a liking for little pigs, and the bears had a liking for the honey in the bee-trees, too. Aristo could find the bee-trees better than the bears—all you had to do was to watch the flight of the bees as they left the clover.

Then there were deer—you could see their tracks any time around the mountain marshes where the springs gushed forth and the watercress grew lush. Still higher up the mountains, beyond where bears ever traveled, there were mountain-sheep, and still higher up were goats. The goats were so wild that hardly any one but Aristo had ever seen them, but he knew they were there.

The King was delighted to have such a lad as companion for his son, and insisted that he should go back to the capital with them and become a member of the Court.

Not he—there were other ambitions. He wanted to go to Athens and study at the school of Plato—Plato, the pupil of the great Socrates.

The King laughed—he had never heard of Plato. That a youth should refuse to become part of the Macedonian Court, preferring the company of an unknown schoolmaster, was amusing—he laughed.

The next year when the King came back to Stagira, Aristo was still there. "And you haven't gone to Athens yet?" said the King.

"No, but I am going," was the firm reply.

"We will send him," said the King to Proxenus, Aristo's guardian.

And so we find Aristo, aged seventeen, tall and straight and bronzed, starting off for Athens, his worldly goods rolled up in a bearskin, tied about with thongs. There is a legend to the effect that Philip went with Aristo, and that for a time they were together at Plato's school. But, anyway, Philip did not remain long. Aristo—or Aristotle, we had better call him—remained with Plato just twenty years.

At Plato's school Aristotle was called by the boys, "the Stagirite," a name that was to last him through life—and longer. In Winter he wore his bearskin, caught over one shoulder, for a robe, and his mountain grace and native beauty of mind and body must have been a joy to Plato from the first. Such a youth could not be overlooked.

To him that hath shall be given. The pupil that wants to learn is the teacher's favorite—which is just as it should not be. Plato proved his humanity by giving his all to the young mountaineer. Plato was then a little over sixty years of age—about the same age that Socrates was when Plato became his pupil. But the years had touched Plato lightly—unlike Socrates, he had endured no Thracian winters in bare feet, neither had he lived on cold snacks picked up here and there, as Providence provided. Plato was a bachelor. He still wore the purple robe, proud, dignified, yet gentle, and his back was straight as that of a youth. Lowell once said, "When I hear Plato's name mentioned, I always think of George William Curtis—a combination of pride and intellect, a man's strength fused with a woman's gentleness."

Plato was an aristocrat. He accepted only such pupils as he invited, or those that were sent by royalty. Like Franz Liszt, he charged no tuition, which plan, by the way, is a good scheme for getting more money than could otherwise be obtained, although no such selfish charge should be brought against either Plato or Liszt. Yet every benefit must be paid for, and whether you use the word fee or honorarium, matters little. I hear there be lecturers who accept invitations to banquets and accept an honorarium mysteriously placed on the mantel, when they would scorn a fee.

Plato's Garden School, where the pupils reclined under the trees on marble benches, and read or talked, or listened to lectures by the Master, was almost an ideal place. Not the ideal for us, because we believe that the mental and the manual must go hand in hand. The world of intellect should not be separated from the world of work. It was too much to expect that in a time when slavery was everywhere, Plato would see the fallacy of having one set of men to do the thinking, and another do the work. We haven't got far from that yet; only free men can see the whole truth, and a free man is one who lives in a country where there are no slaves. To own slaves is to be one, and to live in a land of slavery is to share in the bondage—a partaker in the infamy and the profits.

Plato and Aristotle became fast friends—comrades. With thinking men years do not count—only those grow old who think by proxy. Plato had no sons after the flesh, and the love of his heart went out to the Stagirite: in him he saw his own life projected.

When Aristotle had turned twenty he was acquainted with all the leading thinkers of his time; he read constantly, wrote, studied and conversed. The little property his father left had come to him; the King of Macedon sent him presents; and he taught various pupils from wealthy families—finances were easy. But success did not spoil him. The brightest scholars do not make the greatest success in life, because alma mater usually catches them for teachers. Sometimes this is well, but more often it is not. Plato would not hear of Aristotle's leaving him, and so he remained, the chief ornament and practical leader of the school.

He became rich, owned the largest private library at Athens, and was universally regarded as the most learned man of his time.

In many ways he had surpassed Plato. He delved into natural history, collected plants, rocks, animals, and made studies of the practical workings of economic schemes. He sought to divest the Platonic teaching of its poetry, discarded rhetoric, and tried to get at the simple truth of all subjects.

Toward the last of Plato's career this repudiation by Aristotle of poetry, rhetoric, elocution and the polite accomplishments caused a schism to break out in the Garden School. Plato's head was in the clouds at times; Aristotle's was, too, but his feet were always on the earth.

When Plato died, Aristotle was his natural successor as leader of the school, but there was opposition to him, both on account of his sturdy, independent ways and because he was a foreigner.

He left Athens to become a member of the Court of Hermias, a former pupil, now King of Atarneus.

He remained here long enough to marry the niece of his patron, and doubtless saw himself settled for life—a kingly crown within his reach should his student-sovereign pass away.

And the royal friend did pass away, by the dagger's route. As life-insurance risks I am told that Kings have to pay double premium. Revolution broke out, and as Aristotle was debating in his mind what course to pursue, a messenger with soldiers arrived from King Philip of Macedon, offering safe convoy, enclosing transportation, and asking that Aristotle come and take charge of the education of his son, Alexander, aged thirteen.

Aristotle did not wait to parley: he accepted the invitation. Horses were saddled, camels packed and that night, before the moon arose, the cavalcade silently moved out into the desert.

The offer that had been made twenty-four years before, by Philip's father, was now accepted. Aristotle was forty-two years old, in the prime of his power. Time had tempered his passions, but not subdued his zest in life. He had the curious, receptive, alert and eager mind of a child. His intellect was at its ripest and best. He was a lover of animals, and all outdoor life appealed to him as it does to a growing boy. He was a daring horseman, and we hear of his riding off into the desert and sleeping on the sands, his horse untethered watching over him. Aristotle was the first man to make a scientific study of the horse, and with the help of Alexander he set up a skeleton, fastening the bones in place, to the mighty astonishment of the natives, who mistook the feat for an attempt to make a living animal; and when the beast was not at last saddled and bridled there were subdued chuckles of satisfaction among the "hoi polloi" at the failure of the scheme, and murmurs of "I told you so!"

Eighteen hundred years were to pass before another man was to take up the horse as a serious scientific study; and this was Leonardo da Vinci, a man in many ways very much like Aristotle. The distinguishing feature in these men—the thing that differentiates them from other men—was the great outpouring sympathy with every living creature. Everything they saw was related to themselves—it came very close to them—they wanted to know more about it. This is essentially the child-mind, and the calamity of life is to lose it.

Leonardo became interested in Aristotle's essay on the horse, and continued the subject further, dissecting the animal in minutest detail and illustrating his discoveries with painstaking drawings. His work is so complete and exhaustive that nobody nowadays has time to more than read the title-page. Leonardo's bent was natural science, and his first attempts at drawing were done to illustrate his books. Art was beautiful, of course—it brought in an income, made friends and brought him close to people who saw nothing unless you made a picture of it. He made pictures for recreation and to amuse folks, and his threat to put the peeping Prior into the "Last Supper," posed as Judas, revealed his contempt for the person to whom a picture was just a picture. The marvel to Leonardo was the mind that could imagine, the hand that could execute, and the soul that could see.

And the curious part is that Leonardo lives for us through his play and not through his serious work. His science has been superseded, but his art is immortal.

This expectant mental attitude, this attitude of worship, belongs to all great scientists. The man divines the thing first and then looks for it, just as the Herschels knew where the star ought to be and then patiently waited for it. The Bishop of London said that if Darwin had spent one-half as much time in reading his Bible as in studying earthworms, he would have really benefited the world, and saved his soul alive. To Walt Whitman, a hair on the back of his hand was just as curious and wonderful as the stars in the sky, or God's revelation to man through a printed book.

Aristotle loved animals as a boy loves them—his house was a regular menagerie of pets, and into this world of life Alexander was very early introduced. We hear of young Alexander breaking the wild horse, Bucephalus, and beyond a doubt Aristotle was seated on the top rail of the paddock when he threw the lariat.

Aristotle and his pupil had the first circus of which we know, and they also inaugurated the first Zoological Garden mentioned in history, barring Noah, of course.

So much was Alexander bound up in this menagerie, and in his old teacher as well, that in after-life, in all of his travels, he was continually sending back to Aristotle specimens of every sort of bird, beast and fish to be found in the countries through which he traveled.

When Philip was laid low by the assassin's thrust, it was Aristotle who backed up Alexander, aged twenty—but a man—in his prompt suppression of the revolution. The will that had been used to subdue man-eating stallions and to train wild animals, now came in to repress riot, and the systematic classification of things was a preparation for the forming of an army out of a mob. Aristotle said, "An army is a huge animal with a million claws—it must have only one brain, and that the commander's."

Alexander gave credit again and again to Aristotle for those elements in his character that went to make up success: steadiness of purpose, self-reliance, systematic effort, mathematical calculation, attention to details, and a broad and generous policy that sees the end.

When Aristotle argued with Philip, years before, that horse-breaking should be included in the educational curriculum of all young men, he evidently divined football and was endeavoring to supplant it.

I think history has been a trifle severe on Alexander. He was elected Captain-General of Greece, and ordered to repel the Persian invasion. And he did the business once for all. War is not all fighting—Providence is on the side of the strongest commissariat. Alexander had to train, arm, clothe and feed a million men, and march them long miles across a desert country. The real foe of a man is in his own heart, and the foe of an army is in its own camp—disease takes more prisoners than the enemy. Fever sniped more of our boys in blue than did the hostile Filipinos.

Alexander's losses were principally from men slain in battle; from this, I take it that Alexander knew a deal of sanitary science, and had a knowledge of practical mathematics, in order to systematize that mob of restless, turbulent helots. We hear of Aristotle cautioning him that safety lies in keeping his men busy—they must not have too much time to think, otherwise mutiny is to be feared. Still, they must not be over-worked, or they will be in no condition to fight when the eventful time occurs. And we are amazed to see this: "Do not let your men drink out of stagnant pools—Athenians, city-born, know no better. And when you carry water on the desert marches, it should be first boiled to prevent its getting sour."

Concerning the Jews, Alexander writes to his teacher and says, "They are apt to be in sullen rebellion against their governors, receiving orders only from their high priests, and this leads to severe measures, which are construed as persecution"; all of which might have been written yesterday by the Czar in a message to The Hague Convention.

Alexander captured the East, and was taken captive by the East. Like the male bee that never lives to tell the tale of its wooing, he succeeded and died. Yet he vitalized all Asia with the seeds of Greek philosophy, turned back the hungry barbaric tide, and made a new map of the Eastern world. He built far more cities than he destroyed. He set Andrew Carnegie an example at Alexandria, such as the world had never up to that time seen. At the entrance to the harbor of the same city he erected a lighthouse, surpassing far the one at Minot's Ledge, or Race Rock. This structure endured for two centuries, and when at last wind and weather had their way, there was no Hopkinson Smith who could erect another.

At Thebes, Alexander paid a compliment to letters, by destroying every building in the city except the house of the poet, Pindar. At Corinth, when the great, the wise, the noble, came to pay homage, one great man did not appear. In vain did Alexander look for his card among all those handed in at the door—Diogenes, the Philosopher, oft quoted by Aristotle, was not to be seen.

Alexander went out to hunt him up, and found him sunning himself, propped up against the wall in the Public Square, busy doing nothing.

The philosopher did not arise to greet the conqueror; he did not even offer a nod of recognition.

"I am Alexander—is there not something I can do for you?" modestly asked the descendant of Hercules.

"Just stand out from between me and the sun," replied the philosopher, and went on with his meditations.

Alexander enjoyed the reply so much that he said to his companions, and afterward wrote to Aristotle, "If I were not Alexander, I would be Diogenes," and thus did strenuosity pay its tribute to self-sufficiency.

Aristotle might have assumed important affairs of State, but practical politics were not to his liking. "What Aristotle is in the world of thought I will be in the world of action," said Alexander.

On all of his journeys Alexander found time to keep in touch with his old teacher at home; and we find the ruler of Asia voicing that old request, "Send me something to read," and again, "I live alone with my thoughts, amidst a throng of men, but without companions."

Plutarch gives a copy of a letter sent by Alexander wherein Aristotle is chided for publishing his lecture on oratory. "Now all the world will know what formerly belonged to you and me alone," plaintively cries the young man who sighed for more worlds to conquer, and therein shows he was the victim of a fallacy that will never die—the idea that truth can be embodied in a book. When will we ever learn that inspired books demand inspired readers!

There are no secrets. A book may stimulate thought, but it can never impart it.

Aristotle wrote out the Laws of Oratory. "Alas!" groans Alexander, "everybody will turn orator now." But he was wrong, because Oratory and the Laws of Oratory are totally different things.

A Boston man of excellent parts has just recently given out the Sixteen Perfective Laws of Oratory, and the Nineteen Steps in Evolution.

The real truth is, there are Fifty-seven Varieties of Artistic Vagaries, and all are valuable to the man who evolves them—they serve him as a scaffolding whereby he builds thought. But woe betide Alexander and all rareripe Bostonians who mistake the scaffolding for the edifice.

There are no Laws of Art. A man evolves first, and builds his laws afterward. The style is the man, and a great man, full of the spirit, will express himself in his own way.

Bach ignored all the Laws of Harmony made before his day and set down new ones—and these marked his limitations, that was all. Beethoven upset all these, and Wagner succeeded by breaking most of Beethoven's rules. And now comes Grieg, and writes harmonious discords that Wagner said were impossible, and still it is music, for by it we are transported on the wings of song and uplifted to the stars.

The individual soul striving for expression ignores all man-made laws. Truth is that which serves us best in expressing our lives. A rotting log is truth to a bed of violets, while sand is truth to a cactus. But when the violet writes a book on "Expression as I Have Found It," making laws for the evolution of beautiful blossoms, it leaves the Century Plant out of its equation, or else swears, i' faith, that a cactus is not a flower, and that a Night-Blooming Cereus is a disordered thought from a madman's brain. And when the proud and lofty cactus writes a book it never mentions violets, because it has never stooped to seek them.

Art is the blossoming of the Soul.

We can not make the plant blossom—all we can do is to comply with the conditions of growth. We can supply the sunshine, moisture and aliment, and God does the rest. In teaching, he only is successful who supplies the conditions of growth—that is all there is of the Science of Pedagogics, which is not a science, and if it ever becomes one, it will be the Science of Letting Alone, and not a scheme of interference. Just so long as some of the greatest men are those who have broken through pedagogic fancy and escaped, succeeding by breaking every rule of pedagogy, as Wagner discarded every Law of Harmony, there will be no such thing as a Science of Education.

Recently I read Aristotle's Essays on Rhetoric and Oratory, and I was pained to see how I had been plagiarized by this man who wrote three hundred years before Christ. Aristotle used charts in teaching and indicated the mean by a straight horizontal line, and the extreme by an upright dash. He says: "From one extreme the mean looks extreme, and from another extreme the mean looks small—it all depends upon your point of view. Beware of jumping to conclusions, for beside the appearance you must look within and see from what vantage-ground you gain the conclusions. All truth is relative, and none can be final to a man six feet high, who stands on the ground, who can walk but forty miles at a stretch, who needs four meals a day and one-third of his time for sleep. A loss of sleep, or loss of a meal, or a meal too much, will disarrange his point of view, and change his opinions," And thus do we see that a belief in "eternal punishment" is a mere matter of indigestion.

A certain bishop, we have seen, experienced a regret that Darwin expended so much time on earthworms; and we might also express regret that Aristotle did not spend more. As long as he confined himself to earth, he was eminently sure and right: he was really the first man who ever used his eyes. But when he quit the earth, and began to speculate about the condition of souls before they are clothed with bodies, or what becomes of them after they discard the body, or the nature of God, he shows that he knew no more than we. That is to say, he knew no more than the barbarians who preceded him.

He attempted to grasp ideas which Herbert Spencer pigeonholes forever as the Unknowable; and in some of his endeavors to make plain the unknowable, Aristotle strains language to the breaking-point—the net bursts and all of his fish go free. Here is an Aristotelian proposition, expressed by Hegel to make lucid a thing nobody comprehends: "Essential being as being that meditates with itself, with itself by the negativity of itself, is relative to itself only as it is relative to another; that is, immediate only as something posited and meditated." It gives one a slight shock to hear him speak of headache being caused by wind on the brain, or powdered grasshopper-wings being a cure for gout, but when he calls the heart a pump that forces the blood to the extremities, we see that he anticipates Harvey, although more than two thousand years of night lie between them.

Some of Aristotle reads about like this Geometrical Domestic Equation:

Definitions:

All boarding-houses are the same boarding-houses.

Boarders in the same boarding-house, and on the same flat, are equal to one another.

A single room is that which hath no parts and no magnitude.

The landlady of the boarding-house is a parallelogram—that is, an oblong figure that can not be described, and is equal to anything.

A wrangle is the disinclination to each other of two boarders that meet together, but are not on the same floor.

All the other rooms being taken, a single room is a double room.

Postulates and Propositions:

A pie may be produced any number of times.

The landlady may be reduced to her lowest terms by a series of propositions.

A bee-line is the shortest distance between the Phalanstery and By Allen's.

The clothes of a boarding-house bed stretched both ways will not meet.

Any two meals at a boarding-house are together less than one meal at the Phalanstery.

On the same bill and on the same side of it there should not be two charges for the same thing.

If there be two boarders on the same floor, and the amount of the side of the one be equal to the amount of the side of the other, and the wrangle between the one boarder and the landlady be equal to the wrangle between the landlady and the other boarder, then shall the weekly bills of the two boarders be equal. For, if not, let one bill be the greater, then the other bill is less than it might have been, which is absurd. Therefore the bills are equal.

Quod erat demonstrandum.

The business of the old philosophers was to philosophize. To philosophize as a business is to miss the highest philosophy. To do a certain amount of useful work every day, and not trouble about either the past or the future, is the highest wisdom. The man who drags the past behind him, and dives into the future, spreads the present out thin. Therein lies the bane of most religions. A man goes out into the woods to study the birds: he walks and walks and walks and sees no birds. But just let him sit down on a log and wait, and lo! the branches are full of song.

Those who pursue Culture never catch up with her. Culture takes alarm at pursuit and avoids the stealthy pounce. Culture is a woman, and a certain amount of indifference wins her. Ardent wooing will not secure either wisdom or a woman—except in the case where a woman marries a man to get rid of him, and then he really does not get the woman—he only secures her husk. And the husks of culture are pedantry and sciolism. The highest philosophy of the future will consist in doing each day that which is most useful. Talking about it will be quite incidental and secondary.

After Alexander had completed his little task of conquering the world, it was his intention to sit down and improve his mind. He was going back to Greece to complete the work Pericles had so well begun. To this end Aristotle had left Macedonia and established his Peripatetic School at Athens. Plato was exclusive, and taught in the Garden with its high walls. Aristotle taught in the "peripatos," or porch of the Lyceum, and his classes were for all who wished to attend. Socrates was really the first peripatetic philosopher, but he was a roustabout. Nothing sanctifies like death—and now Socrates had become respectable, and his methods were to be made legal and legitimate.

Socrates discovered the principle of human liberty; he taught the rights of the individual, and as these threatened to interfere with the State, the politicians got alarmed and put him to death. Plato, much more cautious, wrote his "Republic," wherein everything is subordinated for the good of the State, and the individual is but a cog in a most perfectly lubricated machine. Aristotle saw that Socrates was nearer right than Plato—sin is the expression of individuality and is not wholly bad—the State is made up of individuals, and if you suppress the thinking-power of the individual, you will get a weak and effeminate body politic; there will be none to govern. The whole fabric will break down of its own weight. A man must have the privilege of making a fool of himself—within proper bounds, of course. To that end learning must be for all, and liberty both to listen and to teach should be the privilege of every man.

This is a problem that Boston has before it today: Shall free speech be allowed on the Common? William Morris tried it in Trafalgar Square, to his sorrow; but in Hyde Park, if you think you have a message, London will let you give it. But this is not considered good form, and the "Best Society" listen to no speeches in the park. However, there are signs that Aristotle's outdoor school may come back. Phillips Brooks tried outdoor preaching, and if his health had not failed, he might have popularized it. It only wants a man who is big enough to inaugurate it.

Aristotle had various helpers, and arranged to give his lectures and conferences daily in certain porches or promenades. These lectures covered the whole range of human thought—logic, rhetoric, oratory, physics, ethics, politics, esthetics, and physical culture. These outdoor talks were called exoteric, and there gradually grew up esoteric lessons, which were for the rich or luxurious and the dainty. And there being money in the esoteric lessons, these gradually took the place of the exoteric, and so we get the genesis of our modern private school or college, where we send our children to be taught great things by great men, for a consideration.

Will the exoteric, peripatetic school come back?

I think so.

I believe that university education will soon be free to every boy and girl in America, and this without going far from home. Esoteric education is always more or less of a sham. Our public-school system is purely exoteric, only we stop too soon. We also give our teachers too much work and too little pay. Stop building warships, and use the money to double the teachers' salaries, making the profession respectable, raise the standard of efficiency, and the free university with the old Greek Lyceum will be here.

America must do this—the Old World can't. We have the money, and we have the men and the women; all that is needed is the desire, and this is fast awakening.

When Alexander died, of acute success, aged thirty-two, Aristotle's sustaining prop was gone. The Athenians never thought much of the Macedonians—not much more than Saint Paul did, he having tried to convert both and failed.

Athens was jealous of the power of Alexander: that a provincial should thus rule the Mother-Country was unforgivable. It was as if a Canadian should make himself King of England!

Everybody knew that Aristotle had been the tutor of Alexander, and that they were close friends. And that a Macedonian should be the chief school-teacher in Athens was an affront. The very greatness of the man was his offense: Athens had none to match him, and the world has never since matched him, either. How to get rid of the Macedonian philosopher was the question.

And so our old friend, heresy, comes in again. A poem was found, written by Aristotle many years before, on the death of his friend, King Hermias, wherein Apollo was disrespectfully mentioned. It was the old charge against Socrates come back—the hemlock was brewing. But life was sweet to Aristotle; he chose discretion to valor, and fled to his country home at Chalcis in Eubœa.

The humiliation of being driven from his work, and the sudden change from active life to exile, undermined his strength, and he died in a year, aged sixty-two.

In morals the world has added nothing new to the philosophy of Aristotle: gentleness, consideration, moderation, mutual helpfulness, and the principle that one man's privileges end where another man's rights begin—these make up the sum. And on them, all authorities agree, and have for twenty-five hundred years.

The family relations of Aristotle were most exemplary. The unseemly wrangles of Philip and his wife were never repeated in the home of Aristotle. Yet we will have to offer this fact in the interests of stirpiculture: the inconstant Philip and the termagant Olympias brought into the world Alexander; whereas the sons of Aristotle lived their day and died, without making a ripple on the surface of history.

As in the scientific study of the horse, no progress was made from the time of Aristotle to that of Leonardo, so Hegel says there was no advancement in philosophy from the time of Aristotle to that of Spinoza.

Eusebius called Aristotle "Nature's Private Secretary."

Dante spoke of him as the "Master of those who know."

Sir William Hamilton said, "In the range of his powers and perceptions, only Leonardo can be compared with him."

MARCUS AURELIUS

We are made for co-operation, like feet, like hands, like eyelids, like the rows of the upper and lower teeth. To act against one another then is contrary to Nature, and it is acting against one another to be vexed and turn away.

—*The* *Meditations*

MARCUS AURELIUS

Annius Verus was one of the great men of Rome. He had been a soldier, governor of provinces, judge, senator and consul. Sixty years had passed over his head and whitened his hair, but the lines of care that were on his fine face ten years before had now given way to a cherubic double chin, and his complexion was ruddy as a baby's. The entire atmosphere of the man was one of gentleness, repose and kindly good-will. Annius Verus was grateful to the gods, for the years had brought him much good fortune, and better still, knowledge. "Being old I shall know ... the last of life for which the first was made!"

Religion isn't a thing outside of a man, taught by priests out of a book. Religion is in the heart of man, and its chief quality is resignation and a grateful spirit. Annius Verus was religious in the best sense, and his life was peaceful and happy.

And surely Annius Verus should have been content—he was a Roman Consul, rich, powerful, honored by the wisest and best men in Rome, who considered it a privilege to come and dine at his table. His villa was on Mount Cœlius, a suburb of Rome. The house was surrounded by a big stone wall enclosing a tract of about ten acres, where grew citron, orange and fig trees, and giant cedars of Lebanon lifted their branches to the clouds.

At least it seemed to little Marcus, grandson of the Consul, as if they reached the clouds. There was a long ladder running up one of these big cedar trees to a platform or "crow's-nest" nearly a hundred feet from the ground. No boy was allowed to climb up there until he was twelve years old, and when Marcus was ten, time got stuck, he thought, and refused to budge. But this was only little Marcus' idea, for he finally got to be twelve years old, and then he climbed the long ladder to the lookout in the tree and looked down on the Eternal City that lay below in the valley and stretched away over the seven hills. Often the boy would take a book and climb up there to read; and when the good grandfather missed him, he knew where to look, and standing under the tree the old man would call: "Come down, Marcus, come down and kiss your old grandfather—it is lonesome down here! Come down and read to your grandfather who loves his little Marcus!"

Such an appeal as this was irresistible, and the boy, slight, slim and agile, would clamber over the side of the crow's-nest and down the ladder to the outstretched arms.

The boy's father had died when he was only three months old, and the grandfather had adopted the child as his heir, and brought Lucilla, the widowed mother, and her baby to live in his house.

Years before, the Consul's wife had passed away, and Faustina, his daughter, became the lady of the house. Lucilla and Faustina didn't get along very well together—no house is big enough for two families, some man has said. Lucilla was gentle, gracious, spiritual, modest and refined; Faustina was beautiful and not without intellect, but she was proud, domineering and fond of admiration. But be it said to the credit of the good old Consul, he was able to suffuse the whole place with love, and even if Faustina had a tantrum now and then, it did not last long.

There were always visitors in the household—soldiers home on furloughs, governors on vacations, lawyers who came to consult the wise and judicial Verus.

One visitor of note was a man by the name of Aurelius Antoninus. He was about forty years old as Marcus first remembered him—tall and straight, with a full, dark beard, and short, curly hair touched with gray. He was a quiet, self-contained man, and at first little Marcus was a bit afraid of him. Aurelius Antoninus had been a soldier, but he showed such a studious mind, and was so intent on doing the right thing that he was made an undersecretary, then private secretary to the Emperor, and finally he had been sent away to govern a rebellious province, and put down mutiny by wise diplomacy instead of by force of arms.

Aurelius Antoninus was inclined towards the Stoics, although he didn't talk much about it. He usually ate but two meals a day, worked with the servants, and wrote this in his diary, "Men are made for each other: even the inferior for the superior, and these for the sake of one another."

This philosophy of the Stoics rather appealed to the widow Lucilla, also, and she read Zeno with Aurelius Antoninus. Verus did not object to it—he had been a soldier and knew the advantages of doing without things and of being able to make the things you needed, and of living simply and being plain and direct in all your acts and speech. But Faustina laughed at it all—to her it was preposterous that one should wear plain clothing and no jewelry when he could buy the costliest and best; and why one should eschew wine and meat and live on brown bread and fruit and cold water, when he could just as well have spiced and costly dishes—all this was clear beyond her. Various fetes and banquets were given by Faustina, to which the young nobles were invited. She was a beautiful woman and never for a moment forgot it, and by some mistake or accident she got herself betrothed to three men at the same time. Two of these fought a duel and one was killed. The third man looked on and hoped both would be killed, for then he could have the woman. Faustina got this third man to challenge the survivor, and then by one of those strange somersaults of fate the unexpected occurred.

Faustina and Aurelius Antoninus were married.

It was a most queer mismating, for the man was plain, sincere and honorable, and she was almost everything else. Yet she had wit and she had beauty, and Aurelius had been living in the desert so long he imagined that all women were gentle and good. The Consul was very glad to unite his house with so fine and excellent a man as Aurelius; Lucilla cried for two days and more and little Marcus cried because his mother did, and neither cried because Faustina had gone away.

But grief is transient.

In a little over a year Antoninus and Faustina came back to Rome, and brought with them a little girl baby, Faustina Second. Marcus was very much interested in this baby, and made great plans about how they would play together when she got older.

Among other visitors at the house of the old Consul often came the Emperor himself. Hadrian and Verus were Spaniards and had been soldiers together, and now Hadrian often liked to get away from the cares of State, and in the evening hide himself from the office-seekers and flattering parasites, in the quiet villa on Mount Cœlius—he liked it here even better than at his own wonderful gardens at Tivoli. And little Marcus wasn't afraid of him, either. Marcus would sit on the Emperor's knee and listen to tales about hunting wild boars and bears, or men as wild. Then they would play tag or I-spy among the bushes and trees; and once Marcus dared the Emperor to climb the long ladder to the lookout in the big cedar. Hadrian accepted the challenge and climbed to the crow's-nest and cut his initials in the trunk of the tree.

Instead of calling the boy Marcus Verus, the Emperor gave him the name "Verissimus," which means "the open-eyed truthful one," and this name stuck to Marcus for life.

Between Antoninus and Marcus there grew up a very close friendship. Antoninus could scale the ladder up the tall cedar, three rungs at a time, and come down hand over hand without putting his foot on a rest.

He and Marcus built another crow's-nest thirty feet above the first. They drew up the lumber by ropes, and Antoninus being sinewy and strong climbed up first, and with thongs and nails they fixed the boards in place, and made a rope ladder such as sailors make, that they could pull up after them so no one could reach them. When the kind old Emperor came to the villa they showed him what they had done. He said he would not try to climb up now as he had a touch of rheumatism. But a light was fixed in the upper lookout, drawn up by a cord, so they could signal to the Emperor down at the palace.

Then Antoninus taught Marcus to ride horseback and pick up a spear off the ground, with his horse at a gallop. This was great sport for the Consul and the Emperor, who looked on, but they did not try it then, but said they would later on when they were feeling just right.

And beside all this Aurelius Antoninus taught Marcus to read from Epictetus, and told him how this hunchback slave, Epictetus, who was owned by a man who had been a slave himself, was one of the sweetest, gentlest souls who had ever lived. Together they read the Stoic-slave philosopher and made notes from him. And so impressed was Marcus that, boy though he was, he adopted the simple robe of the Stoics, slept on a plank, and made his life and language plain, truthful and direct.

This was all rather amusing to those near him—to all except Antoninus and the boy's mother. The others said, "Leave him alone and he'll get over it."

Faustina was still fond of admiration—the simple, studious ways of her husband were not to her liking. He was twenty years her senior, and she demanded gaiety as her right. Her delight was to tread the borderline of folly, and see how close she could come to the brink and not step off. Julius Cæsar's wife was put away on suspicion, but Faustina was worse than that! She would go down to the city to masquerades, leaving her little girl at home, and be gone for three days.

When she returned Aurelius Antoninus spoke no word of anger or reproof. Her father said to her, "Beware! your husband's patience has a limit. If he divorces you, I shall not blame him; and even if he should kill you, Roman law will not punish him!"

But long years after, Marcus, in looking back on those days, wrote: "His patience knew no limit; he treated her as a perverse child, and he once said to me: 'I pity and love her. I will not put her away—this were selfish. How can her follies injure me? We are what we are, and no one can harm us but ourselves. The mistakes of those near us afford us an opportunity for self-control—we will not imitate their errors, but rather strive to avoid them. In this way what might be a great humiliation has its benefits.'"

Let no one imagine, however, that the tolerance of Antoninus was the soft acquiescence of weakness. After his death Marcus wrote: "Whatsoever excellent thing he had planned to do, he carried out with a persistency that nothing could divert. If he punished men, it was by allowing them to be led by their own folly—his foresight, wisdom and calm deliberation were beyond those of any man I ever knew."

The studious, direct and manly ways of Marcus were not cast aside when he put on the toga virilis, as Faustina had predicted. In spite of the difference in their ages, Antoninus and Marcus mutually sustained each other.

Little Faustina was much more like her father than her mother, and very early showed her preference for her father's society. Marcus was her playmate and taught her to ride a pony astride, just as her father had taught him. The three would often ride over to the village of Lorium, twelve miles from Rome, where Antoninus had a summer villa. At Lanuvium, near at hand, the Emperor spent a part of his time, and he would occasionally join the party and listen to Marcus recite from Cicero and Cæsar.

When Marcus was sixteen, Hadrian appointed him prefect of festivities in Rome, to take the place of the regular officer, a man of years, who was out of the city. So well did Marcus fill the place and make up his report, that when they again met, the old Emperor kissed his cheek, calling him, "My brave Verissimus," and said, "If I had a son, I would want him just like you."

Not long after this the Emperor was taken violently ill. He called his counselors about his bedside and directed that Aurelius Antoninus should be his successor, and that, further, Antoninus should adopt Marcus Verus, so that Marcus should succeed Aurelius Antoninus.

Hadrian loved Marcus for his own sake, and he loved him, too, for the sake of the grandfather, his old soldier comrade, Annius Verus; and beside that he was intent on preserving the Spanish strain.

In a short time Hadrian passed away, and Aurelius Antoninus was crowned Emperor of Rome, and Marcus Verus, aged seventeen, slim, slender and studious, took the name, Marcus Aurelius.

The new reign did not begin under very favorable auspices. There was a prejudice against the Spanish blood, and Hadrian had alienated some of the aristocrats by measures they considered too democratic.

Aurelius Antoninus knew of these prejudices toward his predecessor and he boldly met them by carrying the ashes of Hadrian to the Senate, demanding that the dead Emperor should be enrolled among the gods. So earnest and convincing was his eulogy of the great man gone, that a vote was taken and the resolution passed without a dissenting voice. This gives us a slight clew to the genesis of the gods, and also reveals to us the character of Antoninus. He so impressed the Senate that this honorable body thought best to waive all matters of difference, and in pretty compliment they voted to bestow on the new Emperor the degree of "Pius." Antoninus Pius was a man born to rule—in little things, lenient, but firm at the right time. Faustina still had her little social dissipations, but as she was not allowed to mix in affairs of State, her pink person was not a political factor.

Marcus Aurelius was only seventeen years old: his close studies had robbed him of a bit of the robust health a youth should have. But horseback-riding and daily outdoor games finally got him back into good condition. He was the secretary and companion of the Emperor wherever he went.

Great responsibilities confronted these two strong men. In point of intellect and aspiration they were far beyond the people they governed—so far, indeed, that they were almost isolated. There was a multitude of slaves and consequently there was a feeling everywhere that useful work was degrading. The tendency of the slave-owner is always toward profligacy and conspicuous waste. To do away with slavery was out of the question—that was a matter of time and education—the ruler can never afford to get much in advance of his people. The court was infected with parasites in the way of informers and busybodies who knew no way to thrive except through intrigue. Superstitions were taught by hypocritical priests in order to make the people pay tithes; and attached to the state religion were soothsayers, fortune-tellers, astrologers, gamblers and many pretenders who waxed fat by ministering to ignorance and depravity. These were the cheerful parasites mentioned as "money-changers" a hundred years before, that infested the entrance to every temple.

Many long consultations did the Emperor and his adopted son have concerning the best policy to pursue. They could have issued an edict and swept the wrongs out of existence, but they knew that folly sprouts from a disordered brain, and so they did not treat a symptom: the disease was ignorance, the symptom, superstition. For themselves they kept an esoteric doctrine, and for the many they did what they could.

Twenty-three years of probation lay before Marcus Aurelius—years of study, work, and patient endeavor. He shared in all the honors of the Emperor and bore his part of the burden as well. Never did he thirst for more power—the responsibilities of the situation saddened him—there was so much to be done and he could do so little. Well does Dean Farrar call him "a seeker after God."

The office of young Marcus Aurelius at first was that of Questor, which literally means a messenger, but the word with the Romans meant more—an emissary or an ambassador. When Marcus was eighteen he read to the Senate all speeches and messages from the Emperor; and in a few years more he wrote the messages as well as delivered them. And all the time his education was being carried along by competent instructors.

One of these teachers, Fronto, has come down to us, his portrait well etched on history's tablets, because he saved all the letters written him by Marcus Aurelius; and his grandchildren published them in order to show the excellence of true scientific teaching. That old Fronto was a dear old dear, these letters do fully attest. When Marcus went away on a little journey, even to Lorium, he wrote a letter to Fronto telling about the trip—the sheep by the wayside, the dogs that herded them, the shower they saw coming across the Campagna, and incidentally a little freshman philosophy mixed in, for Fronto had cautioned his pupil always to write out a great thought when it came, for fear he would never have another. Marcus was a sprightly letter-writer, and must have been a quick observer, and Fronto's gentle claims that he made the man are worthy of consideration. As a literary exercise the daily theme, prompted by love, can never be improved upon. The way to learn to write is to write. And Pronto, who resorted to many little tricks in order to get his pupil to express himself, was a teacher whose name should be written high. The correspondence-school has many advantages—Fronto purposely sent his pupil away or absented himself, that the carefully formulated or written thought might take the place of the free and easy conversation. In one letter Marcus ends: "The day was perfect but for one thing—you were not here. But then if you were here, I would not now have the pleasure of writing to you, so thus is your philosophy proved: that all good is equalized, and love grows through separation!" This sounds a bit preachy, but is valuable, as it reveals the man to whom it is written: the person to whom we write dictates the message.

Fronto's habit of giving a problem to work out was quite as good a teaching plan as anything we have to offer now. Thus: "An ambassador of Rome visiting an outlying province attended a gladiatorial contest. And one of the fighters being indisposed, the ambassador replied to a taunt by putting on a coat of mail and going into the ring to kill the lion. Question, was this action commendable? If so, why, and if not, why not?"

The proposition was one that would appeal at once to a young man, and thus did Fronto lead his pupils to think and express.

Another teacher that Marcus had was Rusticus, a blunt old farmer turned pedagog, who has added a word to our language. His pupils were called Rusticana, and later plain rustics. That Rusticus developed in Marcus a deal of plain, sturdy commonsense there is no doubt. Rusticus had a way of stripping a subject of its gloss and verbiage—going straight to the vital point of every issue. For the wisdom of Marcus' legal opinions Rusticus deserves more than passing credit.

For the youth who was destined to be the next Emperor of Rome, there was no dearth of society if he chose to accept it. Managing mammas were on every corner, and kind kinsmen consented to arrange matters with this heiress or that. For the frivolities of society Marcus had no use—his hours were filled with useful work or application to his books. His father and Fronto we find were both constantly urging him to get out more in the sunshine and meet more people, and not bother too much about the books.

How best to curtail over-application, I am told, is a problem that seldom faces a teacher.

As for society as a matrimonial bazaar, Marcus Aurelius could not see that it had its use. He was afraid of it—afraid of himself, perhaps. He loved the little Faustina. They had been comrades together, and played "keep house" under the olive-trees at Lorium; and had ridden their ponies over the hills. Once Marcus and Faustina, on a ride across the country, bought a lamb out of the arms of a shepherd, and kept it until it grew great curling horns, and made visitors scale the wall or climb trees. Then three priests led it away to sacrifice, and Marcus and Faustina fell into each other's arms and rained tears down each other's backs, and refused to be comforted. What if their father was an Emperor, and Marcus would be some day! It would not bring back Beppo, with his innocent lamblike ways, and make him get down on his knees and wag his tail when they fed him out of a pail! Beppo always got on his knees to eat, and showed his love and humility before he grew his horns and reached the age of indiscretion; then he became awfully wicked, and it took three stout priests to lead him away and sacrifice him to the gods for his own good!

But gradually the grass grew on Beppo's make-believe grave in the garden, and Fronto's problems filled the vacuum in their hearts. Fronto gave his lessons to Marcus, and Marcus gave them to Faustina—thus do we keep things by giving them away.

But problems greater than pet sheep grown ribald and reckless were to confront Marcus and Faustina. They had both been betrothed to others, years before, and this they now resented. They talked of this much, and then suddenly ceased to talk of it, and each evaded mentioning it, and pretended they never thought of it. Then they explosively began again—began as suddenly to talk of it, and always when they met they mentioned it. Folks called them brother and sister—they were not brother and sister, only cousins.

Finally the matter was brought to Antoninus, and he pretended that he had never thought about it; but in fact he had thought of little else for a long time. And Antoninus said that if they loved each other very much, and he was sure they did, why, it was the will of the gods that they should marry, and he never interfered with the will of the gods; so he kissed them both and cried a few foolish tears, a thing an Emperor should never do.

So they were married at the country seat at Lorium, out under the orange-trees as was often the custom, for orange-trees are green the year 'round, and bear fruit and flowers at the same time, and the flowers are very sweet, and the fruit is both beautiful and useful—and these things symbol constancy and fruitfulness and good luck, and that is why we yet have orange-blossoms at weddings and play the "Lohengrin March," which is orange-trees expressed in sweet sounds.

Marcus was only twenty, and Faustina could not have been over sixteen—we do not know her exact age. There are stories to the effect that the wife of Marcus Aurelius severely tried her husband's temper at times, but these tales seem to have arisen through a confusion of the two Faustinas. The elder Faustina was the one who set the merry pace in frivolity, and once said that any woman with a husband twenty years her senior must be allowed a lover or two—goodness gracious!

As far as we know, the younger Faustina was a most loyal and loving wife, the mother of a full dozen children. Coins issued by Marcus Aurelius stamped with the features of his wife, and the inscription Concordia, Faustina and Venus Felix, attest the felicity, or "felixity," of the marriage.

Their oldest boy, Commodus, was very much like his grandmother, Faustina, and a man who knows all about the Law of Heredity tells me that children are much more apt to resemble their grandparents than their father and mother.

I believe I once said that no house is big enough for two families, but this truth is like the Greek verb—it has many exceptions. In the same house with Emperor Antoninus Pius dwelt Lucilla, mother of Marcus, and Marcus and his wife. And they were all very happy—but life was rather more peaceful after the death of Faustina, the elder, which occurred a few years after her husband became Emperor.

She could not endure prosperity.

But her husband mourned her death and made a public speech in eulogy of her, determined that only the best should be remembered of one who had been the wife of an Emperor and the mother of his children. As far as we know, Antoninus never spoke a word concerning his wife except in praise, not even when she left his house to be gone for months.

It was Ouida, she of the aqua-fortis ink, who said, "A woman married to a man as good as Antoninus must have been very miserable, for while men who are thoroughly bad are not lovable, yet a man who is not occasionally bad is unendurable." And so Ouida's heart went out in sympathy and condolence to the two Faustinas, who wedded the only two men mentioned in Roman history who were infinitely wise and good.

In one of his essays, Richard Steele writes this, "No woman ever loved a man through life with a mighty love if the man did not occasionally abuse her." I give the remark for what it is worth. However, Montesquieu somewhere says that the chief objection to heaven is its monotony; so possibly there may be something in the Ouida-Steele philosophy—but of this I really can't say, knowing nothing about the subject, myself.

Happy is the man who has no history. The reign of Antoninus Pius was peaceful and prosperous. No great wars nor revulsions occurred, and the times made for education and excellence. Antoninus worked to conserve the good, and that he succeeded, Gibbon says, there is no doubt. He left the country in better condition than he found it, and he could have truthfully repeated the words of Pericles, "I have made no person wear crape."

But there came a day when Antoninus was stricken by the hand of death. The captain of the guard came to him and asked for the password for the night. "Equanimity," replied the Emperor, and turning on his side, sank into sleep, to awake no more. His last word symbols the guiding impulse of his life. Well does Renan say: "Simple, loving, full of sweet gaiety, Antoninus was a philosopher without saying so, almost without knowing it. Marcus was a philosopher, but often consciously, and he became a philosopher by study and reflection, aided and encouraged by the older man. You can not consider the one man and leave the other out, and the early contention that Antoninus was, in fact, the father of Marcus has at least a poetic and spiritual basis in truth."

There was much in Renan's suggestions. The greatest man is he who works his philosophy up into life—this is better than to talk about it. We only discuss that to which we have not attained, and the virtues we talk most of are those beyond us. The ideal outstrips the actual. But it is no discredit that a man pictures more than he realizes—such a one is preparing the way for others. Marcus Antoninus has been a guiding star—an inspiration—to untold millions.

Marcus Aurelius was forty years old when he became Emperor of Rome. At the age of forty a man is safe, if ever: character is formed, and what he will do or become, can be safely presaged.

More than once Rome has repudiated the man in the direct line of accession to the throne, and before Marcus Aurelius took the reins of government he asked the Senate to ratify the people's choice, and thus make it the choice of the gods, and this was done.

As Emperor, we find Marcus endeavored to carry out the policy of his predecessor. He did not favor expansion, but hoped by peace and propitiation to cement the empire and thus work for education, harmony and prosperity.

It is interesting to see how Marcus Aurelius in the year One Hundred Sixty-four was cudgeling his brains concerning problems about which we yet argue and grow red in the face. The Emperor was also Chief Justice, and questions were being constantly brought to him to decide. From him there was no appeal, and his decisions made the law upon which all lesser judges based their rulings. And curiously enough we are dealing most extensively in judge-made law even today.

One vexed question that confronted Marcus was the lessening number of marriages, with a consequent increase in illegitimate births and a gradual dwindling of the free population. He seems to have disliked this word illegitimate, for he says, "All children are beautiful blessings—sent by the gods." But people who were legally married objected to this view, and said to recognize children born out of wedlock as entitled to all the privileges of citizenship is virtually to do away with legal marriage. As a compromise, Marcus decided to recognize all people as married who said they were married. This is exactly our common-law marriage as it exists in various States today.

However, a man could put away his wife at will, and by recording the fact with the nearest pretor, the act was legalized. It will thus be seen that if a man could marry at will and put away his wife at will, there was really no marriage beyond that of nature. To meet the issue, and prevent fickle and unjust men from taking advantage of women, Marcus decided that the pretor could refuse to record the desired divorce, if he saw fit, and demand reasons. We then for the first time get a divorce trial, and on appeal to Marcus, he decided that if the man were in the wrong, he must still support the injured wife.

Then, for the first time, we find women asking for a divorce. Now, nearly three-fourths of all divorces are granted to women; but at first, that a woman should want marital freedom caused a howl of merriment. Marcus was the first Roman Emperor to allow women the right of petition, and the privilege, too, of practising law, for Capitolanus cites various instances of women coming to ask for justice, and women friends coming with them to help plead their case, and the Emperor of Rome, leaning his tired head on his arm, listening for hours with great patience. We also hear of petitions for damages being presented for failure to keep a promise to marry—the action being brought against the girl's father. This would be thought a trifle strange, but an action against a woman for breach of promise is quite in order yet.

Recently the Honorable Henry Ballard of Vermont won heavy damages against a coy and dallying heiress who had played pitch and toss with a good man's heart. The case was carried to the United States Supreme Court and judgment sustained.

The question of marriage and divorce now in the United States is almost precisely where it was in Rome in the time of Marcus Aurelius. No two States have the same marriage-laws, and marriages which are illegal in one State may be made legal in another. Yet with us, any court of jurisdiction may declare any marriage illegal, or set any divorce aside. What makes marriage and what constitutes divorce are matters of opinion in the mind of the judge. We have gone a bit further than Marcus, though, in that we allow couples to marry if they wish, yet divorce is denied if both parties desire it. The fact that they want it is construed as proof that they should not have it. We meet the issue, however, by connivance of the lawyers, who are officers of the court, and a legal fiction is inaugurated by allowing a little bird to tell the judge what decision will be satisfactory to both sides. And in States or countries where no divorce is allowed, marriage can be annulled if you know how—see Ruskin versus Ruskin, Coleridge, J.

Our zealous New Thought friends, who clamor to have marriage made difficult and divorce easy, forget that the whole question has been threshed over for three thousand years, and all schemes tried. The Romans issued marriage-licenses, but before doing so a pretor passed on the fitness of the candidates for each other. This was so embarrassing to many coy couples that they just waived formal proceedings and set up housekeeping. To declare these people lawbreakers, Marcus Aurelius said, would put half of Rome in limbo, just as, if we should technically enforce all laws, it would send most members of the Legislature to the penitentiary. So the Emperor declared de-facto marriage de jure, and for a short time succeeded in striking out the word illegitimate as applied to a person, on the ground that, in justice, no act of a parent could be charged up against and punished in the offspring.

Men who make laws have forever to watch most closely and dance attendance on Nature. Laws which fly in the face of Nature are gently waived or conveniently forgotten. Should Chief Justice Fuller issue an injunction restraining all men from coming within a quarter of a mile of a woman, on penalty of death, we would all place ourselves in contempt in an hour; and should the army try to enforce the order, we would smother Justice Fuller in his wool-sack and hang his effigy on a sour-apple tree. Law isn't worth the paper it is written on unless it embodies the will and natural tendencies of the governed. Where poaching is popular, no law can stop it. Marriage is easy, and divorce difficult, because this is Nature's plan. The natural law of attraction brings men and women together, and it is difficult to separate them. Natural things are easy, and artificial ones difficult. Most couples who desire freedom only think they do: what they really want is a vacation; but they would not separate for good if they could. It is hard to part—people who have lived together grow to need each other. They want some one to quarrel with.

Cæsar Augustus, in his close study of character, introduced a limited divorce. That is, in case of a family quarrel, he ordered the couple to live apart for six months as a penalty. Quintilian says that usually before the expired time the man and woman were surreptitiously living together again, at which the court quietly winked, and finally this form of penalty had to be abandoned because it made the courts ridiculous.

Men and women do not get married because marriage is legal, nor do they continue living together because divorce is difficult. They marry because they desire to, and they do not separate because they do not want to. The task that confronts the legislator is to find out what the people want to do, and then legalize it.

In Rome, the custom of the parties divorcing themselves was prevalent, and the courts were called upon to ratify the act, just to give the matter respectability. Below a certain stratum in society, the formality of legal marriage and divorce was waived entirely, just as it is largely, now, among our colored population in the South. During the French Revolution, the same custom largely obtained in France. And about the year One Hundred Fifty in Rome there was danger that the people would overlook the majesty of the law entirely in their domestic affairs. This condition is what prompted Marcus Aurelius to recognize as legal the common-law marriage and say if a couple called themselves husband and wife, they were. And for a time, if they said they were divorced, they were. But as a mortgage owned by a man on his own property cancels the debt, and legally there is no mortgage, so if the people could get married at will and divorce themselves at their convenience, there really was no legal marriage. Thus the matter was argued. So Marcus adopted the plan of making marriage easy and divorce difficult, and this has been the policy in all civilized countries ever since.

It is very evident, however, that Marcus Aurelius looked forward to a time when men and women would be wise enough, and just enough, to arrange their own affairs, without calling on the police to ratify either their friendships or their misunderstandings. He says:

"Love is beautiful, and that a man and a woman loving each other should live together is the will of God, but if there comes a time when they can not live in peace, let them part. To have no relationship is not a disgrace; to have wrong relations is, for disgrace means lack of grace, discord, and love is harmony."

Marcus Aurelius tried the plan of probationary marriages; and to offset this he also introduced the Augustinian plan of probationary divorces—that is, the interlocutory decree. This scheme has recently been adopted in several States in America with the avowed intent of preventing fraud in divorce procedure, but actually the logic of the situation is the same now as in the time of Marcus Aurelius—it postpones the final decree so as to prevent the couple from becoming the victims of their own rashness, and to give them an opportunity to become reconciled if possible.

So anxious was Marcus Aurelius to decide justly with his people that he found himself swamped with cases of every sort and description. He tried to pass upon each case by its merits, regardless of law and precedent. Then other judges construed his decisions as law, and the lesser courts cited the upper ones, until Gibbon says, "There grew up such a mass of judge-made laws that a skilful lawyer could prove anything, and legal practise swung on the ability to cite similar cases and call attention to desired decisions."

In America we are now back exactly to the same condition. A lawyer in New York State requires over fourteen thousand law-books if he would cover all the ground; and his business is to make it easy for the judge to dispense justice and not dispense with law. That is to say, before a judge can decide a case, he must be able to back up his opinion by precedent. Judges are not elected to deal out justice between man and man; they are elected to decide on points of law. Law is often a great disadvantage to a judge—it may hamper justice—and in America there must surely soon come a day when we will make a bonfire of every law-book in the land, and electing our judges for life, we will make the judiciary free. We will then require our lawyers and judges to read, and pass examinations on Browning's "Ring and the Book," and none other. And if we would follow the Aurelian suggestion of remitting all direct taxes to every citizen who had not been plaintiff in a lawsuit for ten years, we would gradually get something approaching pure justice. The people must be educated to decide quietly and calmly their own disputes, and this can be done only by placing an obvious penalty on litigation. Progress in the future will consist in having less law, and fulfilment will be reached when we have no law at all—each man governing himself, and being willing that his neighbor shall do the same. Trouble arises largely from each man regarding himself as his brother's keeper, and ceasing to be his friend. Marcus Aurelius, the wise judge, saw that most litigation is foolish and absurd—both parties are at fault, and both right. And to bring about the good time when men shall live in peace, he began earnestly to govern himself. His ideal was a state where men would need no governing. Hence his "Meditations," a book which Dean Farrar says is not inferior to the New Testament in its lofty aim and purity of conception.

Every great book is an evolution: Marcus had been getting ready to write this immortal volume for nearly half a century. And now in his fifty-seventh year he found himself in the desert of Asia at the head of the army, endeavoring to put down an insurrection of various barbaric tribes. Later, the seat of war was shifted to the north. The enemy struck and retreated, and danced around him as the Boers fought the English in South Africa.

But Marcus Aurelius had time to think, and so with no books near and all memoranda far away, he began to write out his best thoughts. At first he expressed just for his own satisfaction, but later, as the work progressed, we see that its value grew upon him, and it was his intention to put it in systematic form for posterity. And while working at this task, the exposures of field and camp, and the business of war, in which he had no heart, worked upon him so adversely that he sickened and died, aged fifty-nine.

His body was carried back to Rome and placed by the side of that of his beloved adopted father, Antoninus Pius. And so he sleeps, but the precious legacy of the "Meditations," written during those last two years of travel, turmoil and strife, is ours.

A few quotations seem in order:

Remember, on every occasion which leads thee to vexation, to apply this principle: not that this is a misfortune, but that to bear it nobly is good fortune.

Things do not touch the soul, for they are eternal, and remain immovable; but our perturbations come only from the opinion which is within.... The Universe is transformation; life is opinion.

To the jaundiced, honey tastes bitter; and to those bitten by mad dogs, water causes fear; and to little children, the ball is a fine thing. Why then am I angry? Dost thou think that a false opinion has less power than the bile in the jaundiced, or the poison in him who is bitten by a mad dog?

How easy it is to repel and to wipe away every impression which is troublesome and unsuitable, and immediately to be in all tranquillity!

All things come from the universal Ruling Power, either directly or by way of consequence. And accordingly the lion's gaping jaws, and that which is poisonous, and every hurtful thing, as a thorn, as mud, are after-products of the grand and beautiful. Do not therefore imagine that they are of another kind from that which thou dost venerate, but form a just opinion of the source of all.

Pass through the rest of life like one who has entrusted to the gods, with his whole soul, all that he has, making himself neither the tyrant nor the slave of any man.

Never value anything as profitable to thyself which shall compel thee to break thy promise, to lose thy self-respect, to hate any man, to suspect, to curse, to act the hypocrite, to desire anything which needs walls and curtains.

I am thankful to the gods that I was subjected to a ruler and a father who was able to take away all pride from me, and to bring me to the knowledge that it is possible for a man to live in a palace without wanting either guards or embroidered dresses, or torches and statues, and such-like show; but that it is in such a man's power to bring himself very near to the fashion of a private person, without being, for this reason, either meaner in thought or more remiss in action, with respect to the things which must be done for the public interest in a manner that befits a ruler.

What more dost thou want when thou hast done a man a service? Art thou not content that thou hast done something conformable to thy nature, and dost thou seek to be paid for it? Just as if the eye demanded a recompense for seeing, or the feet for walking. As a horse when he has run, a dog when he has traced the game, a bee when it has made the honey, so a man, when he has done a good act, does not call out for others to come and see, but goes on to another act, as a vine goes on to produce again the grapes in season.

Accustom thyself to attend carefully to what is said by another, and as much as it is possible, be in the speaker's mind.

Some things are hurrying into existence, and others are hurrying out of it; and of that which is coming into existence, part is already extinguished. Motions and changes are continually renewing the world, just as the uninterrupted course of time is always renewing the infinite duration of ages.

Understand that every man is worth just so much as the things are worth about which he busies himself.

Wickedness does no harm at all to the universe—it is only harmful to him who has it in his power to be released from it.

Nothing is more wretched than a man who traverses everything in a round, and pries into the things beneath the earth, as the poet says, and seeks by conjecture what is in the minds of his neighbors, without perceiving that it is sufficient to attend to the deity within him, and to reverence it sincerely.

The prayers of Marcus Aurelius to the gods are for one thing only—that their will be done. All else is vain, all else is rebellion against the universe itself. Our form of worship should be like this: Everything harmonizes with me which is harmonious to thee, O Universe. Nothing for me is too early nor too late, which is in due time for thee. Everything is fruit to me which thy seasons bring, O Nature: from thee are all things, in thee are all things, to thee all things return.

In the morning when thou risest unwillingly, let this thought be present—I am rising to the work of a human being. Why, then, am I dissatisfied if I am going to do the things for which I exist, and for which I was brought into the world? Or have I been made for this, to lie in the bedclothes and keep myself warm? But this is more pleasant. Dost thou exist, then, to take thy pleasure, and not for action or exertion? Dost thou not see the little plants, the little birds, the ants, the spiders, the bees, working together to put in order their several parts of the universe? And art thou unwilling to do the work of a human being, and dost thou not make haste to do that which is according to thy nature?

Judge every word and deed which are according to Nature to be fit for thee, and be not diverted by the blame which follows.... But if a thing is good to be done or said, do not consider it unworthy of thee.

Since it is possible that thou mayest depart from life this very moment, regulate every act and thought accordingly.... Death certainly, and life, honor and dishonor, pain and pleasure, all these things equally happen to good men and bad, being things which make us neither better nor worse. Therefore they are neither good nor evil.

To say all in a word, everything which belongs to the body is a stream, and what belongs to the soul is a dream and vapor; and life is a warfare, and a stranger's sojourn, and after fame is oblivion. What, then, is that which is able to enrich a man? One thing, and only one—philosophy. But this consists in keeping the guardian spirit within a man free from violence and unharmed, superior to pains and pleasures, doing nothing without a purpose, nor yet falsely, and with hypocrisy ... accepting all that happens and all that is allotted ... and finally waiting for death with a cheerful mind.

If thou findest in human life anything better than justice, truth, temperance, fortitude, and, in a word, than thine own soul's satisfaction in the things which it enables thee to do according to right reason, and in the condition that is assigned to thee without thy own choice; if, I say, thou seest anything better than this, turn to it with all thy soul, and enjoy that which thou hast found to be the best. But ... if thou findest everything else smaller and of less value than this, give place to nothing else.... Simply and freely choose the better, and hold to it.

Men seek retreats for themselves, houses in the country, seashores, and mountains; and thou too art wont to desire such things very much. But this is altogether a mark of the most common sort of men, for it is in thy power whenever thou shalt choose to retire into thyself. For nowhere either with more quiet or more freedom from trouble does a man retire than into his own soul, particularly when he has within him such thoughts that by looking into them he is immediately in perfect tranquillity—which is nothing else than the good ordering of the mind.

Unhappy am I, because this has happened to me? Not so, but happy am I though this has happened to me, because I continue free from pain; neither crushed by the present nor fearing the future.

Be cheerful, and seek no external help, nor the tranquillity which others give. A man must stand erect, not be kept erect by others.

Be like the promontory against which the waves continually break, but it stands firm and tames the fury of the water around it.

It is not fit that I should give myself pain, for I have never intentionally given pain even to another.

IMMANUEL KANT

The canons of scientific evidence justify us neither in accepting nor rejecting the ideas upon which morality and religion repose. Both parties to the dispute beat the air; they worry their own shadow; for they pass from Nature into the domain of speculation, where their dogmatic grips find nothing to lay hold upon. The shadows which they hew to pieces grow together in a moment like the heroes in Valhalla, to rejoice again in bloodless battles. Metaphysics can no longer claim to be the cornerstone of religion and morality. But if she can not be the Atlas that bears the moral world she can furnish a magic defense. Around the ideas of religion she throws her bulwark of invisibility; and the sword of the skeptic and the battering-ram of the materialist fall harmless on vacuity.

IMMANUEL KANT

We find that most men fit easily into types. You describe to me one Durham cow and you picture all Durham cows. So it is with men: they belong to breeds, which we politely call denominations, sects or parties. Tell me the man's sect, and I know his dress, his habit of life, his thought. His dress is the uniform of his party, and his thought is that which is ordered and prescribed. Dull indeed is the intellect which can not correctly prophesy the opinions to which this man will arrive on any subject.

Durham cows are not exactly alike, I well know, but a trifle more length of leg, a variation in color, or an off-angle of the horn, and that cow is forever barred from exhibition as a Durham. She is fit only for beef, and the first butcher that makes a bid takes her, hide and horns.

Members of sects do not think exactly alike, but there are well-defined limits of thought and action, beyond which they dare not stray lest the butcher bag them. In joining a sect they have given bonds to uniformity, and have signed their willingness to think and act like all other members of the sect.

Herbert Spencer deals with this "jiner" propensity in man, and describes it as a manifestation of the herding instinct in animals. It is a combination for mutual protection—a social contract, each one waiving a part of his personality in order to secure a supposed benefit. A herd of cattle can stand against a pack of wolves, but a cow alone is doomed.

Few men indeed can stand against the pack. Wise are the many who seek safety in numbers! Think of those who have stood out alone and expressed their individuality, and you count on your fingers God's patriots dead and turned to dust.

The paradox of things is shown in that the entrenched many, having found safety in aggregation, pay their debt of homage to the bold few who lived their lives and paid the penalty by death.

Across the disk of existence, each decade, there glide five hundred million souls, and disappear forever in the dim and dusk of the eternity that lies behind. Out of the bare handful that are remembered, we cherish only the memories of those who stood alone and expressed their honest, inmost thought. And this thought is, always and forever, the thought of liberty. Exile, ostracism, death, have been their fate, and on the smoke of martyr-fires their souls mounted to immortality.

Future generations often confuse these men with Deity, the Maker of the Worlds. And thus do we arrive at truth by indirection, for in very fact these were the Sons of God, vitalized by Divinity, part and parcel of the Power that guides the planets on their way and holds the worlds in space. Upon their tombs we carve a single word: *Savior*.

Kant was sixty years old before he was known to any extent beyond his native town; but so fast then did his fame travel that at his death it was recognized that the greatest thinker of the world had passed away. Kant founded no school; but Fichte, Schelling, Hegel, Herde and Schopenhauer were all his children—and all but Schopenhauer showed their humanity by denouncing him, for men are prone to revile that which has benefited them most. Kant marks an epoch and all thinkers who came after him are his debtors. His philosophy has passed into the current coin of knowledge.

Kant's lifelong researches revolve around four propositions:
1. Who am I?
2. What am I?
3. What can I do?
4. What can I know?

The answer to Number Four is that I can not know anything. That is to say, the wise man is the man who knows that he does not know. And this disposes of Number One and Number Two, leaving only Number Three for our consideration. It took, however, a good many years and a vast amount of study and writing for Kant to thus simplify. For years he toiled with algebraic formulas and syllogistic theorems before he concluded that the best wisdom of life lies in simplification, not complexity.

"What can I do?" resolves itself into, "What must I do?" And the answer is: You must do four things in order to retain your place as a normal being upon this earth: eat, work, associate with your kind, rest. Just four things we must do, and outside of this everything is incidental, accidental, irrelevant and inconsequential. Then how to eat, work, associate and rest wisely and best constitutes life. Every man should be free to work out these four equations for himself, his freedom ending where another man's rights begin. To these four questions we should bring our highest reason, our ripest experience and our best endeavor. As for himself we know that Kant made a schedule of life which evolved a sickly boy into a reasonably strong man who banished pain, sorrow and regret from his existence and lived a long life of deep, quiet satisfaction, sane to the end, watching every symptom of approaching dissolution with keen interest, and at the last passing into quiet sleep, his spirit gliding peacefully away, perhaps to answer those two great questions which he said were unanswerable here: "Who am I?" "What am I?"

Immanuel Kant was born in Seventeen Hundred Twenty-four at the City of Konigsberg, in the northeastern corner of Prussia. There he received his education; there he was a teacher for nearly half a century; and there, in his eightieth year, he died. He was never out of East Prussia and never journeyed sixty miles from his birthplace during his whole life. Professor Josiah Royce of Harvard, himself in the sage business, and perhaps the best example that America has produced of the pure type of philosopher, says, "Kant is the only modern thinker who in point of originality is worthy to be ranked with Plato and Aristotle." Like Emerson, Kant regarded traveling as a fool's paradise; only Emerson had to travel much before he found it out, while Kant gained the truth by staying at home. Once a lady took him for a carriage ride, and on learning from the footman that they were seven miles from home he was so displeased that he refused to utter a single orphic on the way back; and further, the story is that he never after entered a vehicle, and living for thirty years was never again so far from the lodging he called home.

In his lectures on physical geography Kant would often describe mountains, rivers, waterfalls, volcanoes, with great animation and accuracy, yet he had never seen any of these. Once a friend offered to take him to Switzerland, so he could actually see the mountains; but he warmly declined, declaring that the man who was not satisfied until he could touch, taste and see was small, mean and quibbling as was Thomas, the doubting disciple. Moreover, he had samples of the strata of the Alps, and this was enough, which reminds us of the man who had a house for sale and offered to send a prospective purchaser a sample brick.

Mind was the great miracle to Kant—the ability to know all about a thing by seeing it with your inward eye. "The Imagination hath a stage within the brain upon which all scenes are played," and the play to Kant was greater than the reality. Or, to use his own words: "Time and Space have no existence apart from Mind. There is no such thing as Sound unless there be an ear to receive the vibrations. Things and places, matter and substance come under the same law, and exist only as mind creates them."

The parents of Kant were very lowly people. His father was a day laborer—a leather-cutter who never achieved even to the honors and emoluments of a saddler. There were seven children in the family, and never a servant crossed the threshold. One daughter survived Immanuel, and in her eighty-fourth year she expressed regrets that her brother had proved so recreant to the teachings of his parents as practically to alienate him from all his relatives. One brother became a Lutheran minister and lived out an honored career; the others vanish and fade away into the mist of forgetfulness.

So far as we know, all the children were strong and well except this one. At birth he weighed but five pounds, and his weakness was pitiable. He was the kind of child the Spartans used to make way with quickly, for the good of the State. He had a big, bulging head, thin legs, a weak chest, and one shoulder was so much higher than the other that it amounted almost to a deformity.

As the years went by, the parents saw he was not big enough to work, but hope was not dead—they would make a preacher of him! To this end he was sent to the "Fredericianium," a graded school of no mean quality. The master of this school was a worthy clergyman by the name of Schultz, who was attracted to the Kant boy, it seems, on account of his insignificant size. It was the affection of the shepherd for the friendless ewe lamb. A little later the teacher began to love the boy for his big head and the thoughts he worked out of it. Brawn is bought with a price—young men who bank on it get it as legal tender. Those who have no brawn have to rely on brain or go without honors. Immanuel Kant began to ask his school-teacher questions that made the good man laugh.

At sixteen Kant entered Albertina University. And there he was to remain his entire life—student, tutor, teacher, professor.

He must have been an efficient youth, for before he was eighteen he realized that the best way to learn is to teach. The idea of becoming a clergyman was at first strong upon him; and Pastor Schultz occasionally sent the youth out to preach, or lead religious services in rural districts. This embryo preacher had a habit of placing a box behind the pulpit and standing on it while preaching. Then we find him reasoning the matter out in this way: "I stand on a box to preach so as to impress the people by my height or to conceal my insignificant size. This is pretense and a desire to carry out the idea that the preacher is bigger every way than common people. I talk with God in pretended prayer, and this looks as if I were on easy and familiar terms with Deity. Is it like those folks who claim to be on friendly terms with princes: If I do not know anything about God, why should I pretend I do?"

This desire to be absolutely honest with himself gradually grew until he informed the Pastor that he had better secure young men for preachers who could impress people without standing on a box. As for himself, he would impress people by the size of his head, if he impressed them at all. Let it here be noted that Kant then weighed exactly one hundred pounds, and was less than five feet high. His head measured twenty-four inches around, and fifteen and one-half inches over "firmness" from the opening of the ears. To put it another way, he wore a seven-and-a-half hat.

It is a great thing for a man to pride himself on what he is and make the best of it. The pride of craftsman betokens a valuable man. We exaggerate our worth, and this is Nature's plan to get the thing done.

Kant's pride of intellect, in degree, came from his insignificant form, and thus do all things work together for good. But this bony little form was often full of pain, and he had headaches, which led a wit to say, "If a head like yours aches, it must be worse than to be a giraffe and have a sore throat."

Young Kant began to realize that to have a big head, and get the right use from it, one must have vital power enough to feed it.

The brain is the engine—the lungs and digestive apparatus the boiler. Thought is combustion.

Young Kant, the uncouth, became possessed of an idea that made him the butt of many gibes and jeers. He thought that if he could breathe enough, he would be able to think clearly, and headaches would be gone. Life, he said, was a matter of breathing, and all men died from one cause—a shortness of breath. In order to think clearly, you must breathe.

We believe things first and prove them later; our belief is usually right, when derived from experience, but the reasons we give are often wrong. For instance, Kant cured his physical ills by going out of doors, and breathing deeply and slowly with closed mouth. Gradually his health began to improve. But the young man, not knowing at that time much about physiology, wrote a paper proving that the benefit came from the fresh air that circulated through his brain. And of course in one sense he was right. He related the incident of this thesis many years after in a lecture, to show the result of right action and wrong reasoning.

The doctors had advised Kant he must quit study, but when he took up his breathing fad, he renounced the doctors, and later denounced them. If he were going to die, he would die without the benefit of either the clergy or the physicians.

He denied that he was sick, and at night would roll himself in his blankets and repeat half-aloud, "How comfortable I am, how comfortable I am," until he fell asleep.

Near his house ran a narrow street, just a half-mile long. He walked this street up and back, with closed mouth, breathing deeply, waving a rattan cane to ward away talkative neighbors, and to keep up the circulation in his arms. Once and back—in a month he had increased this to twice and back. In a year he had come to the conclusion that to walk the length of that street eight times was the right and proper thing—that is to say, four miles in all. In other words, he had found out how much exercise he required—not too much or too little. At exactly half-past three he came out of his lodging, wearing his cocked hat and long, snuff-colored coat, and walked. The neighbors used to set their clocks by him. He walked and breathed with closed mouth, and no one dare accost him or walk with him. The hour was sacred and must not be broken in upon: it was his holy time—his time of breathing.

The little street is there now—one of the sights of Konigsberg, and the cab-drivers point it out as the Philosopher's Walk. And Kant walked that little street eight times every afternoon from the day he was twenty to within a year of his death, when eighty years old.

This walking and breathing habit physiologists now recognize as eminently scientific, and there is no sensible physician but will endorse Kant's wisdom in renouncing doctors and adopting a regimen of his own. The thing you believe in will probably benefit you—faith is hygienic.

The persistency of the little man's character is shown in the breathing habit—he believed in himself, relied on himself, and that which experience commended, he did.

This firmness in following his own ideas saved his life. When we think of one born in obscurity, living in poverty, handicapped by pain, weakness and deformity; never traveling; and then by sheer persistency and force of will rising to the first place among thinking men of his time, one is almost willing to accept Kant's dictum, "Mind is supreme, and the Universe is but the reflected thought of God."

Kant was great enough to doubt appearances and distrust popular conclusions. He knew that fallacies of reasoning follow fast upon actions—reason follows by slow freight. It is quite necessary that we should believe in a Supreme Power, but quite irrelevant that we should prove it.

Truth for the most part is unpopular, and the proof of this statement lies in the fact that it is so seldom told. Preachers tell people what they wish to hear, and indeed this must be so as long as the congregation that hears the preaching pays for it. People will not pay for anything they do not like. Hence, preaching leads naturally to sophistication and hypocrisy, and the promise of endless bliss for ourselves and a hell for our enemies comes about as a matter of course. What men will listen to and pay for is the real science of theology. That is to say, the science of theology is the science of manipulating men. Success in theology consists in finding a fallacy that is palatable and then banking on it. Again and again Kant points out that a clergyman's advice is usually worthless, because pure truth is out of his province—unaccustomed, undesirable, inexpedient.

And Kant thought this was true also of doctors—doctors care more about pleasing their patients than telling them truth. "In fact," he said, "no doctor with a family to support can afford to tell his patients that his symptoms are no token of a disease—rather uncomfortable feelings are proof of health, for dead men don't have them." Most of the aches, pains and so-called irregularities are remedial moves on the part of Nature to keep the man well. Kant says that doctors treat symptoms, not diseases, and often the treatment causes the disease; so no man can tell what proportion of diseases is caused by medicine and what by other forms of applied ignorance.

As for lawyers, our little philosopher considered them, for the most part, sharks and wreckers. A lawyer looks over an estate, not with the idea of keeping it intact, but of dissolving it, and getting a part of it for himself. Not that men prefer to do what is wrong, but self-interest can always produce sufficient reasons to satisfy the conscience. Lawyers, being attaches of courts of justice, regard themselves as protectors of the people, when really they are the plunderers of the people, and their business is quite as much to defeat justice as to administer it. The evasion of law is as truly a lawyer's work as compliance with law. Then our philosopher explains that if law and justice were synonymous, this state of affairs would be most deplorable; but as it is, no particular harm is worked, save in the moral degradation of the lawyers. The connivance of lawyers tames the rank injustices of law; hence, to a degree, we live in a land where there is neither law nor justice—save such justice as can be appropriated by the man who is diplomat enough to do without lawyers and wise enough to have no property. Justice, however, to Kant is a very uncertain quantity, and he is rather inclined to regard the idea that men are able to administer justice as on a par with the assumption of the priest that he is dealing with God.

Kant once said, "When a woman demands justice, she means revenge."

A pupil here interposed, and asked the master if this was not equally true of men, and the answer was, "I accept the amendment—it certainly is true of all men I ever saw in courtrooms."

"Does death end all?"

"No," said Kant; "there is the litigation over the estate."

Kant's constant reiteration that he had no use for doctors, lawyers and preachers, we can well imagine did not add to his popularity. As for his reasoning concerning lawyers, we can all, probably, recall a few jug-shaped attorneys who fill the Kant requirements—takers of contingent fees and stirrers-up of strife: men who watch for vessels on the rocks and lure with false lights the mariner to his doom. But matters since Kant's day have changed considerably for the better. There is a demand now for a lawyer who is a businessman and who will keep people out of trouble instead of getting them in. And we also have a few physicians who are big enough to tell a man there is nothing the matter with him, if they think so, and then charge him accordingly—in inverse ratio to the amount of medicine administered.

And while we no longer refer to the clergyman as our spiritual adviser, except, perhaps, in way of pleasantry, he surely is useful as a social promoter.

The parents of Kant were Lutherans—punctilious and pious. They were descended from Scotch soldiers who had come over there two hundred years before and settled down after the war, just as the Hessians settled down and went to farming in Pennsylvania, their descendants occasionally becoming Daughters of the Revolution, because their grandsires fought with Washington.

This Scotch strain gave a sturdy bias to the Kants—these Lutherans were really rebels, and as every one knows, there are only two ways of dealing with a religious Scotchman—agree with him or kill him.

Most people said that Kant was supremely stubborn—he himself called it "firmness in the right." Once, when a couple of calumniators were thinking up all the bad things they could say about him, one of them exclaimed, "He isn't five feet high!"

"Liar!" came the shrill voice of the Philosopher, who had accidentally overheard them, "Liar! I am exactly five feet!" And he drew himself up, and struck his staff proudly and defiantly on the ground.

Which reminds one of the story told of Professor Josiah Royce, who once rang up six fares on the register when he wished to stop a Boston street-car. When the conductor protested, the philosopher called him "up-start," "curmudgeon" and "nincompoop," and showed the fallacy of his claim that thirty cents had been lost, since nobody had found it. Moreover, he offered to prove his proposition by algebraic equation, if one of the gentlemen present had chalk and blackboard on his person.

Once Kant was looking at the flowers in a beautiful garden. But instead of looking through the iron pickets, he stooped over and was squinting through the key-hole of the lock. A student coming along asked him why he didn't look through the pickets and thus get a perfect view.

"Go on, you fool," was the stern reply; "I am studying the law of optics—the unobstructed vision reveals too much—the vivid view is only gotten through a small aperture."

All of which was believed to be a sudden inspiration in way of reply that came to the great professor when caught doing an absent-minded thing. That Kant was not above a little pious prevarication is shown by a story he himself tells. He was never inside of a church once during the last fifty years of his life. But when he became Chancellor of the University, one of his duties was to lead a procession to the Cathedral, where certain formal religious services were held. Kant tried to have the exercises in a hall, but failing in this, he did his duty, and marched like a pigmy drum-major at the head of the cavalcade.

"Now he will have to go in," the scoffers said.

But he didn't. Arriving at the church-door, he excused himself, pleading an urgent necessity, walked around to the back of the church, sacrificed, like Diogenes, to all the gods at once, and made off for home, quietly chuckling to himself at the thought of how he had circumvented the enemy.

Every actor has just so many make-ups and no more. Usually the characters he assumes are variations of a single one. Steele Mackaye used to say, "'There are only five distinct dramatic situations." The artist, too, has his properties. And the recognition of this truth caused Massillon to say, "The great preacher has but one sermon, yet out of this he makes many—by giving portions of it backwards, or beginning in the middle and working both ways, or presenting patchwork pieces, tinted and colored by his mood." All public speakers have canned goods they fall back upon when the fresh fruit of thought grows scarce.

The literary man also has his puppets, pet phrases, and situations to his liking. Victor Hugo always catches the attention by a blind girl, a hunchback, a hunted convict or some mutilated and maimed unfortunate.

In his lectures, Kant used to please the boys by such phrases as this, "I dearly love the muse, although I must admit that I have never been the recipient of any of her favors." This took so well that later he was encouraged to say, "The Old Metaphysics is positively unattractive, but the New Metaphysics is to me most lovely, although I can not boast that I have ever been honored by any of her favors."

A large audience caused Kant to lose his poise—he became self-conscious—but in his own little lecture-room, with a dozen, or fifty at the most (because this was the capacity of the room), he was charming. He would fix his eye on a single boy, and often upon a single button on this boy's coat, and forgetting the immediate theme in hand, would ramble into an amusing and most instructive monolog of criticism concerning politics, pedagogy or current events. In his writing he was exact, heavy and complex, but in these heart-to-heart talks, Herder, who attended Kant's lectures for five years, says, "The man had a deal of nimble wit, and here Kant was at his best."

So we have two different men—the man who wrote the "Critique" and the man who gave the lectures and clarified his thought by explaining things to others. It was in the lectures that he threw off this: "Men are creatures that can not do without their kind, yet are sure to quarrel when together." This took fairly well, and later he said, "Men can not do without men, yet they hate each other when together." And in a year after, comes this: "A man is miserable without a wife, and is seldom happy after he gets one." No doubt this caused a shout of applause from the students, college boys being always on the lookout for just such things; and coming from a very confirmed old bachelor it was peculiarly fetching.

To say that Kant was devoid of wit, as many writers do, is not to know the man. About a year after the "Critique of Pure Reason" appeared, he wrote this: "I am obliged to the learned public for the silence with which it has honored my book, as this silence means a suspension of judgment and a wise determination not to voice a premature opinion." He knew perfectly well that the "learned public" had not read his book, and moreover, could not, intelligently, and the silence betokened simply a stupid lack of interest. Moreover, he knew there was no such thing as a learned public. Kant's remark reveals a keen wit, and it also reveals something more—the pique of the unappreciated author who declares he doesn't care what the public thinks of him, and thereby reveals the fact that he does.

Here are a couple of remarks that could only have been made in the reign of Frederick the Great, and under the spell of a college lecture: "The statement that man is the noblest work of God was never made by anybody but man, and must therefore be taken 'cum grano salis.'" "We are told that God said He made man in His own image, but the remark was probably ironical."

Schopenhauer says: "The chief jewel in the crown of Frederick the Great is Immanuel Kant. Such a man as Kant could not have held a salaried position under any other monarch on the globe at that time and have expressed the things that Kant did. A little earlier or a little later, and there would have been no such person as Immanuel Kant. Rulers are seldom big men, but if they are big enough to recognize and encourage big men, they deserve the gratitude of mankind!"

SWEDENBORG

When a man's deeds are discovered after death, his angels, who are inquisitors, look into his face, and extend their examination over his whole body, beginning with the fingers of each hand. I was surprised at this, and the reason was thus explained to me:

Every volition and thought of man is inscribed on his brain; for volition and thought have their beginnings in the brain, thence they are conveyed to the bodily members, wherein they terminate. Whatever, therefore, is in the mind is in the brain, and from the brain in the body, according to the order of its parts. So a man writes his life in his physique, and thus the angels discover his autobiography in his structure.

—*Swedenborg's*   *"Spirit*   *World"*

SWEDENBORG

A bucolic citizen of East Aurora, on being questioned by a visitor as to his opinion of a certain literary man, exclaimed: "Smart? Is he smart? Why, Missus, he writes things nobody can understand!"

This sounds like a paraphrase (but it isn't) of the old lady's remark on hearing Henry Ward Beecher preach. She went home and said, "I don't think he is so very great—I understood everything he said!"

Paganini wrote musical scores for the violin, which no violinist has ever been able to play. Victor Herbert has recently analyzed some of these compositions and shown that Paganini himself could never have played them without using four hands and handling two bows at once. So far, no one can play a duet on the piano; the hand can span only so many keys, and the attempt of Robert Schumann to improve on Nature by building an artificial extension to his fingers was vetoed by paralysis of the members. Two bodies can not occupy the same space at the same time; mathematics has its limit, for you can not look out of a window four and a half times. The dictum of Ingersoll that all sticks and strings have two ends has not yet been disproved; and Herbert Spencer discovered, for his own satisfaction, fixed limits beyond which the mind can not travel. His expression, the Unknowable, reminds one of those old maps wherein vast sections were labeled, Terra Incognita.

If we read Emanuel Swedenborg, we find that these vast stretches in the domain of thought which Herbert Spencer disposed of as the Unknowable have been traversed and minutely described. Swedenborg's books are so learned that even Herbert Spencer could not read them: his scores are so intricate, his compositions so involved, that no man can play them.

The mystic who sees more than he can explain is universally regarded as an unsafe and unreliable person. The people who consult him go away and do as they please, and faith in his prophecies weaken as his opinions and hopes vary from theirs. We stand by the clairvoyant just as long as he gives us palatable things, and no longer, and nobody knows this better than your genus clairvoyant. When his advice is contrary to our desires, we pronounce him a fraud and go our way. When enterprises of great pith and moment are to be carried through, we give the power into the hands of the worldling infidel, rather than the spiritual seer.

The person on intimate terms with another world seldom knows much about this, and when Robert Browning tells of Sludge, the Medium, he symbols his opinion of all mediums. A medium, if sincere, is one who has abandoned his intellect and turned the bark of reason rudderless, adrift. This is entirely apart from the very common reinforcement of usual psychic powers with fraud, which, beginning in self-deception, puts out from port without papers and sails the sea with forged letters of marque and reprisal.

There are mediums in every city who tell us they are guided by Shakespeare, Dante, Milton, Luther, Tennyson or Henry Ward Beecher. So we are led to believe that the chief business of great men in the spiritual realm is to guide commonplace men in this, and cause them to take pen in hand.

All publishers are perfectly familiar with these productions written by people who think they are psychic when they are only sick. And I have never yet seen a publisher's reader who had found anything in inspirational writing but words, words, words. High-sounding paraphrases and rolling sentences do not make literature; and so far as we know, only the fallible, live and loving man or woman can breathe into the nostrils of a literary production the breath of life. All the rest is only lifeless clay.

That mystery enshrouds the workings of the mind, and that some people have remarkable mental experiences, none will deny. People who can not write at all in a normal mood will, under a psychic spell, produce high-sounding literary reverberations, or play the piano or paint a picture. Yet the literature is worthless, the music indifferent, and the picture bad; but, like Doctor Johnson's simile of the dog that walked on its hind legs, while the walking is never done well, we are amazed that it can be done at all.

The astounding assumption comes in when we leap the gulf and attribute these peculiar rappings and all this ability of seeing around a corner to disembodied spirits. The people with credulity plus, however, always close our mouths with this, "If it isn't spirits, what in the world is it?" And we, crestfallen and abashed, are forced to say, "We do not know."

The absolute worthlessness of spiritual communication comes in when we are told by the medium, caught in a contradiction, that spirits are awful liars. On this point all mediums agree: many disembodied spirits are much given to untruth, and the man who is a liar here will be a liar there.

Swedenborg was so annoyed with this disposition on the part of spirits to prevaricate that he says, "I usually conduct my affairs regardless of their advice." When a spirit came to him and said, "I am the shade of Aristotle," Swedenborg challenged him, and the spirit acknowledged he was only Jimmy Smith. This is delightfully naive and surely reveals the man's sanity: he was deceived by neither living nor dead: he accepted or rejected communications as they appealed to his reason: he kept his literature and his hallucinations separate from his business, and never did a thing which did not gibe with his reason. In this way he lived to be eighty, earnest, yet composed, serene, steering safely clear from Bedlam, by making his commonsense the court of last appeal.

Emerson says that the critic who will render the greatest gift to modern civilization is the one who will show us how to fuse the characters of Shakespeare and Swedenborg. One stands for intellect, the other for spirituality. We need both, but we tire of too much goodness, virtue palls on us, and if we hear only psalms sung, we will long for the clink of glasses and the brave choruses of unrestrained good-fellowship. A slap on the back may give you a thrill of delight that the touch of holy water on your forehead can not lend.

Shakespeare hasn't much regard for concrete truth; Swedenborg is devoted to nothing else. Shakespeare moves jauntily, airily, easily, with careless indifference; Swedenborg lives earnestly, seriously, awfully. Shakespeare thinks that truth is only a point of view, a local issue, a matter of geography; Swedenborg considers it an exact science, with boundaries fixed and cornerstones immovable, and the business of his life was to map the domain.

If you would know the man Shakespeare, you will find him usually in cap and bells. Jaques, Costard, Trinculo, Mercutio, are confessions, for into the mouths of these he puts his wisest maxims. Shakespeare dearly loved a fool, because he was one. He plays with truth as a kitten gambols with a ball of yarn.

So Emerson would have us reconcile the holy zeal for truth and the swish of this bright blade of the intellect. He himself confesses that after reading Swedenborg he turns to Shakespeare and reads "As You Like It" with positive delight, because Shakespeare isn't trying to prove anything. The monks of the olden time read Rabelais and Saint Augustine with equal relish.

Possibly we take these great men too seriously—literature is only incidental, and what any man says about anything matters little, except to himself. No book is of much importance; the vital thing is: What do you yourself think?

When we read Shakespeare in a parlor class there are many things we read over rapidly—the teacher does not stop to discuss them. The remarks of Ophelia or the shepherd talk of Corin are indecent only when you stop and linger over them; it will not do to sculpture such things—let them forever remain in gaseous form. When George Francis Train picked out certain parts of the Bible and printed them, and was arrested for publishing obscene literature, the charge was proper and right. There are things that need not to be emphasized—they may all be a part of life, but in books they should be slurred over as representing simply a passing glimpse of nature.

And so the earnest and minute arguments of Swedenborg need not give us headache in efforts to comprehend them. They were written for himself, as a scaffolding for his imagination. Don't take Jonathan Edwards too seriously—he means well, but we know more. We know we do not know anything, and he never got that far.

The bracketing of the names of Shakespeare and Swedenborg is eminently well. They are Titans both. In the presence of such giants, small men seem to wither and blow away. Swedenborg was cast in heroic mold, and no other man since history began ever compassed in himself so much physical science, and with it all on his back, made such daring voyages into the clouds.

The men who soar highest and know most about another world usually know little about this. No man of his time was so competent a scientist as Swedenborg, and no man before or since has mapped so minutely the Heavenly Kingdom.

Shakespeare's feet were really never off the ground. His excursion in "The Tempest" was only in a captured balloon. Ariel and Caliban he secured out of an old book of fables.

Shakespeare knew little about physics; economics and sociology never troubled him; he had small Latin and less Greek; he never traveled, and the history of the rocks was to him a blank.

Swedenborg anticipated Darwin in a dozen ways; he knew the classic languages and most of the modern; he traveled everywhere; he was a practical economist, and the best civil engineer of his day.

Shakespeare knew the human heart—where the wild storms arise and where the passions die—the Delectable Isles where Allah counts not the days, and the swamps where love turns to hate and Hell knocks on the gates of Heaven. Shakespeare knew humanity, but little else; Swedenborg knew everything else, but here he balked, for woman's love never unlocked for him the secrets of the human heart.

Emanuel Swedenborg was born at Stockholm, Sweden, in Sixteen Hundred Eighty-eight. His father was a bishop in the Lutheran Church, a professor in the theological seminary, a writer on various things, and withal a man of marked power and worth. He was a spiritualist, heard voices and received messages from the spirit world. It will be remembered that Martin Luther, in his monkish days, heard voices, and was in communication with both angels and devils. Many of his followers, knowing of his strange experiences, gave themselves up to fasts and vigils, and they, too, saw things. Abstain from food for two days and this sense of lightness and soaring is the usual result. So strong is example, and so prone are we to follow in the footsteps of those we love, that one "psychic" is sure to develop more. Little Emanuel Swedenborg, aged seven, saw angels, too, and when his father had a vision, he straightway matched it with a bigger one.

Then we find the mother of the boy getting alarmed, and peremptorily putting her foot down and ordering her husband to cease all celestial excursions.

Emanuel was set to work at his books and in the garden, and no more rappings was he to hear, nor strange white lights to see, until he was fifty-six years old.

Sweden is the least illiterate country on the globe, and has been for three hundred years. Her climate is eminently fitted to produce one fine product—men. The winter's cold does not subdue nor suppress, but tends to that earnest industry which improves the passing hours. The Scandinavians make hay while the sun shines; but in countries where the sun shines all the time men make no hay. In Florida, where flowers bloom the whole year through, even the bees quit work and say, "What's the use?"

Emanuel Swedenborg climbed the mountains with his father, fished in the fjords, collected the mosses on the rocks, and wrote out at length all of their amateur discoveries. The boy grew strong in body, lithe of limb, clear of eye—noble and manly.

His affection for his parents was perfect. When fifteen he addressed to them letters of apostrophe, all in studied words of deference and curious compliment, like, say, the letters of Columbus to Ferdinand and Isabella. His purity of purpose was sublime, and the jewel of his soul was integrity.

At college he easily stood at the head of his class. He reduced calculus to its simplest forms, and made abstractions plain. Even his tutors could not follow him. Once the King's actuary was called upon to verify some of his calculations. This brought him to the notice of the King, and thereafter he was always on easy and familiar terms with royalty. There is no hallucination in mathematics—figures do not lie, although mathematicians may, but this one never did.

We look in vain for college pranks, and some of those absurd and foolish things in which young men delight. We wish he could unbend, and be indiscreet, or even impolite, just to show us his humanity. But no, he is always grave, earnest, dignified, and rebukingly handsome. The college "grind" with bulging forehead, round shoulders, myopic vision and shambling gait is well known in every college, and serves as the butt of innumerable practical jokes. But no one took liberties with Emanuel Swedenborg either in boyhood or in after-life. His countenance was stern, yet not forbidding; his form tall, manly and muscular, and his persistent mountain-climbing and outdoor prospecting and botanizing gave him a glow of health which the typical grubber after facts very seldom has.

Thus we find Emanuel Swedenborg walking with stately tread through college, taking all the honors, looked upon by teachers and professors with a sort of awe, and pointed out by his fellow students in subdued wonder. His physical strength became a byword, yet we do not find he ever exercised it in contests; but it served as a protection, and commanded respect from all the underlings.

At twenty we find him falling violently in love, the one sole love-affair of his lone life. Instead of going to the girl he placed the matter before her father, and secured from him a written warrant for the damsel, returnable in three years' time. This document he carried with him, pored over it, slept with it under his pillow. As for the girl, timid, sensitive, aged fifteen, she fled on his approach, and shook with fear if he looked at her. He made his love plain by logical formulas, and proved his passion by geometrical permutations—by charts and diagrams. A seasoned widow might have broken up the icy fastness of his soul and melted his forbidding nature in the crucible of feeling, but this poor girl just wanted some one to hold her little hand and say peace to her fluttering heart. How could she go plump herself in his lap, pull his ears and tell him he was a fool? Finally, the girl's brother, seeing her distress, stole the precious warrant from Swedenborg's coat, tore it up, and Swedenborg knew his case was hopeless. He brought calculus to bear, and proved by the law of averages that there were just as good fish in the sea as ever were caught.

At twenty-one Swedenborg graduated at the University of Upsala. He took the degree of Doctor of Philosophy, and was sent on a tour of the European capitals to complete his education. He visited Hamburg, Paris, Vienna and then went to London, where he remained a year. He bore letters from the King of Sweden that admitted him readily into the best society, and as far as we know he carried himself with dignity, filled with a zeal to know and to become.

One prime object in his travel was to learn the language of the country that he was in, and so we hear of his writing home, "In Hamburg I speak only German; at Paris I talk and think in French; in London no one doubts but that I am an Englishman." This not only reveals the young man's accomplishments, but shows that sublime confidence in himself which never forsook him.

The desire of his father was that he should enter the diplomatic service of the government, and the interest the King took in his welfare shows that the way was opening in that direction. But in the various cities where he traveled he merely used his consular letters to reach the men in each place who knew most of mathematics, anatomy, geology, astronomy and physics. He hunted out the thinkers and the doers, and it seems he had enough specific gravity of soul so he was never turned away.

When big men meet for the first time, they try conclusions just as surely as do the patriarchs of the herds. Instantly there is a mental duel, before scarcely a word is spoken, and the psychic measurements then and there taken are usually about correct.

The very silence of a superior person is impressive. And knowing this, we do not wonder that Swedenborg would sometimes call unannounced on men in high station, and forgetting his letters, would ask for an interview. The audacity of the request would break down the barriers, and his calm, quiet self-possession would do the rest. The man wanted nothing but knowledge. Returning home at twenty-seven, he wrote out two voluminous reports of his travels, one for his father and one for the King. These reports were so complete, so learned, so full of allusion, suggestion and advice, that it is probable they were never read.

He was made Assessor of the School of Mines, an office which we would call that of Assayer, and his business was to give scientific advice as to the value of ores and the best ways to mine and smelt them.

About this time we hear of Swedenborg writing to his brother explaining that he was working on the model of a boat that would navigate below the surface of the sea, and do great damage to the enemy; a gun that would discharge a thousand bullets a minute; a flying machine that would sail the air like a gull; a mechanical chariot that would go twenty miles an hour on a smooth road without horses; and a plan of mathematics which would quickly and simply enable us to compute and express fractions. We also hear of his inventing a treadmill chariot, which carried the horse on board the vehicle, but the horse once ran away and attained such a velocity in the streets of Stockholm that people declared the whole thing was a diabolical invention, and in deference to popular clamor Swedenborg discontinued his experiments along this line.

One is amazed that this man in the early days of the Eighteenth Century should have anticipated the submarine boat, and guessed what could be done by the expansion of steam; prophesied a Gatling gun, and made a motor-car that carried the horse, working on a treadmill and propelling the vehicle faster than the horse could go on the ground; and if the inventor had had the gasoline he surely would have made an automobile.

His diversity of inventive genius was finally focalized on building sluiceways and canals for the government, and he set Holyoke an example by running the water back and forth in canals and utilizing the power over and over again.

Later he was called upon to break a blockade by transferring ships overland a distance of fourteen miles. This he successfully did by the use of a roller railway, and as a reward for the feat was duly knighted by the King.

The one idea that he worked out in detail and gave to the world, and which the world has not improved upon, is our present decimal system.

As the years passed, Swedenborg became rich. He lived well, but not lavishly. We hear of his having his private carriages and being attended by servants on his travels.

He lectured at various universities, and on account of his close association with royalty, as well as on account of his own high character and strong personality, he was a commanding figure wherever he went. His life was full to the brim.

And we naturally expect that a man of wealth, with all the honors belonging to any one person, should take on a comforting accumulation of adipose, and encyst himself in the conventionalities of church, state and society.

And this was what the man himself saw in store, for at forty-six he wrote a book on science, setting forth his ideas and making accurate prophecies as to what would yet be brought about. He regrets that a multiplicity of duties and failing health forbid his carrying out his plans, and further adds, "As this is probably the last book I shall ever write, I desire here to make known to posterity these thoughts which so far as I know have never been explained before."

The real fact was that at this time Swedenborg's career had not really begun, and if he had then died, his fame would not have extended beyond the country of his birth.

Mr. Poultney Bigelow, happening to be in Brighton, England, a few years ago, was entertained at the home of a worthy London broker. The family was prosperous and intelligent, but clung closely to all conventional and churchly lines. As happens often in English homes, the man does most of the thinking and sets metes and bounds to all conversation as well as reading. The mother refers to him as "He," and the children and servants look up to him and make mental obeisance when he speaks.

"I hear Herbert Spencer lives in Brighton—do you ever see him?" ventured the guest of the hostess, in a vain reaching 'round for a topic of mutual interest. "Spencer—Spencer? Who is Herbert Spencer?" asked the good mother.

But "He" caught the run of the talk and came to the rescue: "Oh, Mother, Spencer is nobody you are interested in—just a writer of infidelic books!"

The next day Bigelow called on Spencer and saw upon his table a copy of "Science and Health," which some one had sent him. He smiled when the American referred to the book, and in answer to a question said: "It is surely interesting, and I find many pleasing maxims scattered through it. But we can hardly call it scientific, any more than we can call Swedenborg's 'Conjugal Love' scientific." And the author of "First Principles" showed he had read Mrs. Eddy's book, for he turned to the chapter on "Marriage," calling attention to the statement that marriage in its present status is a permitted condition—a matter of expediency—and children will yet be begotten by telepathic correspondence. "The unintelligibility of the book recommends it to many and accounts for its vogue. Swedenborg's immortality is largely owing to the same reason," and the man who once loved George Eliot smiled not unkindly, and the conversation drifted to other themes.

This comparison of Swedenborg with Mary Baker Eddy is not straining a point. No one can read "Science and Health" intelligently unless his mind is first prepared for it by some one whose mind has been prepared for it by some one else. It requires a deal of explanation; and like the Plan of Salvation, no one would ever know anything about it if it wasn't elucidated by an educated person.

Books strong in abstraction are a convenient rag-bag for your mental odds and ends. Swedenborg's philosophy is "Science and Health" multiplied by forty. He lays down propositions and proves them in a thousand pages.

Yet this must be confessed: The Swedenborgians and the Christian Scientists as sects rank above most other denominations in point of intellectual worth. In speaking of the artist Thompson, Nathaniel Hawthorne once wrote: "This artist is a man of thought, and with no mean idea of art, a Swedenborgian, or, as he prefers to call it, a member of the New Church. I have generally found something marked in men who adopt that faith. He seems to me to possess truth in himself, and to aim at it is his artistic endeavor."

Swedenborg's essay on "Conjugal Love" contains four hundred thousand words and divides the theme into forty parts, each of these being subdivided into forty more. The delights of paradise are pictured in the perfect mating of the right man with the right woman. In order to explain what perfect marriage is, Swedenborg works by the process of elimination and reveals every possible condition of mismating. Every error, mistake, crime, wrong and fallacy is shown in order to get at the truth. Swedenborg tells us that he got his facts from four husbands and four wives in the Spirit Land, and so his statements are authentic. Emerson disposes of Swedenborg's ideal marriage as it exists in heaven, as "merely an indefinite bridal-chamber," and intimates that it is the dream of one who had never been disillusioned by experience.

In Maudsley's fine book, "Body and Mind," the statement is made that during Swedenborg's stay in London his life was decidedly promiscuous. Fortunately the innocence and ignorance of Swedenborg's speculations are proof in themselves that his entire life was absolutely above reproach. Swedenborg's bridal-chamber is the dream of a school-girl, presented by a scientific analyst, a man well past his grand climacteric, who imagined that the perpetuation of sexual "bliss" was a desirable thing.

Emerson hints that there is the taint of impurity in Swedenborg's matrimonial excursions, for "life and nature are right, but closet speculations are bound to be vicious when persisted in." Max Müller's little book, "A Story of German Love," showing the intellectual and spiritual uplift that comes from the natural and spontaneous friendship of a good man and woman, is worth all the weighty speculations of all the virtuous bachelors who ever lived and raked the stagnant ponds of their imagination for an ideal.

The love of a recluse is not God's kind—only running water is pure; the living love of a live man and woman absolves itself, refines, benefits, and blesses, though it be the love of Aucassin and Nicolete, Plutarch and Laura, Paola and Francesca, Abelard and Heloise, and they go to hell for it.

From his thirty-fourth year to his forty-sixth Swedenborg wrote nothing for publication. He lectured, traveled, and advised the government on questions of engineering and finance, and in various practical ways made himself useful. Then it was that he decided to break the silence and give the world the benefit of his studies, which he does in his great work, "Principia." Well does Emerson say that this work, purporting to explain the birth of worlds, places the man side by side with Aristotle, Leonardo, Bacon, Selden, Copernicus and Humboldt.

It is a book for giants, written by one. Although the man was a nominal Christian, yet to him, plainly, the Bible was only a book of fables and fairy-tales. The Mosaic account of Creation is simply waived, as we waive Jack the Giant-Killer when dealing with the question of capital punishment.

That Darwin read Swedenborg with minute care, there is no doubt. In the "Principia" is a chapter on mosses wherein it is explained how the first vestige of lichen catches the dust particles of disintegrating rock, and we get the first tokens of a coming forest. Darwin never made a point better; and the nebular hypothesis and the origin of species are worked out with conjectures, fanciful flights, queer conceits, poetic comparisons, far-reaching analogies, and most astounding leaps of imagination.

The man was warming to his task—this was not to be his last book—the heavens were opening before him, and if he went astray it was light from heaven that dazzled him. No one could converse with him, because there was none who could understand him; none could refute him, because none could follow his winding logic, which led to heights where the air was too rarefied for mortals to breathe. He speculated on magnetism, chemistry, astronomy, anatomy, geology and spiritism. He believed a thing first and then set the mighty machinery of his learning to bear to prove it. This is the universal method of great minds—they divine things first. But no other scientist the world has ever known divined as much as this man. He reminds us of his own motor-car, with the horse inside running away with the machine and none to stop the beast in its mad flight. To his engine there is no governor, and he revolves like the screw of a steamship when the waves lift the craft out of the water.

There is no stimulant equal to expression. The more men write the more they know. Swedenborg continued to write, and following the "Principia" came "The Animal Kingdom," "The Economy of the Universe," and more vast reaches into the realm of fact and fancy. His books were published at his own expense, and the work was done under his own supervision at Antwerp, Amsterdam, Venice, Vienna, London and Paris. In all these cities he worked to get the benefit of their libraries and museums.

Popularity was out of the question—only the learned attempted to follow his investigations, and these preferred to recommend his books rather than read them. And as for heresy, his disbelief in popular superstitions was so veiled in scientific formulas that it went unchallenged. Had he simplified truth for the masses his career would have been that of Erasmus. His safety lay in his unintelligibility. He was gracious, gentle, suave, with a calm self-confidence that routed every would-be antagonist.

It was in his fifty-sixth year that the supreme change came over him. He was in London, in his room, when a great light came to him. He was prostrated as was Saint Paul on the road to Damascus; he lost consciousness, and was awakened by a reassuring voice. Christ came to him and talked with him face to face; he was told that he would be shown the inmost recesses of the Spirit World, and must write out the revelation for the benefit of humanity.

There was no disturbance in the man's general health, although he continued to have visions, trances and curious dreams. He began to write—steadily, day by day the writings went on—but from this time experience was disregarded, and for him the material world slept; he dealt only with spiritual things, using the physical merely for analogy, and his geology and botany were those of the Old Testament.

Returning to Stockholm he resigned his government office, broke his engagements with the University, repudiated all scientific studies, and devoted himself to his new mission—that is, writing out what the spirits dictated, and what he saw on his celestial journeys.

That there are passages of great beauty and insight in his work, is very sure, and by discarding what one does not understand, and accepting what seems reasonable and right, a practical theology that serves and benefits can be built up. The value of Swedenborg lies largely in what you can read into him.

The Swedish Protestant Church in London chose him as their bishop without advising with him. Gradually other scattering churches did the same, and after his death a well-defined cult, calling themselves Swedenborgians, arose and his works were ranked as holy writ and read in the churches, side by side with the Bible.

Swedenborg died in London, March Twenty-ninth, Seventeen Hundred Seventy-two, aged eighty-four years. Up to the very day of his passing away he enjoyed good health, and was possessed of a gentle, kind and obliging disposition that endeared him to all he met. There is an idea in the minds of simple people that insanity is always accompanied by violence, ravings and uncouth and dangerous conduct. Dreams are a temporary insanity—reason sleeps and the mind roams the universe, uncurbed and wildly free. On awakening, for an instant we may not know where we are, and all things are in disorder; but gradually time, location, size and correspondences find their proper place and we are awake.

Should, however, the dreams of the night continue during the day, when we are awake and moving about, we would say the man was insane. Swedenborg could become oblivious to every external thing, and dream at will. And to a degree his mind always dictated the dreams, at least the subject was of his own volition. If it was necessary to travel or transact business, the dreams were postponed and he lived right here on earth, a man of good judgment, safe reason and proper conduct.

Unsoundness of mind is not necessarily folly. Across the murky clouds of madness shoots and gleams, at times, the deepest insight into the heart of things. And the fact that Swedenborg was unbalanced does not warrant us in rejecting all he said and taught as false and faulty. He was always well able to take care of himself and to manage his affairs successfully, even to printing the books that contain the record of his ravings. Follow closely the lives of great inventors, discoverers, poets and artists, and it will be found that the world is debtor to so-called madmen for many of its richest gifts. Few, indeed, are they who can burst the bonds of custom and condition, sail out across the unknown seas, and bring us records of the Enchanted Isles. And who shall say where originality ends and insanity begins? Swedenborg himself attributed his remarkable faculties to the development of a sixth sense, and intimates that in time all men will be so equipped. Death is as natural as life, and possibly insanity is a plan of Nature for sending a searchlight flash into the darkness of futurity. Insane or not, thinking men everywhere agree that Swedenborg blessed and benefited the race—preparing the way for the thinkers and the doers who should come after him.

SPINOZA

Men are so made as to resent nothing more impatiently than to be treated as criminal on account of opinions which they deem true, and charged as guilty for simply what wakes their affection to God and men. Hence, laws about opinions are aimed not at the base but at

the noble, and tend not to restrain the evil-minded but rather to irritate the good, and can not be enforced without great peril to the Government.... What evil can be imagined greater for a State, than that honorable men, because they have thoughts of their own and can not act a lie, are sent as culprits into exile! What more baneful than that men, for no guilt or wrongdoing, but for the generous largeness of their mind, should be taken for enemies and led off to death, and that the torture-bed, the terror of the bad, should become, to the signal shame of authority, the finest stage for the public spectacle of endurance and virtue!
—*Benedict* *Spinoza*

SPINOZA

The word philosophy means the love of truth: "philo," love; "soph," truth; or, if you prefer, the love of that which is reasonable and right. Philosophy refers directly to the life of man—how shall we live so as to get the most out of this little Earth-Journey!

Life is our heritage—we all have so much vitality at our disposal—what shall we do with it?

Truth can be proved in just one way, and no other—that is, by living it. You know what is good, only by trying. Truth, for us, is that which brings good results—happiness or reasonable content, health, peace and prosperity. These things are all relative—none are final, and they are good only as they are mixed in right proportion with other things. Oxygen, we say, is life, but it is also death, for it attacks every living thing with pitiless persistency. Hydrogen is good, but it makes the very hottest fire known, and may explode if you try to confine it.

Prosperity is excellent, but too much is very dangerous to most folks; and to seek happiness as a final aim is like loving love as a business—the end is desolation, death. Good health is best secured and retained by those who are not anxious about health. Absolute good can never be known, for always and forever creeps in the suspicion that if we had acted differently a better result might have followed.

And that which is good for one is not necessarily good for another.

But there are certain general rules of conduct which apply to all men, and to sum these up and express them in words is the business of the philosopher. As all men live truth, in degree, and all men express some truth in language, so to that extent all men are philosophers; but by common assent, we give the title only to the men who make other men think for themselves.

Whistler refers to Velasquez as "a painter's painter." John Wesley said, "No man is worthy to be called a teacher, unless he be a teacher of teachers." The great writer is the one who inspires writers. And in this book I will not refer to a man as a philosopher unless he has inspired philosophers.

Preachers and priests in the employ of a denomination are attorneys for the defense. God is not found in a theological seminary, for very seldom is the seminary seminal—it galvanizes the dead rather than vitalizes the germs of thought in the living. No man understands theology—it is not intended to be understood; it is merely believed. Most colleges are places where is taught the gentle art of sophistication; and memorizing the theories of great men gone passes for knowledge.

Words are fluid and change their meaning with the years and according to the mind and mood of the hearer. A word means all you read into it, and nothing more. The word "soph" once had a high and honorable distinction, but now it is used to point a moral, and the synonym of sophomore is soft.

Originally the sophist was a lover of truth; then he became a lover of words that concealed truth, and the chief end of his existence was to balance a feather on his nose and keep three balls in the air for the astonishment and admiration of the bystanders.

Education is something else.

Education is growth, development, life in abundance, creation.

We grow only through exercise. The faculties we use become strong, and those we fail to use are taken away from us.

This exercise of our powers through which growth is attained affords the finest gratification that mortals know. To think, reason, weigh, sift, decide and act—this is life. It means health, sanity and length of days. Those live longest who live most.

The end of college education to the majority of students and parents is to secure a degree, and a degree is valuable only to the man who needs it. Visiting the office of the "Outlook," a weekly, religious newspaper, I noticed that the titles, Rev., Prof, and Dr., and the degrees, M. D., D. D., LL. D., Ph. D., were carefully used by the clerks in addressing envelopes and wrappers. And I said to the manager, "Why this misuse of time and effort? The ink thus wasted should be sold and the proceeds given to the poor!" And the man replied, "To omit these titles and degrees would cost us half our subscription-list." And so I assume that man is a calculating animal, not a thinking one.

And the point of this sermonette is that truth is not monopolized by universities and colleges; nor must we expect much from those who parade degrees and make professions. It is one thing to love truth and it is another thing to lust after honors.

The larger life—the life of love, health, self-sufficiency, usefulness and expanding power—this life in abundance is often taught best out of the mouths of babes and sucklings. It is not esoteric, nor hidden in secret formulas, nor locked in languages old and strange.

No one can compute how much the bulwarked learned ones have blocked the path of wisdom. Socrates, the barefoot philosopher, did more good than all the Sophists with their schools. Diogenes, who lived in a tub, searched in vain for an honest man, owned nothing but a blanket and a bowl, and threw the bowl away when he saw a boy drinking out of his hand, even yet makes men think, and so blesses and benefits the race. Jesus of Nazareth, with no place to lay his tired head, associating with publicans and sinners, and choosing his closest companions from among ignorant fishermen, still lives in the affections of millions of people, a molding force for good untold. Friedrich Froebel, who first preached the propensity to play as a pedagogic dynamo, as the tides of the sea could be used to turn the countless wheels of trade, is yet only partially accepted, but has influenced every teacher in Christendom and stamped his personality upon the walls of schoolrooms unnumbered. Then comes Richard Wagner, the political outcast, writing from exile the music that serves as a mine for much of our modern composing, marching down the centuries to the solemn chant of his "Pilgrims' Chorus"; William Morris, Oxford graduate and uncouth workingman in blouse and overalls, arrested in the streets of London for haranguing crowds on Socialism, let go with a warning, on suspended sentence—canceled only by death—making his mark upon the walls of every well-furnished house in England or America; Jean Francois Millet, starved out in art-loving Paris, his pictures refused at the Salon, living next door to abject want in Barbizon, dubbed the "wild man of the woods," dead and turned to dust, his pictures commanding such sums as Paris never before paid; Walt Whitman, issuing his book at his own expense, publishers having refused it, this book excluded from the mails, as Wanamaker immortalized himself by serving a like sentence on Tolstoy; Walt Whitman, riding on top of a Broadway 'bus all day, happy in the great solitude of bustling city streets, sending his barbaric yawp down the ages, singing pæans to those who fail, chants to Death—strong deliverer—and giving courage to a fear-stricken world; Thoreau, declining to pay the fee of five dollars for his Harvard diploma "because it wasn't worth the price," later refusing to pay poll-tax and sent to jail, thus missing, possibly, the chance of finding that specimen of Victoria regia on Concord River—Thoreau, most virile of all the thinkers of his day, inspiring Emerson, the one man America could illest spare; Spinoza, the intellectual hermit, asking nothing, and giving everything—all these worked their philosophy up into life and are the type of men who jostle the world out of its ruts—creators all, one with Deity, sons of God, saviors of the race.

Washington Irving once spoke of Spain as the Paradise of Jews. But it must be borne in mind that he wrote the words in Granada, which was essentially a Moorish province. The Moors and the Jews are both Semitic in origin—they trace back to a common ancestry. It was the Moslem Moors that welcomed the Jews in both Venetia and Spain, not the Christians. The wealth, energy and practical business sense of the Jews recommended them to the grandees of Leon, Aragon and Castile. To the Jews they committed their exchequer, the care of their health, the setting of their jewels, and the fashioning of their finery. In this genial atmosphere many of the Jews grew great in the study of science, literature, history, philosophy and all that makes for mental betterment. They increased in numbers, in opulence and in culture. Their thrift and success set them apart as a mark for hate and envy.

It was a period of ominous peace, of treacherous repose.

A senseless and fanatical cry went up, that the Moors—the infidels—must be driven from Spain. The iniquities and inhuman barbarities visited upon the Mohammedan Moors would make a book in itself, but let it go at this: Ferdinand and Isabella drove the Mohammedans from Spain. In the struggle, the Jews were overlooked—and anyway, Christians do not repudiate the Old Testament, and if the Jews would accept Christ, why, they could remain!

It looked easy to the gracious King and Queen of Spain—it was really generous: two religions were unnecessary, and Christianity was beautiful and right. If the Jews would become Catholics, all barriers would be removed—the Jews would be recognized as citizens and every walk of life would be open to them.

This manifesto to the Jews is still quoted by Churchmen to show the excellence, tolerance, patience and love of the Spanish rulers. Turn your synagogues over to the Catholics—come and be one with us—we will all worship the one God together—come, these open arms invite—no distinctions—no badges—no preferences—no prejudices—come!

In quoting the edict it is not generally stated that the Jews were given thirty days to make the change.

The Jews who loved their faith fled; the weak succumbed, or pretended to. If a Jew wished to flee the country he could, but he must leave all his property behind. This caused many to remain and profess Christianity, only awaiting a time when their property could be turned into gold or jewels and be borne upon the person. This fondness for concrete wealth is a race instinct implanted in the Jewish mind by the inbred thought that possibly tomorrow he must fly.

After attending service at a Catholic Church, Jews would go home and in secret read the Talmud and in whispers chant the Psalms of David.

Laws were passed making such action a penal offense—spies were everywhere. No secret can be kept long, and in the Province of Seville over two thousand Jews were hanged or burned in a single year. When Ferdinand and Isabella gave Torquemada, Deza and Lucio orders to make good Catholics of all Jews, they had not the faintest idea what would be the result. Every Jew that was hurried to the stake was first stripped of his property.

No Jew was safe, especially if he was rich—his sincerity or insincerity had really little to do in the matter. The prisons were full, the fagots crackled, the streets ran blood, and all in the name of the gentle Christ.

Then for a time the severity relaxed, for the horror had spent itself. But early in the Seventeenth Century the same edicts were again put forth.

Fortunately, priesthood had tried its mailed hand on the slow and sluggish Dutch, with the result that the Spaniards were driven from the Netherlands. Holland was the home of freedom. Amsterdam became a Mecca for the oppressed. The Jews flocked thither, and among others who, in Sixteen Hundred Thirty-one, landed on the quay was a young Jew by the name of Michael d'Espinoza. With him was a Moorish girl that he had rescued from the clutch of a Spanish grandee, in whose house she had been kept a prisoner.

By a happy accident, this beautiful girl of seventeen had escaped from her tormentors and was huddling, sobbing, in an alley as the young Jew came hurrying by on his way to the ship that was to bear him to freedom. It was near day-dawn—there was no time to lose—the young man only knew that the girl, like himself, was in imminent peril. A small boat waited near—soon they were safely secreted in the hold of the ship. Before sundown the tide had carried the ship to sea, and Portugal was but a dark line on the horizon.

Other refugees were on board the boat; they came from their hiding-places—and the second day out a refugee rabbi called a meeting on deck. It was a solemn service of thanksgiving and the songs of Zion were sung, the first time for some in many months, and only friends and the great, sobbing, salt sea listened.

The tears of the Moorish girl were now dried—the horror of the future had gone with the black memories of the past. Other women, not quite so poor, contributed to her wardrobe, and there and then, after she had been accepted into the Jewish faith, she and Michael d'Espinoza, aged twenty-two, were married.

The ship arrived at Amsterdam in safety. In a year, on November Twenty-fourth, Sixteen Hundred Thirty-two, in a little stone house that still stands on the canal bank, was born Benedict Spinoza.

Benedict Spinoza was brought up in the faith and culture of his people. Beyond his religious training at the synagogue, there was a Jewish High School at Amsterdam which he attended. This school might compare very favorably with our modern schools, in that it included a certain degree of manual training. Besides this he had received special instruction from several learned rabbis. In matters of true education, the Jews have ever been in advance of the Gentile world—they bring their children up to be useful. The father of Benedict was a maker of lenses for spectacles, and at this trade the boy was very early set to work. Again and again in the writings of Spinoza, we find the argument that every man should have a trade and earn his living with his hands, not by writing, speaking or philosophizing. If you can earn a living at your trade, you thus make your mind free.

This early idea of usefulness led to a sympathy with another religious body, of which there were quite a number of members in Holland: the Mennonites. This sect was founded by Menno Simons, a Frieslander, contemporary of Luther; only this man swung on further from Catholicism than Luther and declared that a paid priesthood was what made all the trouble. Religion to him was a matter of individual inspiration. When an institution was formed, built on man's sense of relation with his Maker, property purchased, and paid priests employed, instantly there was a pollution of the well of life. It became a money-making scheme, and a grand clutch for place and power followed: it really ceased to be religion at all, so long as we define religion in its spiritual sense. "A priest," said Menno, "is a man who thrives on the sacred relations that exist between man and God, and is little better than a person who would live on the love-emotions of men and women."

This certainly was bold language, but to be exact, it was persecution that forced the expression. The Catholics had placed an interdict on all services held by Protestant pastors, and the deprivation proved to Menno that paid preaching and costly churches and trappings were really not necessary at all. Man could go to God without them, and pray in secret. Spirituality is not dependent on either church or priest.

The Mennonites in Holland escaped theological criticism by disclaiming to be a church, and calling their institution a college, and themselves "Collegiants."

All the Mennonites asked was to be let alone. They were plain, unpretentious people, who worked hard, lived frugally, refused to make oaths, to accept civil office, or to go to war. They are a variant of the impulse that makes Quakers and all those peculiar people known as Primitive Christians, who mark the swinging of the pendulum from pride and pretense to simplicity and a life of modest usefulness.

The sincerity, truthfulness and virtue of the Mennonites so impressed itself upon even the ruthless Corsican, that he made them exempt from conscription.

Before Spinoza was twenty, he had come into acquaintanceship with these plain people. His relationship with the rabbis and learned men of Israel had given him a culture that the Mennonites did not possess; but these plain people, by the earnestness of their lives, showed him that the science of theology was not a science at all. Nobody understands theology: it is not meant to be understood—it is for belief. Spinoza compared the Mennonites, who confessed they knew nothing, but hoped much, to the rabbis, who pretended they knew all. His praise of the Mennonites, and his criticisms of the growing love for power in Judaism, were carried to the Jewish authorities by some young men who had come to him in the guise of learners. Moreover, the report was abroad that he was to marry a Gentile—the daughter of Van den Ende, the infidel.

On order, he appeared at the synagogue, and defended his position. His ability in argument, his knowledge of Jewish law, his insight into the lessons of history, were alarming to the assembled rabbis. The young man was quiet, gentle, but firm. He expressed the belief that God might possibly have revealed Himself to other peoples beside the Jews.

"Then you are not a Jew!" was the answer.

"Yes, I am a Jew, and I love my faith."

"But it is not all to you?"

"I confess that occasionally I have found what seems to be truth outside of the Law."

The rabbis tore their raiment in mingled rage and surprise at the young man's temerity.

Spinoza did not withdraw from the Jewish Congregation—he was thrust out. Moreover, a fanatical Jew, in the warmth of his religious zeal, attempted to kill him. Spinoza escaped, his clothing cut through by a dagger-thrust, close to the heart.

The curse of Israel was upon him—his own brothers and sisters refused him shelter, his father turned against him, and again was the icy unkindness of kinsmen made manifest. The tribe of Spinoza lives in history, saved from the fell clutch of oblivion by the man it denied with an oath and pushed in bitterness from its heart. Spinoza fled to his friends, the Mennonites, plain market-gardeners who lived a few miles out of the city.

Spinoza had not meant to leave the Jews—the racial instinct was strong in him, and the pride of his people colored his character to the last. But the attempts to bribe him and coerce him into a following of fanatical law, when this law did not appeal to his commonsense, forced him into a position that his enemies took for innate perversity. When an eagle is hatched in a barnyard brood and mounts on soaring pinions toward the sun, it is always cursed and vilified because it does not remain at home and scratch in the compost. Its flight skyward is construed as proof of its vile nature.

How can people who do not think, and can not think, and therefore have no thoughts to express, sympathize with one whose highest joy comes from the expression of his thought?

Deprive a thinker of the privilege to think and you take from him his life. The joy of existence lies in self-expression. What if we should order the painter to quit his canvas, the sculptor to lay aside his tools, the farmer to leave the soil? Do these things, and you do no more than you do when you force a thinker to follow in the groove that dead men have furrowed. The thirst for knowledge must be slaked or the soul sickens and slow death follows.

In Spinoza's time the literature of Greece and Rome was locked in the Latin language, which the Jews were forbidden to acquire. Young Spinoza longed to know what Plato, Aristotle, Cicero, Seneca and Vergil had taught, but these authors were considered anathema by the rabbinical councils. Spinoza desired to be honest, and so asked for a special dispensation in his favor, as he was to be a teacher—could he study the Latin language?

And the answer was, "Read your Joshua, first chapter and eighth verse, 'This book of the law shall not depart out of thy mouth, but thou shalt meditate therein day and night.'"

From this time on Spinoza was more or less under the ban, and rumors of his heresy were rife. It is possible, if it had not been for one person, that the growing desire for knowledge, the reaching out for better things, the dissatisfaction with his environment, might have passed in safety and the restless young rabbi slipped back into the conventional Jew. Youth always has its periods of unrest—sometimes more, sometimes less.

Spinoza had made the acquaintance of Van den Ende, a teacher of Greek and Latin, an erratic, argumentative rationalist, who had his say on all topics of the time, and fixed his place in history by being shot as a revolutionary, just outside the walls of the Bastile.

But at this time Van den Ende was fairly prosperous and Amsterdam was the freest city in Christendom.

Van den Ende had a daughter, Clara Maria, a little younger than Spinoza, who surely was a most superior woman. She was the companion of her father in his studies. It speaks well for the father and it speaks well for the daughter that they were comrades and that his highest thought was expressed to her. I can conceive of no finer joy coming to a man than, as his hair whitens, to have a daughter who understands him at his best, who enters into his life, sympathizes with his ideals, ministers to his mental needs, who is his companion and friend. Only a great man ever has such a daughter. Madame De Stael, who delighted in being called "the daughter of Necker," was such a woman, and the splendor of her mind was no less her father's glory than was the fact that he was the greatest financier of his time.

Clara Van den Ende was her father's helper and companion, and when he was busied in other tasks she took charge of his classes.

Auerbach has written a charming story with Clara Van den Ende and Spinoza as a central theme. In the tale is pictured with skilful psychology the awakening of the sleeping soul of Spinoza as he was introduced from a cheerless home, devoid of art and freedom, into the beauties of undraped Greece and the fine atmosphere of a forum where nothing human was considered alien.

From a love for Vergil, Cicero and Horace, to a love for each other, was a very natural sequence. A growing indifference for the censure of Judaism was quite a natural result. Auerbach would have us believe that no man alone ever stood out against the revilings of kinsmen and the stupidity of sectarians: we move in the line of least resistance and only a very great passion makes it possible for a man calmly to face the contumely of an angry world.

Zangwill, in his vivid sketch, "The Maker of Lenses," makes this single love-episode in the life of Spinoza the controlling impulse of his life, probably reasoning on the premise that men who mark epochs are ever and always, without exception, those with the love nature strongly implanted in their hearts. So thoroughly does Zangwill believe in the one passion of Spinoza's life, that a score of years after the chief incident of it had transpired, he pictures the philosopher trembling at mention of the woman's name, coughing to conceal his agitation and clutching the doorpost for support. And this a man who smilingly faced a mob that howled for his life, and was only moved to philosophize on the nature of human intellect when a flying stone grazed his cheek!

But the lady had ambitions—the lens-maker was penniless, and probably always would be—his passion was passive—he lacked the show and dash that made other women jealous. And so Oldenburg, a rival with love and jewels, won the heart that could not be won by love alone. That the lady soon knew she had erred did not help her case—Spinoza loved his ideal, and he had thought it was the woman.

Follow Zangwill's stories of the Ghetto and your heart is wrung by the injustice, cruelty and inhumanity visited upon the Jews by the people who worship a Jew as God and make daily supplications to a Jewess.

But read between the lines and you will see that Israel Zangwill, child of the Ghetto, knows that the Peculiar People are peculiar through persecution, and not necessarily so through innate nature. Zangwill knows that no religion is pure except in its stage of persecution, and that Judaism, grown rich and powerful, would oppress and has oppressed. Martyr and persecutor shift places easily.

The Jew arrives in a city at night, and in the morning takes down the shutters and is doing business. The Jew winds his way into the life of every city and becomes at once an integral part of it—a part, yet separate and distinct, for his social and religious life is not colored by his environment.

Children imitate unconsciously. The golden rule is not natural to children: it has to be taught them. They do unto others as others have done unto them, and have no question as to right or wrong. We are all children, and have to think hard before we are conscious of any feeling of the brotherhood of man. As soon as the Jews relaxed in Amsterdam—got their breath, and felt secure—they did unto others as they had been done by—they persecuted.

A Jew must be a Jew, and as they had been watched with suspicion in Spain and Portugal by the Christians, so now they watched each other for heresies. They compelled strictest obedience to every form and ceremony. To the Jew the Law forms the firmament above and the earth beneath. All is law to him, and his part and work in this life is obedience to law.

The Jewish religion is a concrete, unbroken mass of laws. The Jew is bounded on the east by law; on the north by law; on the west by law; on the south by law. There are set rules and laws that govern his getting up, his going to bed, his eating, drinking, sleeping, and praying. There is no phase of human relationship that is not covered by the Mishna and Gemara. Being learned in the Law means being learned in the proper way to kill chickens, to dress ducks, wear your vestments, go to prayers, and what to say when you meet two Christians in an alley. If a Jew quarrels with a neighbor and goes to his Rabbi for advice, the learned man gets down his Talmud and finds the page. The relation of wife and husband, child and parent, brother and sister, lover and sweetheart, are covered by law, fixed, immovable. The learned men of Judah are men learned in the Law, not learned in the science of life, and commonsense. When these learned men meet they argue for six days and nights together as to interpretations of the Law concerning whether it is right to make a fire in your cook-stove on the Sabbath if a Christian is starving for food on your doorstep, or what will become of you if you eat pork to save your life.

Rational Jews are those who do what they think is right, but Orthodox Jews are those who do what the Law prescribes. When Jesus plucked the ears of corn on the Sabbath day, he proved himself a Rational Jew—he set his own opinion higher than Law and thereby made himself an outcast. Jewish Law provides curdling curses for just such offenses.

Plato's Republic was a scheme of life regulated absolutely by law; every contingency was provided for. And Plato's plan was founded on the hypothesis that it is the duty of wise men to do the thinking and regulate the conduct of those who are supposed not to be wise enough to think and to act for themselves. But Plato's idea lacked the "Thus saith the Lord," with which Moses and Aaron enforced their edicts. So Plato's Republic is still on paper, for no set of rules minutely regulating conduct has ever been enforced except as the ruler made his subjects believe he received his instructions direct from God.

Yet all the Jewish Laws are founded with an eye to a sanitary and hygienic good—they are built on the basis of expediency. And that rule of the Gemara which provides that if you have gravy on the table, you can not also have butter, without sin, seems more of a move in the direction of economics than a matter of ethics. Laws are good for the people who believe that a blind obedience to a good thing is better than to work your way alone and find out for yourself what is best and right. The Jewish Law is based, like all religious codes, on the assumption that man by nature is vile, and really prefers wrong to right.

The thought that all men prefer the good, and think at the moment they are doing what is best, no matter what they do, was first sharply and clearly expressed by Spinoza. Truth, he said, could only be reached through freedom—a man must even have the privilege of thinking wrong so long as his actions do not jeopardize the life and immediate safety of others.

For a people whose every act is governed by fixed laws there can be no progression. Mistakes are the rungs of the ladder by which we reach the skies. The man who allows the dead to regulate his life, and accepts their thinking as final, satisfied to repeat what he is taught, remains forever in the lowlands. His wings are leaden.

The Jews—most law-bound and priest-ridden of all peoples—are at home everywhere because they have no home. They mix in the life of every nation and remain forever separate and apart. They will run with you, ride with you, trade with you, but they will not eat with you nor pray with you. They build no Altars to the Unknown God, out of courtesy to visitors and guests from distant climes. Mohammedans recognize the divinity of Jesus, the Buddhists look upon him as one of many Christs, the Universalist sees good in every faith, but the Jew regards all other religions than his own as pestilence. If by chance, or in the line of business, he finds himself in a heathen temple or Christian Church, his Gemara orders that he shall present himself at his own temple for purification.

Read Leviticus, Numbers and Deuteronomy, and you behold on every page curses, revilings, threats and bitter scorn for all outside the pale. Orders by Jehovah to burn, kill and utterly destroy are frequent. And we must remember that every people make their god in their own image. A man's God is himself at his best; his devil is himself at his worst.

The very expression, "The Chosen People," would be an insult to every man outside the pale, were it not such a petulant and childish boast that its serious assumption makes us smile.

Well does Moses Mendelssohn, the Jew, say: "The Ghetto is an arrangement first contrived by Jews for keeping infidels out of a sacred precinct. When the infidels were strong enough they turned the tables and forbade the Jews to leave their Ghetto except at certain hours. For the misery, poverty and squalor of the Ghetto the Jew is not to blame—if he could, he would have the Ghetto a place of opulence, beauty and all that makes for the good. Every undesirable thing he would bestow on the outsider. In the twilight days of Jewish power, the Jew, with bigotry, arrogance and intolerance unsurpassed, regulated the infidels and fixed their goings and comings as they now do his, and he would do it again if he had the power. The Jew never changes—once a Jew always a Jew."

This was written by a man who was not only a Jew, but a man. He was a Jew in pride of race—in racial instinct, but he was great enough to know that all men are God's children, and that to set up a fixed, dogmatic standard regulating every act of life has its serious penalties. He was a Jew so big that he knew that the cruelty and inhumanity visited upon the Jews by Christians was first taught to these Christians by Jews—it is all in the Old Testament. The villainy you have taught me I will execute. It shall go hard, but I will better the instruction.

The Christians who had persecuted Jews were really orthodox Jews in disguise, and were actuated more by the Jewish Law expressed in the Old Testament, than by the life of Jesus, who placed man above the Sabbath and taught that the good is that which serves.

And so Benedict Spinoza, the Rabbi, gentle, spiritual, kind, heir to the Jewish faith, learned in all the refinements of Jewish Law, knowing minutely the history of the race, knowing that for which the curses of Judaism were reserved, perceiving with unblinking eyes the absurdity and folly of all dogmatic belief, gradually withdrew from practising and following "Law," preferring his own commonsense. There were threats, then attempts to bribe, and again threats and finally excommunication and curses so terrible that if they were carried out, a man would walk the earth an exile—unknown by brothers and sisters, shunned by the mother that gave him birth, a moral leper to his father, despised, rejected, turned away, spit upon by every being of his kind.

And here is the document:

By the sentence of the angels, by the decree of the saints, we anathematize, cut off, curse, and execrate Baruch Spinoza, in the presence of these sacred books with the six hundred and thirteen precepts which are written therein, with the anathema wherewith Joshua anathematized Jericho; with the cursing wherewith Elisha cursed the children; and with all the cursings which are written in the Book of the Law; cursed be he by day, and cursed by night; cursed when he lieth down, and cursed when he riseth up; cursed when he goeth out, and cursed when he cometh in; the Lord pardon him never; the wrath and fury of the Lord burn upon this man, and bring upon him all the curses which are written in the Book of the Law. The Lord blot out his name under heaven. The Lord set him apart for destruction from all the tribes of Israel, with all the curses of the firmament which are written in the Book of the Law. There shall no one speak to him, no man write to him, no man show him any kindness, no man stay under the same roof with him, no man come nigh him.

When the Jewish congregation had placed its ban upon Spinoza, he dropped the Jewish name Baruch, for the Latin Benedictus. In this action he tokened his frame of mind: he was going to persist in his study of the Latin language, and his new name stood for peace or blessing, just as the other had, being essentially the same as our word benediction. The man's purpose was firm. To perfect himself in Latin, he began a study of Descartes' "Meditations," and this led to proving the Cartesian philosophy by a geometrical formula. In his quiet home among the simple Mennonites, five miles from Amsterdam, there gradually grew up around him a body of students to whom he read his writings. The Cartesian philosophy swings around the proposition that only through universal doubt can we at last reach truth. Spinoza soon went beyond this and made his plea for faith in a universal Good.

Five years went by—years of work at his lenses, helping his friends in their farm work, and several hours daily devoted to study and writing. Spinoza's manuscripts were handed around by his pupils. He wrote for them, and in making truth plain to them he made it clear to himself. The Jews at Amsterdam kept track of his doings and made charges to the Protestant authorities to the effect that Spinoza was guilty of treason, and his presence a danger to the State. Spies were about, and their presence becoming known to the Mennonites, caused uneasiness. To relieve his friends of a possible unpleasant situation, the gentle philosopher packed up his scanty effects and moved away. He went to the village of Voorburg, two miles from The Hague.

Here he lived for seven years, often for six months not going farther than three miles from home. He studied, worked and wrote, and his writings were sent out to his few friends who circulated them among friends of theirs, and in time the manuscripts came back soiled and dog-eared, proof that some one had read them. Persecution binds human hearts, and at this time there was a brotherhood of thinkers throughout the capitals and University towns of Europe. Spinoza's name became known gradually to these—they grew to look for his monthly contribution, and in many places when his manuscript arrived little bands of earnest students would meet, and the manuscript would be read and discussed. The interdict placed on free thought made it attractive. Spinoza became recognized by the esoteric few as one of the world's great thinkers, although the good people with whom he lived knew him only as a model lodger, who kept regular hours and made little trouble. Occasionally visitors would come from a distance and remain for hours discussing such abstract themes as the freedom of the will or the nature of the over-soul. And these visitors caused the rustic neighbors to grow curious, and we find Spinoza moving into the city and renting a modest back room. By a curious chance, his landlady, fifty years before, had been a servant in the household of Grotius, and once had locked that great man in a trunk and escorted him, right side up, across the border into Switzerland to escape the heresy-hunters who were looking for human kindling. This kind landlady, now grown old, and living largely in the past, saw points of resemblance between her philosophic boarder and the great Grotius, and soon waxed boastful to the neighbors. Spinoza noticed that he was being pointed out on the streets. His record had followed him. The Jews hated him because he was a renegade; the Christians hated him because he was a Jew, and both Catholics and Protestants shunned him when they ought not, and greeted him with howls when they should have let him alone.

He again moved his lodgings to the suburbs of the city, where he lived with the family of Van der Spijck, a worthy Dutch painter who smoked his pipe in calm indifference to the Higher Criticism. For their quiet and studious lodger Van der Spijck and his wife had a profound regard. They did not understand him, but they believed in him. Often he would go to church with them and coming home would discuss the sermon with them at length. The Lutheran pastor who came to call on the family invited Spinoza to join his flock, and they calmly discussed the questions of baptism and regeneration by faith together; but genius only expresses itself to genius, and the pastor went away mystified. Van der Spijck did not produce great art, yet his pictures are now in demand because he was the kind and loyal friend of Spinoza, and his heart, not his art, fixes his place in history.

In his sketch, Zangwill has certain of his old friends, members of the Van den Ende family, hunt out the philosopher in his obscure lodgings and pay him a social visit. Then it was that he turned pale, and stammeringly tried to conceal his agitation at mention of the name of the only woman he had ever loved.

The image of that one fine flaming up of divine passion followed him to the day of his death. It was too sacred for him to discuss—he avoided women, kept out of society, and forever in his sad heart there burned a shrine to the ideal. And so he lived, separate and apart. A single little room sufficed—the work-bench where he made his lenses near the window, and near at hand the table covered with manuscript where he wrote. Renan says that when he died, aged forty-three, his passing was like a sigh, he had lived so quietly—so few knew him—there were no earthly ties to break.

The worthy Van der Spijcks, plain, honest people, had invited him to go to church with them. He smilingly excused himself—he had thoughts he must write out ere they escaped. When the good man and his wife returned in an hour, their lodger was dead.

A tablet on the house marks the spot, and but a short distance away in the open square sits his form in deathless bronze, pensively writing out an idea which we can only guess—or is it a last love-letter to the woman to whom he gave his heart and who pushed from her the gift?

Spinoza had courage, yet great gentleness of disposition. His habit of mind was conciliatory: if strong opinions were expressed in his presence concerning some person or thing, he usually found some good to say of the person or an excuse for the thing. He was one of the most unselfish men in history—money was nothing to him, save as it might minister to his very few immediate wants or the needs of others.

He smilingly refused a pension offered him by a French courtier if he would but dedicate a book to the King; and a legacy left him by an admiring student, Simon de Vries, was declined for the reason that it was too much and he did not wish the care of it. Later, he compromised with the heirs by accepting an income of one hundred and twenty-five dollars a year. "How unreasonable," he exclaimed, "they want me to accept five hundred florins a year—I told them I would take three hundred, but I will not be burdened by a stiver more." If he was financially free from the necessity of earning his living at his trade, he feared the quality of his thought might be diluted. You can not think intently and intensely all of the time. Those who try it never are able to dive deep nor soar high.... Good digestion demands a certain amount of coarse food—refined and condensed aliment alone kills. Man should work and busy himself with the commonplace, rest himself for his flight, and when the moment of transfiguration comes, make the best of it.

All he asked was to be given the privilege to work and to think. As for expressing his thoughts, he made no public addresses and during his life only one of his books was printed. This was the "Tractatus Theologico-Politicus," which mentioned "Hamburg" on the title page, but with the author's name wisely omitted. Trite enough now are the propositions laid down—that God is everywhere and that man is brother to the tree, the rock, the flower. Emerson states the case in his "Over-Soul" and "Spiritual Laws" in the true, calm Spinozistic style—as if the gentle Jew had come back to earth and dictated his thought, refined, polished and smooth as one of his own little lenses, to the man of Concord. Benedictus Concordia, blessing and peace be with thee!

But the lynx-eyed censors soon discovered this single, solitary book of Spinoza's, and although they failed to locate the author, Spinoza had the satisfaction of seeing the work placed on the Index and a general interdict issued against it by Christendom and Judea as well. It was really of some importance. It was so thoroughly in demand that it still circulated with false title pages. In the Lenox Library, New York, is a copy of the first edition, finely bound, and lettered thus: "A Treatise on the Sailing of Ships against the Wind," which shows the straits booksellers were put to in evading the censors, and also reveals a touch of wit that doubtless was appreciated by the Elect.

His modesty, patience, kindness and freedom from all petty whim and prejudice set Spinoza apart as a marked man. Withal he was eminently religious, and the reference to him by Novalis as "the God-intoxicated man" seems especially applicable to one who saw God in everything.

Renan said at the dedication of The Hague monument to Spinoza, "Since the days of Epictetus and Marcus Aurelius we have not seen a life so profoundly filled with the sentiment of the divine."

When walking along the streets of The Hague and coarse voices called after him in guttural, "Kill the renegade!" he said calmly, "We must remember that these men are expressing the essence of their being, just as I express the essence of mine."

Spinoza taught that the love of God is the supreme good; that virtue is its own reward, and folly its own punishment; and that every one ought to love his neighbor and obey the civil powers.

He made no enemies except by his opinions. He was infinitely patient, sweet in temper—had respect for all religions, and never offended by parading his heresies in the faces of others.

Nothing but the kicks of scorn and the contumely that came to Spinoza could possibly have freed him to the extent he was free from Judaistic bonds.

He had disciples who called him "Master," and who taught him nothing but patience in answering their difficulties.

One is amazed at the hunger of the mind at the time of Spinoza. Men seemed to think, and dare to grasp for "New Thought" to a marvelous extent.

Spinoza says that "evil" and "good" have no objective reality, but are merely relative to our feelings, and that "evil" in particular is nothing positive, but a privation only, or non-existence.

Spinoza says that love consecrates every indifferent particular connected with the object of affection. Good is that which we certainly know to be useful to us. Evil is that which we certainly know stands in the way of our command of good.

Good is that which helps. Bad is that which hinders our self-maintenance and active powers.

A passage from Spinoza which well reveals his habit of thought and which placed the censors on his track runs as follows:

The ultimate design of the State is not to dominate men, to restrain them by fear, to make them subject to the will of others, but, on the contrary, to permit every one, as far as possible, to live in security. That is to say, to preserve intact the natural right which is his, to live without being harmed himself or doing harm to others. No, I say, the design of the State is not to transform men into animals or automata from reasonable beings; its design is to arrange matters that citizens may develop their minds and bodies in security, and to make free use of their reason. The true design of the State, then, is liberty. Whoever would respect the rights of the sovereign ought never to act in opposition to his decrees; but each has a right to think as he pleases and to say what he thinks, provided that he limits himself to speaking and to teaching in the name of pure reason, and that he does not attempt, in his private capacity, to introduce innovations into the State. For example, a citizen demonstrates that a certain law is repugnant to sound reason, and believing this, he thinks it ought to be abrogated. If he submits his opinion to the judgment of the sovereign, to which alone it belongs to establish and to abolish laws, and if, in the meantime, he does nothing contrary to law, he certainly deserves well of the State as being a good citizen.

Let us admit that it is possible to stifle liberty of men and to impose on them a yoke, to the point that they dare not even murmur, however feebly, without the consent of the sovereign: never, it is certain, can any one hinder them from thinking according to their own free will. What follows hence? It is that men will think one way and speak another; that, consequently, good faith, so essential a virtue to a State, becomes corrupted; that adulation, so detestable, and perfidy, shall be held in honor, bringing in their train a decadence of all good and sound habitudes. What can be more fatal to a State than to exile, as malcontents, honest citizens, simply because they do not hold the opinion of the multitude, and because they are ignorant of the art of dissembling! What can be more fatal to a State than to treat as enemies and to put to death men who have committed no other crime than that of thinking independently! Behold, then, the scaffold, the dread of the bad man, which now becomes the glorious theater where tolerance and virtue blaze forth in all their splendor, and covers publicly with opprobrium the sovereign majesty! Assuredly, there is but one thing which that spectacle can teach us, and that is to imitate these noble martyrs, or, if we fear death, to become the abject flatterers of the powerful. Nothing hence can be so perilous as to relegate and submit to divine right things which are purely speculative, and to impose laws upon opinions which are, or at least ought to be, subject to discussion among men. If the right of the State were limited to repressing acts, and speech were allowed impunity, controversies would not turn so often into seditions.

AUGUSTE COMTE

In the name of the Past and of the Future, the servants of Humanity—both its philosophical and its practical servants—come forward to claim as their due the general direction of the world. Their object is to constitute at length a real Providence in all departments—moral, intellectual and material.

—*Auguste* *Comte*

AUGUSTE COMTE

A little city girl asked of her country cousin, when honey was the topic up for discussion, "Does your papa keep a bee?"

Let the statement go unchallenged, that a single bee has neither the disposition nor the ability to make honey.

Bees accomplish nothing save as they work together, and neither do men.

Great men come in groups.

Six men, three living at the village of Concord, Massachusetts, and three at Cambridge, fifteen miles away, supplied America really all her literature, until Indiana suddenly loomed large on the horizon, and assumed the center of the stage, like the spirit of the Brocken.

Five men made up the Barbizon school of painting, which has influenced the entire art education of the world. And that those who have been influenced and helped most, deny their redeemer with an oath, is a natural phenomenon psychologists look for and fully understand.

Greece had a group of seven thinkers, in the time of Pericles, who made the name and fame of the city deathless.

Rome had a similar group in the time of Augustus; then the world went to sleep, and although there were individuals, now and then, of great talent, their lights went out in darkness, for it takes bulk to make a conflagration.

Florence had her group of thinkers and doers when Michelangelo and Leonardo lived only a few miles apart, but never met. Yet each man spurred the other on to do and dare, until an impetus was reached that sent the names of both down the centuries.

Boswell gives us a group of a dozen men who made each other possible—often helped by hate and strengthened by scorn.

The Mutual Admiration Society does not live in piping times of peace, where glowing good-will strews violets; often the sessions of this interesting aggregation are stormy and acrimonious, but one thing holds—the man who arises at this board must have something to say. Strong men, matched by destiny, set each other a pace. Criticism is full and free. The most interesting and the most successful social experiment in America owed its lease of life largely to its scheme of Public Criticism, a plan society at large will adopt when it puts off swaddling-clothes. Public Criticism is a diversion of gossip into a scientific channel. It is a plan of healthful, hygienic, social plumbing.

England produced one group of thinkers that changed the complexion of the theological belief of Christendom—Darwin, Spencer, Wallace, Huxley and Mill. But this group built on the French philosophers, who were taught antithetically by the decaying and crumbling aristocracy of France. Rousseau and Voltaire loved each other and helped each other, as the proud Leonardo helped the humble and no less proud peasant, Michelangelo—by absent treatment.

Victor Hugo says that when the skulls of Voltaire and Rousseau were taken in a sack from the Pantheon and tumbled into a common grave, a spark of recognition was emitted that the gravedigger did not see.

Voltaire was patronized by Frederick the Great, who, though a married man, lived a bachelor life and forbade women his court, and protected Kant with the bulging forehead and independent ways. Kant lived among a group of thinkers he never saw, but reached out and touched finger-tips with them over the miles that his feet never traversed.

To Kant are we indebted for Turgot, that practical and farseeing man of affairs told of in matchless phrase in Thomas Watson's "Story of France," the best book ever written in America, with possibly a few exceptions. Condorcet kept step with him, and Auguste Comte calls Condorcet his spiritual stepfather, and a wit of the time here said, "Then Turgot is your uncle"; and Comte replied, "I am proud of the honor, for if Turgot is my uncle, then indeed am I of royal blood."

Auguste Comte is the one bright particular star amid that milky way of riotous thinkers which followed close upon the destruction of the French Monarchy.

When Napoleon visited the grave of Rousseau, he mused in silence and then said, "Perhaps it might have been as well if this man had never lived."

And Marshal Ney, standing near, said, "It reveals small gratitude for Napoleon Bonaparte to say so." Napoleon smiled and answered, "Possibly the world would be as well off if neither of us had ever lived."

Auguste Comte thought that Napoleon was just as necessary in the social evolution as Rousseau, and that both were needed—and he himself was needed to make the matter plain in print.

Auguste Comte was born at Montpelier, France, in Seventeen Hundred Ninety-eight. His father was receiver of taxes, an office that carried with it much leisure and a fair income. Men of leisure seldom have time to think—if you want a thing done it is safest and best not to pick a publican. Only busy men have time to do things. The men who have good incomes and work little are envied only by those with a mental impediment.

The boy Auguste owed little to his parents for his peculiar evolution, save as his father taught him by antithesis: the children of drunkards make temperance fanatics, and shiftless fathers sometimes have sons who are great financiers.

When nine years of age, the passion to know and to become was upon Auguste Comte. He was small in stature, insignificant in appearance, and had a great appetite for facts. Comte is a fine refutation of the maxim that infant prodigies fall victims to arrested development.

At twelve years of age he was filled with the idea that the social order was all wrong. To the utter astonishment of his parents and tutors, he argued that the world could not be bettered until mankind was taught the lesson that history, languages, theology and polite etiquette were not learning at all; and as long as educated men centered on these things, there was no hope for the race.

The birch was brought in to disannex the boy from his foolishness, but this only seemed to make him cling the closer to what he was pleased to call his convictions.

He read books that wearied the brains of grown-ups, and took a hearty interest in the abstruse, the obscure and the complex.

At thirteen, that peculiar time when the young turn to faith, this perverse rareripe was so filled with doubt that it ran over and he stood in the slop. He offered to publicly debate the question of Freewill with the local curé; and on several occasions stood up in meeting and contradicted the preacher.

His parents, thinking to divert his mind from abstractions to useful effort, sent him to the Polytechnic School at Paris, that excellent institution founded by Napoleon, which served America most nobly as a model for the Boston School of Technology, only the French "Polytechnique" was purely a government institution—a sample of the Twentieth Century sent for the benefit of the Nineteenth.

But institutions are never much beyond the people—they can not be, for the people dilute everything until it is palatable. Laws that do not embody public opinion can never be enforced. No man who expresses himself is really much ahead of his time—if he is, the times snuff him out, and quickly.

In Eighteen Hundred Fourteen, the Polytechnic School was well saturated with the priestly idea of education, and the attempt was made to produce an alumni of cultured men, rather than a race of useful ones.

Revolt was rife in the ranks of the students. It is still debatable whether revolution and riot in colleges are actuated by a passion for truth or a love of excitement. Anyway, the "Techs" laid deep places to the effect that when a certain professor appeared at chapel, a unique reception would be in store for him.

He appeared, and a fusillade of books, rulers and ink-wells shot at his learned head from every quarter of the room. Other professors appeared and sought to restore order. Riot followed—seats were torn up, windows broken, and there was much loud talk and gesticulation peculiarly Gallic.

It was Ninety-three done in little.

Instead of expelling the delinquents, the National Assembly took the matter in hand and simply voted to close the school.

Auguste Comte went home a hero, proud as a Heidelberg student, with a sweeping scar on his chin and the end of his nose gone. "I have dealt the Old Education its deathblow," he solemnly said, mistaking a cane-rush for a revolution.

Against the direct command of his parents, he went back to Paris. He had now reached the mature age of eighteen. He resolved to write out truth as it occurred to him, and incidentally he would gain a livelihood by teaching mathematics.

At Paris, the mental audacity of the youth won him recognition; he picked up a precarious living, and was a frequenter at scientific lectures and discussions, and in gatherings where great themes were up for debate, he was always present.

Benjamin Franklin was his ideal. In his notebook he wrote this: "Franklin at twenty-five resolved he would become great and wise. I now vow the same at twenty." He had five years the start!

Franklin, calm, healthy, judicial, wise—the greatest man America has produced—worked his philosophy up into life. He did not think much beyond his ability to perform. To him, to think was to do. And he did things that to many men were miracles.

Comte once said, "I would have followed the venerable Benjamin Franklin through the street, and kissed the hem of the homespun overcoat, made by Deborah." These men were very unlike. One was big, gentle, calm and kind; the other was small, dyspeptic, excitable and full of challenge. Yet the little man had times of insight and abstraction, when he tracked reasons further than the big, practical man could have followed them.

Franklin's habit of life—the semi-ascetic quality of getting your gratification by doing without things—especially pleased Comte. He lived in a garret on two meals a day, and was happy in the thought that he could endure and yet think and study. The old monastic impulse was upon him, minus the religious features—or stay! why may not science become a religion? And surely science can become dogmatic, and even tyrannically build a hierarchy on a hypothesis no less than theology.

A friend, pitying young Comte's hard lot, not knowing its sweet recompense, got him a position as tutor in the household of a nobleman; like unto the kind man who caught the sea-gulls roosting on an iceberg, and in pity, transferred them to the warm delights of a compost-pile in his barnyard.

Comte held the place for three weeks and then resigned. He went back to the garret and sweet liberty—having had his taste of luxury, but miserable in it all—wondering how a gavotte or a minuet could make a man forget that he was living in a city where thirty thousand human beings were constantly only one meal beyond the sniff of starvation.

At this time Comte came into close relationship with a man who was to have a very great influence in his life—this was Count Henri of Saint-Simon, usually spoken of as Saint-Simon.

Saint-Simon was rich, gently proud, and fondly patronizing. He was a sort of scientific Mæcenas—and be it known that Mæcenas was a poet and philosopher of worth, and one Horace was his pupil.

Saint-Simon was an excellent and learned man who wrote, lectured and taught on philosophic themes. He had a garden-school, modeled in degree after that of Plato. Saint-Simon became much interested in young Comte, invited him to his classes, supplied him books, clothing, and tickets to the opera. Part of the time Comte lived under Saint-Simon's roof, and did translating and copying in partial payment for his meal-ticket. The teacher and the pupil had a fine affection for each other. What Comte needed, he took from Saint-Simon as if it were his own.

In writing to friends at this time, Comte praises Saint-Simon as the greatest man who ever lived—"a model of patience, generosity, learning and love—my spiritual father!" There was fifty years' difference in their ages, but they studied, read and rambled the realm of books together, with mutual pleasure and profit.

The central idea of the "Positive Philosophy" is that of the three stages through which man passes in his evolution. This was gotten from Saint-Simon, and together they worked out much of the thought that Comte afterward carried further and incorporated in his book.

But about this time, Saint-Simon, in one of his lectures, afterward printed, made use of some of the thoughts that Comte had expressed, as if they were his own—and possibly they were. There is no copyright on an idea, no caveat can be filed on feeling, and at the last there is no such thing as originality, except as a matter of form.

Young Comte now proved his humanity by accusing his teacher of stealing his radium. A quarrel followed, in which Comte was so violent that Saint-Simon had to put the youth out of his house.

The wrangles of Grub Street would fill volumes: both sides are always right, or wrong—it matters little, and is simply a point of view. But the rancor of it all, if seen from heaven, must serve finely to dispel the monotony of the place—a panacea for paradisiacal ennui.

From lavish praise, Comte swung over to words of bitterness and accusation. Having sat at the man's table and partaken of his hospitality for several years, he was now guilty of the unpardonable offense of ridiculing and berating him.

He speaks of the Saint as a "depraved quack," and says that the time he spent with him was worse than wasted. If Saint-Simon was the rogue and pretender that Comte avers, it is no certificate of Comte's insight that it took him four years to find it out.

In Eighteen Hundred Twenty-five Comte married. The ceremony was performed civilly, on a sudden impulse of what Schopenhauer would call "the genius of the genus." The lady was young, agreeable; and having no opinions of her own, was quite willing to accept his. Comte congratulated himself that here was virgin soil, and he laid the flattering unction to his soul that he could mold the lady's mind to match his own. She would be his helpmeet. Comte had not read Ouida, who once wrote that when God said, "I will make a helpmeet for him," He was speaking ironically.

Comte had associated but very little with women—he had theories about them. Small men, with midget minds, know femininity much better than do the great ones. Traveling salesmen, with checkered vests, gauge women as Herbert Spencer never could.

Comte's wife was pretty and she was astute—as most pretty women are. John Fiske, in his lecture on "Communal Life," says that astute persons add nothing of value to the community in which they live—their mission being to be the admired glass of fashion for the non-cogitabund. The value of astuteness is that it protects us from the astute.

Samuel Johnson and his wife had their first quarrel on the way from the church, and Auguste Comte and his wife tiffed going down the steps from the notary's. Comte had no use for ecclesiastical forms, and the lady agreed with him until after the notary had earned his fee. Then she suddenly had qualms, like those peculiar ladies told of by Robert Louis Stevenson, who turn the Madonna's face to the wall.

The couple went to Montpelier on their wedding-tour, to visit Comte's parents. The new wife agreed with the old folks on but one point—the marriage should be solemnized by a priest. Having won them on this point, they stood a solid phalanx against the husband; but the lady took exceptions to Montpelier on all other grounds—she hated it thoroughly and said so.

Instead of molding her to his liking, Comte was being kneaded into animal crackers for her amusement.

Then we find him writing to a friend, confessing that his hopes were ashes; but in his misery he grows philosophical and says, "It is all good, for now I am driven back to my work, and from now on my life is dedicated to science."

No doubt the lady was as much disappointed in the venture as was the husband, but he, being literary, eased his grief by working it up into art, while her side of the story lies buried deep in silence glum.

In choosing the names of philosophers for this series, no thought was given in the selection beyond the achievements of the men. But it now comes to me with a slight surprise that seven out of the twelve were unmarried, and probably it would have been as well— certainly for the wives—if the other five had remained bachelors, too. Xantippe would have been the gainer, even if Socrates did miss his discipline.

To center on science and devote one's thought to philosophy produces a being more or less deformed. There is great danger in specialization: Nature sacrifices the man in order to get the thing done. Abstract thought unfits one for domestic life; for, to a degree, it separates a man from his kind.

The proper advice to a woman about to marry a philosopher would be, "Don't!"

The advantage of a little actual hardship in one's life is that it makes existence real and not merely literary. Comte was inclined to thrive on martyrdom. His restless, eager mind invented troubles, if there were no real ones, but he was wise enough to know this, as he once said: "The trials of life are all of one size—imaginary pains are as bad as real ones, and men who have no actual troubles usually conjure forth a few. Thus far, happily, I am not reduced to this strait."

We thus see that the true essence of philosophy was there. Comte got a gratification by dissecting, analyzing and classifying his emotions. All was grist that came to his mill.

When he was twenty-eight the Positive Philosophy had assumed such proportions in his mind that he announced a course of twelve lectures on the subject.

He was jealous of his discoveries, and was intent on getting all the credit that was due him. Money he cared little for; power and reputation to him were the only gods worth appeasing. The thought of domestic joy was forever behind, but philosophy came as a solace. A prospectus was sent out and tickets were issued. The landlady where he boarded offered her parlor and her boarder, second floor back, for the benefit of science. Several zealous denizens of the Latin Quarter made a canvass, and enough tickets were sold so that the philosopher felt that at last the world was really at his feet.

When the afternoon for the first lecture arrived, no carriages blocked the street, and as only about half of those who had purchased tickets appeared, the difficulties of the landlady and her nervous boarder were much lessened.

There was one man at this first lecture who was profoundly impressed, and if we had his testimony, and none other, we might well restrain our smiles. That man was Alexander von Humboldt. In various passages Humboldt does Comte the honor of quoting from him, and in one instance says, "He has summed up certain phases of truth better than they have ever been expressed before."

Little did the landlady guess that her crusty, crabbed boarder was firing a shot that would be heard 'round the world, and surely the gendarme on that particular beat never heard it—so small and commonplace are the beginnings of great things!

Comte was so saturated with this theme—so immersed in it—that it consumed him like a fever. Three lectures were given, but at the third, without warning, the man's nerves snapped—he stopped, sat down, and the audience filed out perplexed, thinking they had merely seen an exhibition of one of the eccentricities of genius. The philosopher's mind was a blank, and kind friends sent him away to a hospital.

It was two years before he regained his reason. The enforced rest did him good. Nervous Prostration is heroic treatment on the part of Nature. It is an intent to do for the man what he will never do for himself.

Unkind critics, hotly intent on refuting the Positive Philosophy, seized upon the fact of Comte's mental trouble and made much of it. "Look you!" said they, "the man is insane!"

This is convenient, but not judicial. Comte's philosophy stands or falls on its own merits, and what the author did before, after, or during the writing of his theses matters not. Madmen are not mad all the time, and the fact that Sir Isaac Newton was for a time unbalanced does not lessen our regard for the "Principia," nor consign to limbo the law of gravitation. Ruskin's work is not the less thought of because the man had his pathetic spells of indecision. Martin Luther had visions of devils before he saw the truth, and Emerson's love for Longfellow need not be disparaged because he looked down on his still, white face and said, "A dear gentle soul, but I really can not remember his name."

Men write on physiology, and then die, but this does not disprove the truth they expressed, but failed, possibly, to fully live. The great man always thinks further than he can travel—even the rest of us can do that. We can think "Chicago" in a second, but to go there takes time, strength and money.

When Comte's mental trouble was at its height, and two men were required to care for him, Lamennais persuaded his wife to have their marriage solemnized by the Church, and this was done. This performance was such a violation of sanctity and decency that in after-years Comte could not believe it was true, until he consulted the church records. "They might as well have had me confirmed," said Comte, grimly. And we can well guess that the action did not increase his regard for either his wife or the Church. The trick seems quite on a par with that of the astute colored gentleman who anxiously asks for love-powders at the corner drugstore; or the good wives who purchase harmless potions from red-dyed rogues to place in the husband's coffee to cure him of the liquor habit.

However, the incident gives a clew to the mental processes of Madame Comte—she would accomplish by trickery what she had failed to do by moral suasion, and this in the name of religion!

Two years of enforced rest, and the glowing mind of the philosopher awoke with a start. He rubbed his eyes after his Rip-Van-Winkle sleep, and called for his manuscripts—he must prepare for the fourth lecture!

The rest of the course was given, and in Eighteen Hundred Thirty the first volume of Positive Philosophy was issued.

The sixth and last volume appeared in Eighteen Hundred Forty-two—twelve years of intense application and ceaseless work. This was the happiest time of Comte's life; he had the whole scheme in his head from the start, but he now saw it gradually taking form, and it was meeting with appreciation from a few earnest thinkers, at least. His services were in demand for occasional lectures on scientific subjects. In astronomy, especially, he excelled, and on this theme he was able to please a popular assembly.

The Polytechnic School had now grown to large proportions, and the institution that Comte had helped to slide into dissolution now called him back to serve as examiner and professor.

The constant misunderstandings with his wife had increased to such a point that both felt a separation desirable. Married people do not separate on slight excuse—they go because they must. That Comte thought much more of the lady when they were several hundred miles apart than when they were together, there is no doubt. He wrote to her at regular intervals, one-half of his income was religiously sent to her, and he practised the most painstaking economy in order that he might feel that she was provided for.

One letter, especially, to his wife reveals a side of Comte's nature that shows he had the instinct of a true teacher. He says, "I hardly dare disclose the sweet and softened feeling that comes over me when I find a scholar whose heart is thoroughly in his work."

The Positive Philosophy was taken up by John Stuart Mill, who wrote a fine essay on it. It was Mill who introduced the work to Harriet Martineau. Mr. and Mrs. Mill had intended to translate and condense the philosophy of Comte for English readers, but when Miss Martineau expressed her intention of attempting the task, they relinquished the idea, but backed her up in her efforts.

Miss Martineau condensed the six volumes into two, and what is most strange, Comte thought so well of the work that he wrote a glowing acknowledgment of it.

The Martineaus were of good old Huguenot stock, and the French language came easy to Harriet. For the plain people of France she had a profound regard, and being sort of a revolutionary by prenatal instincts, Comte's work from the start appealed to her. James Martineau had such a bristling personality—being very much like his sister Harriet—that when this sister wrote a review of a volume of his sermons, showing the fatuity and foolishness of the reasoning, and calling attention to much bad grammar, the good man cut her off with a shilling—"which he will have to borrow," said Harriet.

James hugged the idea to his death that his sister had insulted his genius—"But I forgive her," he said, which remark proves that he hadn't, for if he had, he would not have thought to mention the matter. James Martineau was a great man, but if he had been just a little greater he would have taken a profound pride in a sister who was so sharp a shooter that she could puncture his balloon. James Martineau was a theologian; Harriet was a Positivist. But Positivity had a lure for him, and so there is a long review, penned largely with aqua fortis, on Miss Martineau's translation, done by her brother for the "Edinburgh Review," wherein Harriet is not once mentioned.

When Robert Ingersoll's wife would occasionally, under great stress of the servant-girl problem, break over a bit, as good women will, and say things, Robert would remark, "Gently, my dear, gently—I fear me you haven't yet gotten rid of all your Christian virtues."

The Reverend Doctor James Martineau never quite got rid of his Christian virtues, which perhaps proves that a little hate, like strychnin, is useful as a stimulant when properly reduced, for Doctor Martineau died only a few years ago, having nearly rounded out a century run.

Harriet Martineau was in much doubt about how Comte would regard her completed work, but was greatly relieved when he gave it his unqualified approval. On his earnest invitation she visited him in Paris. Fortunately, she did not have to resort to the Herbert Spencer expedient of wearing ear-muffs for protection against loquacious friends. She liked Comte first-rate, until he began to make love to her. Then his stock dropped below par.

Comte was always much impressed by intellectual women. His wife had given him a sample of the other kind, and caused him to swing out and idealize the woman of brains.

So that, when Harriet Martineau admired the Positive Philosophy, it was proof sufficient to Comte of her excellence in all things. She knew better, and started soon for Dover.

Mr. and Mrs. Mill had called on Comte a few months before, and given him a glimpse of the ideal—an intellectual man mated with an intellectual woman. But Comte didn't see that it was plain commonsense that made them great. Comte prided himself on his own commonsense, but the article was not in his equipment, else he would not have put the blame of all his troubles upon his wife. A man with commonsense, married to a woman who hasn't any, does not necessarily forfeit his own.

Mr. or Mrs. Mill would have been great anywhere—singly, separately, together, or apart. Each was a radiant center. Weakness multiplied by two does not give strength, and naught times naught equals naught.

Having finished the Positive Philosophy, Comte's restless mind began to look around for more worlds to conquer.

In the expenditure of money he was careful, and in his accounts exact; but the making of money and its accumulation were things that to him could safely be delegated to second-class minds. A haughty pride of intellect was his, not unmixed with that peculiar quality of the prima donna which causes her to cut fantastic capers and make everybody kiss her big toe.

Comte had done one thing superbly well. England had recognized his merit to a degree that France had not, and to his English friends he now made an appeal for financial help, so he could have freedom to complete another great work he had in his mind. To John Stuart Mill he wrote, outlining in a general way his new book on a social science, to be called "The Positive Polity." It was, in a degree, to be a sequel to the Positive Philosophy.

Mill communicated with Grote, the banker, known to us through his superb history of Greece, and with the help of George Henry Lewes and a mite from Herbert Spencer to show his good-will, a purse equal to about twelve hundred dollars was sent to Comte.

Matters went along for a year, when Comte wrote a brief letter to Mill suggesting that it was about time for another remittance. Mill again appealed to Grote, and Grote, the man of affairs, wrote to his Paris correspondent, who ascertained that Comte, now believing he was free from the bread-and-butter bugaboo, was giving his services to the Polytechnic, gratis, and also giving lectures to the people wherever some one would simply pay for the hall.

To advance money to a man that he might write a book showing how the nation should manage its finances, when the author could not look after his own, reminded Grote of the individual who wrote from the Debtors' Prison to the Secretary of the Exchequer, giving valuable advice. All publishers are familiar with the penniless person who writes a book on "How to Achieve Success," expecting to achieve success by publishing it.

Grote wrote to Mill, expressing the wholesome truth that the first duty of every man was to make a living for himself—a fact which Mill states in "On Liberty." Mill hadn't the temerity to pass Grote's maxim along to Comte, and so sent a small contribution out of his own pocket. This was very much like the Indian who, feeling that his dog's tail should be amputated, cut it off a little at a time, so as not to hurt the animal. We have all done this, and got the ingratitude we deserved.

Comte wrote back a most sarcastic letter, accusing Mill and Grote with having broken faith with him.

He now treated them very much as he had Saint-Simon; and in his lectures seldom failed to tell in pointed phrase what a lot of money-grubbing barbarians inhabited the British Isles. To the credit of Mill be it said that he still believed in the value of the Positive Philosophy, and did all he could to further Comte's reputation and help the sale of his books.

In Eighteen Hundred Forty-five, when Comte was forty-seven years old, he met Madame Clothilde de Vaux. Her husband was in prison, serving a life-sentence for political offenses, and Comte was first attracted to her through pity. Soon this evolved into a violent attachment, and Comte began to quote her in his lectures.

Comte was now most busy with his "Polity" in collaboration with Madame De Vaux. Her part of the work seems to have been to listen to Comte while he read her his amusing manuscript: and she, being a good woman and wise, praised the work in every part. They were together almost daily, and she seemed to supply him the sympathy he had all of his life so much craved.

In one short year Madame De Vaux died, and Comte for a time was inconsolable. Then his sorrow found surcease in an attempt to do for her in prose what Dante had done for Beatrice in poetry. But the vehicle of Comte's thoughts creaked. The exact language of science when applied to a woman becomes peculiarly non-piquant and lacking in perspicacity and perspicuity. No woman can be summed up in an algebraic formula, and when a mathematician does a problem to his lady's eyebrow, he forgets entirely that femininity forever equals x. Those who can write Sonnets from the Portuguese may place their loves on exhibition—no others should. Sweets too sweet do cloy.

For the rest of his life, Comte made every Wednesday afternoon sacred for a visit to the grave of Madame De Vaux, and three times every day, with the precision of a Mussulman, he retired to his room, locked the door, and in silence apostrophized to her spirit. Comte now continued as industrious as ever, but the quality of his writing lamentably declined. His popular lectures to the people on scientific themes were always good, and his work as a teacher was satisfactory, but when he endeavored to continue original research, then his hazards of mind lacked steady flight.

The Positive Polity degenerated into a dogmatic scheme of government where the wisest should rule. The determination of who was wisest was to be left to the wise ones themselves, and Comte himself volunteered to be the first Pope.

The worship of Humanity would be the only religion, and women would shine as the high priests. Comte thought it all out in detail, and arranged a complete scheme of life, and actually wished to form a political party and overthrow the government, founding a gynecocracy on the ruins. His ebbing mind could not grasp the thought that tyranny founded on goodness is a tyranny still, and that a despotic altruism is a despotism nevertheless. Slavery blocks evolution.

So thus rounded out the life of Auguste Comte—beginning in childhood, he traversed the circle, and ended where he began.

He died in his sixtieth year. M. Littre, his most famous pupil, touchingly looked after his wants to the last, ministered to his necessities, advancing money on royalties that were never due. M. Littre occasionally apologized for the meagerness of the returns, and was closely questioned and even doubted by Comte, who died unaware of the unflinching loyalty of a friendship that endured distrust and contumely without resentment. Such love and patience and loyalty as were shown by M. Littre redeem the race.

The best certificate to the worth of Auguste Comte lies in the fact that, in spite of marked personal limitations and much petty querulousness, he profoundly influenced such men as Littre, Humboldt, Mill, Lewes, Grote, Spencer and Frederic Harrison.

To have helped such men as these, and cheered them on their way, was no small achievement. Comte's sole claim for immortality lies in the Positive Philosophy. The word "positive," as used by Comte, is similar in intent to pose, poise—fixed, final. So, besides a positive present good, Comte believed he was stating a final truth; to-wit: that which is good here is good everywhere, and if there is a future life, the best preparation for it is to live now and here, up to your highest and best. Comte protested against the idea of "a preparation for a life to come"—now is the time, and the place is here.

The essence of Positive Philosophy is that man passes through three mental periods—the Theological or fictitious; the Metaphysical or abstract; the Positive or scientific.

Hence, there are three general philosophies or systems of conceptions concerning life and destiny.

The Theological, or first system, is the necessary starting-point of the human intellect. The Positive, or third period, is the ultimate goal of every progressive, thinking man; the second period is merely a state of transition that bridges the gulf between the first and the third.

Metaphysics holds the child by the hand until he can trust his feet—it is a passageway between the fictitious and the actual. Once across the chasm, it is no longer needed. Theology represents the child; Metaphysics the youth; Science the man.

The evolution of the race is mirrored in the evolution of the individual. Look back on your own career—your first dawn of thought began in an inquiry, "Who made all this—how did it all happen?"

And Theology comes in with a glib explanation: the fairies, dryads, gnomes and gods made everything, and they can do with it all as they please. Later, we concentrate all of these personalities in one god, with a devil in competition, and this for a time satisfies.

Later, the thought of an arbitrary being dealing out rewards and punishments grows dim, for we see the regular workings of Cause and Effect. We begin to talk of Energy, the Divine Essence, and the Reign of Law. We speak, as Matthew Arnold did, of "a Power, not ourselves, that makes for righteousness." But Emerson believed in a power that was in himself that made for righteousness.

Metaphysics reaches its highest stage when it affirms "All is One," or "All is Mind," just as Theology reaches its highest conception when it becomes Monotheistic—having one God and curtailing the personality of the devil to a mere abstraction.

But this does not long satisfy, for we begin to ask, "What is this One?" or "What is Mind?"

Then Positivity comes in and says that the highest wisdom lies in knowing that we do not know anything, and never can, concerning a First Cause. All we find is phenomena and behind phenomena, phenomena. The laws of Nature do not account for the origin of the laws of Nature. Spencer's famous chapter on the Unknowable was derived largely from Comte, who attempted to define the limits of human knowledge. And it is worth noting that the one thing which gave most offense in both Comte's and Spencer's works was their doctrine of the Unknowable. This, indeed, forms but a small part of the work of these men, and if it were all demolished there would still remain their doctrine of the known. The bitterness of Theology toward Science arises from the fact that as we find things out we dispense with the arbitrary god, and his business agent, the priest, who insists that no transaction is legal unless he ratifies it.

Men begin by explaining everything, and the explanations given are always first for other people. Parents answer the child, not telling him the actual truth, but giving him that which will satisfy—that which he can mentally digest. To say, "The fairies brought it," may be all right until the child begins to ask who the fairies are, and wants to be shown one, and then we have to make the somewhat humiliating confession that there are no fairies.

But now we perceive that this mild fabrication in reference to Santa Claus, and the fairies, is right and proper mental food for the child. His mind can not grasp the truth that some things are unknowable; and he is not sufficiently skilled in the things of the world to become interested in them—he must have a resting-place for his thought, so the fairy-tale comes in as an aid to the growing imagination. Only this: we place no penalty on disbelief in fairies, nor do we make special offers of reward to all who believe that fairies actually exist. Neither do we tell the child that people who believe in fairies are good, and that those who do not are wicked and perverse.

Comte admits that the theological and metaphysical stages are necessary, but the sooner man can be graduated out of them the better. He brought vast research to bear in order to show the growth and death of theological conceptions. Hate, fear, revenge and doubt are all theological attributes, detrimental to man's best efforts. That moral ideas were an afterthought, and really form no part of theology, Comte emphasized at great length, and shows from much data where these ideas were grafted on to the original tree.

And the sum of the argument is, that all progress of mind, body and material things has come to man through the study of Cause and Effect. And just in degree as he has abandoned the study of Theology as futile and absurd, and centered on helping himself here and now, has he prospered.

Positivism is really a religion. The object of its worship is Humanity. It does not believe in a devil or any influence that works for harm, or in opposition to man. Man's only enemy is himself, on account of his ignorance of this world, and his superstitious belief in another. Our troubles, like diseases, all come from ignorance and weakness, and through our ignorance are we weak and unable to adjust ourselves to conditions. The more we know of this world the better we think of it, and the better are we able to use it for our advancement.

So far as we can judge, the Unknown Cause that rules the world by unchanging laws is a movement forward toward happiness, growth, justice, peace and right. Therefore, the Scientist, who perceives that all is good when rightly received and rightly understood, is really the priest or holy man—the mediator and explainer of the mysteries. As fast as we understand things they cease to be supernatural, for the supernatural is the natural not yet understood. The theological priest who believes in a god and a devil is the real modern infidel. Such a belief is fallacious, contrary to reason, and contrary to all the man of courage sees and knows.

The real man of faith is the one who discards all thought of "how it first happened," and fixes his mind on the fact that he is here. The more he studies the conditions that surround him, the greater his faith in the truth that all is well.

If men had turned their attention to Humanity, discarding Theology, using as much talent, time, money and effort to wring from the skies the secrets of the Unknowable, this world would now be a veritable paradise. It is Theology that has barred the entrance to Eden, by diverting the attention of men from this world to another. Heaven is Here.

All religious denominations now dimly perceive the trend of the times, and are gradually omitting theology from their teachings and taking on ethics and sociology instead. A preacher is now simply Society's walking delegate. We are evolving theology out and sociology in. Theology has ever been the foe of progress and the enemy of knowledge. It has professed to know all and has placed a penalty on advancement. The Age of Enlightenment will not be here until every church has evolved into a schoolhouse, and every priest is a pupil as well as a teacher.

VOLTAIRE

We are intelligent beings; and intelligent beings can not have been formed by a blind, brute, insensible being. There is certainly some difference between a clod and the ideas of Newton. Newton's intelligence came from some greater Intelligence.

—*The Philosophical Dictionary*

VOLTAIRE

The man, Francois Marie Arouet, known to us as Voltaire (which name he adopted in his twenty-first year), was born in Paris in Sixteen Hundred Ninety-four. He was the second son in a family of three children. During his babyhood he was very frail; in childhood sickly and weak; and throughout his whole life he suffered much from indigestion and insomnia.

In all the realm of writers no man ever had a fuller and more active career, touching life at so many points, than Voltaire.

The first requisite in a long and useful career would seem to be, have yourself born weak and cultivate dyspepsia, nervousness and insomnia. Whether or not the good die young is still a mooted question, but certainly the athletic often do. All those good men and true, who at grocery, tavern and railroad-station eat hard-boiled eggs on a wager, and lift barrels of flour with one hand, are carried to early graves, and over the grass-grown mounds that cover their dust, consumptive, dyspeptic and neurotic relatives, for twice or thrice a score of years, strew sweet myrtle, thyme and mignonette.

Voltaire died of an accident—too much Four-o'Clock—cut off in his prime, when life for him was at its brightest and best, aged eighty-three.

The only evidence we have that the mind of Voltaire failed at the last came from the Abbe Gaultier and the Curé of Saint Sulpice. These good men arrived with a written retraction, which they desired Voltaire to sign. Waiting in the anteroom of the sick-chamber they sent in word that they wished to enter. "Assure them of my respect," said the stricken man. But the holy men were not to be thus turned away, so they entered. They approached the bedside, and the Curé of Saint Sulpice said: "M. de Voltaire, your life is about to end. Do you acknowledge the divinity of Jesus Christ?"

And the dying man stretched out a bony hand, making a gesture that they should depart, and murmured, "Let me die in peace."

"You see," said the Curé to the Abbe, as they withdrew, "you see that he is out of his head!"

The father of Voltaire, Francois Arouet, was a notary who looked after various family estates and waxed prosperous on the crumbs that fell from the rich man's table.

He was solicitor to the Duc de Richelieu, the Sullys, and also the Duchesse de Saint-Simon, mother of the philosopher, Saint-Simon, who made the mistake of helping Auguste Comte, thus getting himself hotly and positively denounced by the man who formulated the "Positive Philosophy."

Arouet belonged to the middle class and never knew that he sprang from a noble line until his son announced the fact. It was then too late to deny it.

He was a devout Churchman, upright in all his affairs, respectable, walked with a waddle and cultivated a double chin. M. Arouet pater did not marry until his mind was mature, so that he might avoid the danger of a mismating. He was forty, past. The second son, Francois fils, was ten years younger than his brother Armand, so the father was over fifty when our hero was born. Francois fils used to speak of himself as an afterthought—a sort of domestic postscript—"but," added he musingly, "our afterthoughts are often best."

One of the most distinguished clients of M. Arouet was Ninon de Lenclos, who had the felicity to be made love to by three generations of Frenchmen. Ninon has been likened for her vivacious ways, her flashing intellect, and her perennial youth, to the divine Sara, who at sixty plays the part of Juliet with a woman of thirty for the old nurse. Ninon had turned her three-score and ten, and swung gracefully into the home-stretch, when the second son was born to M. Arouet. She was of a deeply religious turn of mind, for she had been loved by several priests, and now the Abbe de Chateauneuf was paying his devotions to her.

Ninon was much interested in the new arrival, and going to the house of M. Arouet, took to bed, and sent in haste for the Abbe de Chateauneuf, saying she was in sore trouble. When the good man arrived, he thought it a matter of extreme unction, and was ushered into the room of the alleged invalid. Here he was duly presented with the infant that later was to write the "Philosophical Dictionary." It was as queer a case of kabojolism as history records.

Doubtless the Abbe was a bit agitated at first, but finally getting his breath, he managed to say, "As there is a vicarious atonement, there must also be, on occasion, vicarious births, and this is one—God be praised."

The child was then baptized, the good Abbe standing as godfather.

There must be something, after all, in prenatal influences, for as the little Francois grew up he evolved the traits of Ninon de Lenclos and the Abbe much more than those of his father and mother.

When the boy was a little over six years old the mother died. Of her we know absolutely nothing. In her son's writings he refers to her but once, wherein he has her say that "Boileau was a clever book, but a silly man."

The education of the youngster seemed largely to have been left to the Abbe, his godfather, who very early taught him to recite the "Mosiad," a metrical effusion wherein the mistakes of Moses were related in churchly Latin, done first for the divertisement of sundry pious monks in idle hours.

At ten years of age Francois was sent to the College of Louis-le-Grand, a Jesuit school where the minds of youth were molded in things sacred and secular.

In only one thing did the boy really excel, and that was in the matter of making rhymes. The Abbe Chateauneuf had taught him the trick before he could speak plainly, and Ninon had been so pleased with the wee poet that she left him two thousand francs in her will for the purchase of books. As Ninon insisted on living to be ninety, Voltaire discounted the legacy and got it cashed on dedicating a sonnet to the divine Ninon. In this sonnet Voltaire suggests that a life of virtue conduces largely to longevity, as witness the incomparable Ninon de Lenclos, to which sentiment Ninon filed no exceptions.

In one of the school debates young Francois presented his argument in rhyme, and evidently ran in some choice passages from the "Mosiad," for Father le Jay, according to Condorcet, left his official chair, and rushing down the aisle, grabbed the boy by the collar, and shaking him, said, "Unhappy boy! you will one day be the standard-bearer of deism in France!"—a prophecy, possibly, made after its fulfilment.

Young Francois remained at the college until he was seventeen years old. From letters sent by him while there, it is evident that the chief characteristic of his mind was already a contempt for the clergy. Of two of his colleagues who were preparing for the priesthood, he says, "They had reflected on the dangers of a world of the charms of which they were ignorant; and on the pleasures of a religious life of which they knew not the disagreeableness." Already we see he was getting handy in polishing a sentence with the emery of his wit. Continuing, he says: "In a quarter of an hour they ran over all the Orders, and each seemed so attractive that they could not decide. In which predicament they might have been left like the ass, which died of starvation between two bundles of hay, not knowing which to choose. However, they decided to leave the matter to Providence, and let the dice decide. So one became a Carmelite and the other a Jesuit."

Arouet, at first intent on having his son become a priest, now fell back on the law as second choice. The young man was therefore duly articled with a firm of advocates and sent to hear lectures on jurisprudence. But his godfather introduced him into the Society of the Temple, a group of wits, of all ages, who could take snuff and throw off an epigram on any subject. The bright young man, flashing, dashing and daring, made friends at once through his skill in writing scurrilous verse upon any one whose name might be mentioned. This habit had been begun in college, where it was much applauded by the underlings, who delighted to see their unpopular teachers done to a turn. The scribbling habit is a variant of that peculiar propensity which finds form in drawing a portrait on the blackboard before the teacher gets around in the morning. If the teacher does not happen to love art for art's sake, there may be trouble; but verses are safer, for they circulate secretly and are copied and quoted anonymously.

The thing we do best in life is that which we play at most in youth.

Ridicule was this man's weapon. For the benefit of the Society of the Temple he paid his respects to the sham piety and politics of Versailles. He had been educated by priests, and his father was a politician feeding at the public trough. The young man knew the faults and foibles of both priest and politician, and his keen wit told truths about the court that were so well expressed the wastebasket did not capture them. One of these effusions was printed, anonymously, of course, but a copy coming into the hands of M. Arouet, the old gentleman recognized the literary style and became alarmed. He must get the young man out of Paris—the Bastile yawned for poets like this!

A brother of the Abbe de Chateauneuf was Ambassador at The Hague, and the great man, being importuned, consented to take the youth as clerk.

Life at The Hague afforded the embryo poet an opportunity to meet many distinguished people.

In Francois there was none of the bourgeois—he associated only with nobility—and as he had an aristocracy of the intellect, which served him quite as well as a peerage, he was everywhere received. In his manner there was nothing apologetic—he took everything as his divine right.

In this brilliant little coterie at The Hague was one Madame Dunoyer, a writer of court gossip and a social promoter of ability, separated from her husband for her husband's good. Francois crossed swords with her in an encounter of wit, was worsted, but got even by making love to her; and later he made love to her daughter, a beautiful girl of about his own age.

The air became surcharged with gossip. There was danger of an explosion any moment. Madame Dunoyer gave it out that the brilliant subaltern was to marry the girl. The Madame was going to capture the youth, either with her own charms or those of her daughter—or combined. Rumblings were heard on the horizon. The Ambassador, fearing entanglement, bundled young Arouet back to Paris, with a testimonial as to his character, quite unnecessary. A denial without an accusation is equal to a plea of guilty; and that the young man had made the mistake of making violent love to the mother and daughter at the same time there is no doubt. The mother had accused him and he said things back; he even had shown the atrocious bad taste of references in rhyme to the mutual interchange of confidences that the mother and daughter might enjoy. The Ambassador had acted none too soon.

The father was frantic with alarm—the boy had disgraced him, and even his own position seemed to be threatened when some wit adroitly accused the parent of writing the doggerel for his son.

M. Arouet denied it with an oath—while the son refused to explain, or to say anything beyond that he loved his father, thus carrying out the idea that the stupid old notary was really a wit in disguise, masking his intellect by a seeming dulness. No more biting irony was ever put out by Voltaire than this, and the pathos of it lies in the fact that the father was quite unable to appreciate the quip.

It was a sample of filial humor much more subtle than that indulged in by Charles Dickens, who pilloried his parents in print, one as Mr. Micawber and the other as Mrs. Nickleby. Dickens told the truth and painted it large, but Francois Arouet dealt in indiscreet fallacy when he endeavored to give his father a reputation for raillery.

A peculiarly offensive poem, appearing about this time, with the Regent and his daughter, the Duchesse de Berri, for a central theme, a rescript was issued which indirectly testified to the poetic skill of young Arouet. He was exiled to a point three hundred miles from Paris and forbidden to come nearer on penalty, like unto the injunction issued by Prince Henry against the blameless Falstaff. Rumor said that the father had something to do with the matter.

But the exile was not for long. The young poet wrote a most adulatory composition to the Regent, setting forth his innocence. The Regent was a mild and amiable man and much desired peace with all his subjects—especially those who dipped their quills in gall. He was melted by the rhyme that made him out such a paragon of virtue, and made haste to issue a pardon.

The elder Arouet now proved that he was not wholly without humor, for he wrote to a friend, "The exile of my dear son distressed me much less than does this precipitate recall."

In order to protect himself the father now refused a home to the son, and Francois became a lodger at a boarding-house. He wrote plays and acted in them, penned much bad poetry, went in good society and had a very rouge time. Up to this period he knew little Latin and less Greek, but now he had an opportunity to furbish up on both. He found himself an inmate of the Bastile, on the charge of expressing his congratulations to the people of France on the passing of Louis the Fourteenth. In America libel only applies to live men, but the world had not then gotten this far along.

In the prison it was provided that Sieur Arouet fils should not be allowed pens and paper on account of his misuse of these good things when outside. He was given copies of Homer, however, in Greek and Latin, and he set himself at work, with several of the other prisoners, to perfect himself in these languages. We have glimpses of his dining with the governor of the prison, and even organizing theatrical performances, and he was finally allowed writing materials on promise that he would not do anything worse than translate the Bible, so altogether he was very well treated.

In fact, he himself referred to this year spent in prison as "a pious retreat, that I might meditate, and chasten my soul in quiet thought."

He was only twenty-one, and yet he had set Paris by the ears, and his name was known throughout France. "I am as well known as the Regent and will be remembered longer," he wrote—a statement and a prophecy that then seemed very egotistical, but which time has fully justified.

It was in prison that he decided to change his name to Voltaire, a fanciful word of his own coining. His pretended reason for the change was that he might begin life anew and escape the disgrace he had undergone of being in prison. There is reason to believe, however, that he was rather proud of being "detained," it was proof of his power—he was dangerous outside. But his family had practically cast him off—he owed nothing to them—and the change of name fostered a mysterious noble birth, an idea that he allowed to gain currency without contradiction. Moliere had changed his name from Poquolin—and was he not really following in Moliere's footsteps, even to suffering disgrace and public odium?

The play of "Œdipe" was presented by Voltaire at the Theater Francaise, November Eighteenth, Seventeen Hundred Eighteen. This play was written before the author's sojourn in prison, but there he had sandpapered its passages, and hand-polished the epigrams.

It was rehearsed at length with the help of the "guests" at the Bastile, and once Voltaire wrote a note of appreciation to the Prefect of Police, thanking him for his thoughtfulness in sending such excellent and pure-minded people to help him in his work.

These things had been managed so they discreetly leaked out, and the cafes echoed with the name of Voltaire.

Very soon after his release the play was presented to a crowded house. It was a success from the start, for into its lines the audience was allowed to read many veiled allusions to Paris public characters. It ran for forty-five nights, and was the furore. On one occasion when interest seemed to lag, Voltaire, on a sudden inspiration, dressed up as a bumpkin page, and attended the Pontiff, carrying his train, playing various and sundry sly pranks in pantomime, a la Francis Wilson.

In one of the boxes sat a famous beauty, the Duchesse de Villars. "Who is this strange person who is intent upon spoiling the play?" she asked. On being told that he was the author of the drama, her censure turned to approbation and she sent for the young man. His appearance in her box was duly noted. The Regent and his daughter, the Duchesse de Berri, could not resist the temptation to attend the play, and see how much they were satirized. Voltaire did his little train-bearing act for their benefit, with a few extra grimaces, which pleased them very much, and seeing his opportunity, wrote a gracious letter of thanks to His Highness for having deigned to visit his play, winding up with thanks for the years in the Bastile where, "God wot, all of my evil inclinations were duly chastened and corrected."

It had the desired effect—each side feared the other. The Regent wanted the ready writers on his side, and the playwright who was opposed by the party in power could not hope for success. The Regent sent a present of a thousand crowns to Voltaire and also fixed on him a pension of twelve hundred livres a year. At once every passage in the play that could be construed as bearing on royalty was revised into words of adulation, and all went merry as a marriage-bell. Financially the play was a success, and better yet was the pension and the good-will of the young King and his Regent.

Thus at twenty-two did Voltaire have the world at his feet.

When Voltaire was twenty-four, his father died. The will provided that the property should be equally divided between his three children, but it was stipulated that the second son should not come into possession of his share until he was thirty-five, and not then unless he was able to show the Master in Chancery that he was capable of wisely managing his own affairs.

This doubt of the father concerning the son's financial ability has often been commented upon ironically, in view of the pronounced thrift shown by Voltaire in later life.

But who shall say whether the father by that provision in his will did not drive home a stern lesson in economy? Commodore Vanderbilt had so much distrust of his son William's capacity for business that he exiled him to a Long Island farm, on an allowance. Years after, when William had shown his ability to outstrip his father, he rebuked a critic who volunteered a suggestion to the effect that the father had erred in the boy problem. Said William, "My father was right in this, as in most other things—I was a fool, and he knew it."

Voltaire's vacation of a year in the Bastile had done him much good. Then the will of his father, with its cautious provisions, tended to sober the youth to a point where he was docile enough for society's needs.

A good deal of ballast in way of trouble was necessary to hold this man down.

Marriage might have tamed him. Bachelors are of two kinds—those who are innocent of women, and those who know women too well. The second class, I am told, outnumbers the first as ten to one.

Voltaire had been a favorite of various women—usually married ladies, and those older than himself. He had plagiarized Franklin, saying, fifty years before the American put out his famous advice, "If you must fall in love, why, fall in love with a woman much older than yourself, or at least a homely one—for only such are grateful."

In answer to a man who said divorce and marriage were instituted at the same time, Voltaire said: "This is a mistake: there is at least three days' difference. Men sometimes quarrel with their wives at the end of three days, beat them in a week and divorce them at the end of a month."

Voltaire was small and slight in stature, but his bubbling wit and graceful presence more than made amends for any deficiency in way of form and feature. Had he desired, he might have taken his pick among the young women of nobility, but we see the caution of his nature in limiting his love-affairs to plain women, securely married. "Gossip isn't busy with the plain women—that is why I like you," he once said to Madame de Bernieres. What the Madame's reply was, we do not know, but probably she was not displeased. If a woman knows she is loved, it matters little what you say to her. Compliments by the right oblique are construed into lavish praise when expressed in the right tone of voice by the right person.

The Regent had allowed Voltaire another pension of two thousand francs, at the same time intimating that he hoped the writer's income was sufficient so he could now tell the truth. Voltaire took the hint, so subtly veiled, to the effect that if he again affronted royalty by unkind criticisms, his entire pension would be canceled.

From this time on to the end of his life, he was full of lavish praise for royalty. He was needlessly loyal, and dedicated poems and pamphlets to nobility, right and left, in a way that would have caused a smile were not nobility so hopelessly bound in three-quarters pachyderm. He also wrote religious poems, protesting his love for the Church. And here seems a good place to say that Voltaire was a member of the Catholic Church to his death. Many of his worst attacks on the priesthood were put in way of defense for outrageous actions which he enumerated in detail. He kept people guessing as to what he meant and what he would do next.

Immediately after the death of President McKinley there was a fine scramble among the editors of certain saffron sheets—to get in line and shake their ulsters free from all taint of anarchy. Some writers, in order to divert suspicion from themselves, hotly denounced other men as anarchists.

Throughout his life Voltaire had spasms of repentance, prompted by caution, possibly, when he warmly denounced atheists, and swore, i' faith, that one object of his life was to purify the Church and cleanse it of its secret faults.

In his twenty-sixth year, when he was trying hard to be good, he got into a personal altercation with the Chevalier de Rohan, an insignificant man bearing a proud name. The Chevalier's wit was no match for the other's rapier-like tongue, but he had a way of his own in which to get even. He had his servants waylay the luckless poet and chastise him soundly with rattans.

Voltaire was furious; he tried to get the courts to take it up, but the prevailing idea was that he had gotten what he deserved, and the fact that the whole affair occurred after dark and the Chevalier did not do the beating in person, made conviction impossible.

But Voltaire now quit the anapest and dactyl and devoted his best hours to taking fencing lessons. His firm intent was to baptize the soil with Rohan's blood. Voltaire was of enough importance so the secret police knew of all his doings. Suddenly he found himself taking a post-graduate course in the Bastile. I am not sure that the fiery little man was entirely displeased with the procedure. It proved to the world that he was a dangerous character, and it also gave him a respite from the tyranny of the fencing-master, and allowed him to turn to his first, last and only love—literature. In Voltaire's cosmos was a good deal of the Bob Acres quality.

There were plenty of reasons for locking him up—heresy and treason have ever been first cousins—and pamphlets lampooning Churchmen high in office were laid at his door. No doubt some of the anonymous literature was not his—"I would have done the thing better or not at all," he once said in reference to a scurrilous brochure. The real fact was, that that particular pamphlet was done by a disciple, and if Voltaire's writings were vile, then was his offense doubled in that he vitalized a ravenous brood of scribblers. They played Caliban to his Setebos.

Voltaire's most offensive contributions were always attributed by him to this bishop or that, and to various dignitaries who had no existence save in the figment of his own fertile pigment.

He once carried on a controversy between the Bishop of Berlin and the Archbishop of Paris, each man thundering against the other with a monthly pamphlet wherein each one gored the other without mercy, and revealed the senselessness of the other's religion. They flung the literary stinkpot with great accuracy. "The other man's superstition is always ridiculous to us—our own is sacred," said Voltaire, and so he allowed his controversialists to fight it out for his own quiet joy, and the edification of the onlookers.

Then his plan of printing an alleged sermon, giving some unknown prelate due credit on the title-page, starting in with a pious text and a page of trite nothings and gradually drifting off into ridicule of the things he had started in to defend—all this gives a comic tinge to his wail that "some evil-minded person is attributing things to me I never wrote," If an occasional sly Churchman got after him with his own weapon, writing things in his style more hazardous than he dare express, surely he should not have complained.

But this was a fact—the enemy could not follow him long with a literary fusillade—they hadn't the mental ammunition.

Well has Voltaire been called "the father of all those who wear shovel-hats."

A few months in the Bastile, and Voltaire's indeterminate sentence was commuted to exile. He was allowed to leave his country for his country's good. Early in the year Seventeen Hundred Twenty-six he landed in England, evidently knowing nobody there except one merchant, a man of no special prominence.

Voltaire belonged to the nobility by divine right—as much as did Disraeli. Both had an inward contempt for titles, but they knew the hearts of the owners so well that they simply played a game of chess, and the "men" they moved were live knights, bishops, kings and queens, with rollers under the castles. The pawns they pushed here and there were the literary puppets of the time.

The first thing Voltaire had to master in England was the language, and this he did passably inside of three months. He took Grub Street by storm; dawdled at Dodsley's; met Dean Swift, and these worthies respected each other's wit so much that they simply took snuff, grimaced and let it go at that; Pope came in for a visit, and the French poet crossed Twickenham ferry and offered a handmade sonnet in admiration of the "Essay on Man," which he had probably never read. Gay gave Voltaire "The Beggar's Opera," in private, and together they called on Congreve, who interrupted the Frenchman's flow of flattery long enough to say that he wished to be looked on as a gentleman, not a poet. And Voltaire replied that there were many gentlemen but few poets, and if Congreve had had the misfortune to be simply a gentleman he would not have troubled to call on him at all. Congreve, who really regarded himself as the peer of Shakespeare, was won, and sent Voltaire on his way with letters to Horace Walpole of Strawberry Hill. Thomson, who lived at Hammersmith, and wrote his "Seasons" in a "public" next door to Kelmscott, corrected and revised some of Voltaire's attempts at English poetry. Young evolved some of his "Night Thoughts" while on a visit with Voltaire at Bubb Dodington's.

A call on the Duchess of Marlborough led to a dinner at Lord Chesterfield's. Next he met Queen Caroline and assured her that she spoke French like a Parisian. King George the Second quite liked Voltaire, because Voltaire quite liked Lady Sandon, his mistress. Only a Frenchman could have successfully paid court to the King, Queen and Lady Sandon at the same time, as Voltaire did. His great epic poem, "Henriade," that he had been sandpapering for ten years, was now published, dedicated to the Queen. The King headed the subscription-list with more copies than he needed, at five guineas each, on agreement. Voltaire afterward said that he would not be expected to read the poem. The Queen's good offices were utilized—she became for the time a royal book-agent, and her signature and the author's adorned all deluxe copies. A suggestion from the Queen was equal to an order, and the edition was soon worked off.

Voltaire now spent three years in England. He had written his "Life of Charles the Twelfth," several plays, an "English Note-Book," and best of all, had gotten together a thousand pounds good money as proceeds of "Henriade," a stiff and stilted piece of pedantic bombast, written with sweat and lamp-smoke.

The "Letters on the English" were published a few years later in Paris with good results, considering it was only a by-product. It is a deal better-natured than Dickens' "American Note-Book," and had more humor than Emerson's "English Traits." Among other things quite Voltairesque in the "Letters" is this: "The Anglican Church has retained many of the good old Catholic customs—not the least of which is the collection of tithes with great regularity."

The priestly habit of Voltaire's life manifested itself even to the sharp collecting from the world all that the world owed him.

The snug little sum he had secured in England would have shown his ability, but there was something better in store, awaiting his return to France. It seems the Controller of Finance had organized a lottery to help pay the interest on the public debt. A considerable sum of money had been realized, but there was still a large number of tickets unsold, and the drawing was soon to take place. Voltaire knew the officials who had the matter in charge and they knew him. He organized a syndicate that would take all tickets there were left, on guarantee that among the tickets purchased would be the one that called for the principal prize of forty thousand pounds. Just how it was known in advance what ticket would win must be left to those good people who understand these little things in detail. In any event, Voltaire put in every sou he had—and his little fortune was then a matter of about ten thousand dollars. Several of his friends contributed a like sum.

The drawing took place, and the prize of forty thousand pounds was theirs. It is said that Voltaire took twenty-five thousand pounds as his share—the whole scheme was his anyway—and his friends were quite satisfied with having doubled their money in a fortnight. Immediately on securing this money, Voltaire presented himself at the office of the President of Accounts, and asked for the legacy left him by his father. As proof of his financial ability, and as a guarantee of good faith, he opened a hand-satchel and piled on the President's table a small mountain of gold and bank-notes. The first question of the astonished official was, "Will M. de Voltaire have the supreme goodness to explain where he stole all this money?"

This was soon followed by an apology, as the visitor explained the reason of his visit.

The father's legacy amounted to nearly four thousand pounds, and this was at once paid over to Voltaire with a flattering letter expressing perfect faith in his ability to manage his own finances.

There is a popular opinion that Voltaire made considerable money by his pen, but the fact is, that at no period of his life did literature contribute in but a very scanty way to his prosperity.

After the lottery scheme, Voltaire embarked in grain speculations, importing wheat from Barbary for French consumption. In this he made a fair profit, but when war broke out between Italy and France, he entered into an arrangement with Duverney, who had the army commissariat in his hands, to provision the troops. It was not much of a war, but it lasted long enough, as most wars do, for a few contractors to make much moneys. The war spirit is usually fanned by financiers, Kuhn, Loeb and Company giving the ultimatum.

Voltaire cleared about twenty thousand pounds out of his provision contract.

Thus we find this thrifty poet at forty with a fortune equal to a half-million dollars. This money he loaned out in a way of his own—a way as original as his literary style. His knowledge of the upper circles again served him well. Among the proud scions of nobility there were always a few who, through gambling proclivities, and other royal qualities, were much in need of funds. Voltaire picked the men who had only a life interest in their estates, and made them loans, secured by the rentals. The loans were to be paid back in annuities as long as both men lived.

All insurance is a species of gambling—the company offers to make you a bet that your house will burn within a year.

In life-insurance, the company's expert looks you over, and if your waist measurement is not too great for your height, a bargain is entered into wherein you agree to pay so much now, and so much every year as long as you live, in consideration that the company will pay your heirs so much at your death.

The chief value of life-insurance lies in the fact that it insures a man against his own indiscretion, a thing supposedly under his own control—but which never is. Voltaire's scheme banked on the man's weakness, and laid his indiscretion open before the world. It was life-insurance turned wrong side out, and could only have been devised and carried out by a man of courage with an actuary's bias for mathematics.

Instead of agreeing to pay the man so much at death, Voltaire paid him the whole sum in advance, and the man agreed to pay, say, ten per cent interest until either the lender or the borrower died. No principal was to be paid, and on the death of either party, the whole debt was canceled.

Voltaire picked only men younger than himself. It was a tempting offer to the borrower, for Voltaire looked like a consumptive, and it is said that on occasion he evolved a wheezy cough that helped close the deal. The whole scheme, for Voltaire, was immensely successful. On some of the risks he collected his yearly ten per cent for over forty years, or until his death.

On Voltaire's loan of sixteen hundred pounds to the Marquis du Chatelet, however, it is known that he collected nothing either in way of principal or interest. This was as strange a piece of financiering as was ever consummated; and the inside history of the matter, with its peculiar psychology, has never been written. The only two persons who could have told that story in its completeness were Voltaire and the Madame du Chatelet, and neither ever did.

Madame du Chatelet—the divine Emilie—was twenty-seven and Voltaire was thirty-nine when they first met.

He was living in obscure lodgings in Paris for prudential reasons, the executioner having just burned, in the public street, all the copies of his last book that could be found.

The Madame called on him to express her sympathy—and congratulations. She had written a book, but it had not been burned—not even read! She was tall, thin, angular, far from handsome, but had beaming eyes and a face that tokened intellect. And best of all, her voice was low, finely modulated, and was not exercised more than was meet.

She leaned her chin upon her hand and looked at him.

She had met Voltaire when she was a child—at least she said so, and he, being a gentleman, remembered perfectly. She read to him a little manuscript she had just dashed off. It was deep, profound and full of reasons—that is the way learned women write—they write like professors of rhetoric. Really great men write lightly, suggestively, and with a certain amount of indifference, dash, froth and foam. When women evolve literary foam, it is the sweet, cloying, fixed foam of the charlotte russe—not the bubbling, effervescent Voltaire article.

Could M. de Voltaire suggest a way in which her manuscript might be lightened up so the public executioner would deign to notice it?

M. de Voltaire responded by reading to her a little thing of his own.

The next day she called again.

Some say that Madame called on Voltaire to secure a loan on her husband's estate at Civey. No matter—she got the loan.

Doubtless she did not know where she was going—none of us do. We are all sailing under sealed orders.

The Madame had been married eight years. She was versed in Latin and knew Italian literature. She was educated; Voltaire was not. She offered to teach him Italian if he would give her lessons in English.

They read to each other things they had recently written. When men and women read to each other and mingle their emotions, the danger-line is being reached. Literary people of the opposite sex do not really love each other. All they desire is to read their manuscript aloud to a receptive listener.

Thus are the literary germs vitalized—by giving our thoughts to another we really make them our own. Only well-sexed people produce literature—poetry is the pollen of the mind. Meter, rhythm, lilt and style are stamen, pistil and stalk swaying in the warm breeze of springtime.

An order for arrest was out for Voltaire. Pamphlets which he had been refused permission to publish in Paris were printed at Rouen and were setting all Paris by the ears.

With Madame du Chatelet he fled to Civey, where was the tumbledown chateau of the Marquis—the Madame's complaisant husband. Voltaire advanced the Marquis sixteen hundred pounds to put the place in order, and then on his own account fitted up two sumptuous apartments, one for himself and one for Madame. The Marquis went away with his regiment, and occasionally came back and lounged about the chateau. But Voltaire was the real master of the place.

Voltaire was neither domestic nor rural in his tastes, but the Du Chatelet seemed to fill his cup to the brim, and made him enjoy what otherwise would have been exile. He wrote incessantly—poems, essays, plays—and fired pamphlets at a world of fools.

All that he wrote during the day he read to Madame at night. One of her maids has given us a vivid little picture of how Voltaire, at exactly eleven o'clock each night, would come out of hiding, and entering the Madame's room, would partake of the dainty supper that was always prepared for him. The divine Émilie had the French habit of receiving her visitors in bed, and as her hours were much more regular than Voltaire's, she usually enjoyed a nap before he entered. After his supper he would read aloud to her all he had written since they last met. If the piece was dramatic he would act it out with roll of r's, striding walk, grimace and gesticulations gracefully done, for the man was an actor of rare talent.

Emerson says, "Let a man do a thing incomparably well, and the world will make a path to his door, though he live in a forest." There was no lack of society at Civey—the writers, poets and philosophers found their way there. Voltaire fitted up a little private theater, where his plays were given, and concerts and lectures held from time to time.

The divine Émilie's forte was science and mathematics—and on these themes she wrote much, competing for prizes and winning the recognition of various learned societies. It will be seen that the man and the woman were not in competition with each other, which, perhaps, accounts, in degree, for their firm friendship.

Yet they did quarrel, too, as true lovers will, I am told. But their quarreling was all done in English, so the servants and His Inertia, the Marquis, did not know the purpose of it. It is probable that the accounts of their misunderstandings are considerably exaggerated, as the rehearsal of a tragedy by this pair of histrions would be taken by the servants for a sure-enough fight.

And they were always acting—often beginning breakfast with a "stunt." The Madame sang well, and her little impromptu arias pleased her thin little lover immensely and he would improvise and answer in kind, and then take the part of an audience and applaud, calling loudly, "Bravo! Bravo!"

Mornings they would ride horseback through the winding woods, or else hunt for geological and botanical specimens. About all of Voltaire's science he got from the lady and this was true of languages as well.

To a nervous, irritable and intense thinker a certain amount of solitude seems necessary. Voltaire occasionally grew weary of the delicious quiet of Civey, and the indictment against him having been quashed, he would go away to Paris or elsewhere. On these trips if he did not take Madame along she would grow furious, then lacrimose and finally submissive—with a weepy protest. If he failed to write her daily she grew hysterical. Two winters they spent together in Paris and another at Brussels.

A lawsuit involving the estate of the Marquis du Chatelet, that had been in the courts for eighty years, was pushed to a successful issue by Voltaire and Madame. Four hundred fifty thousand dollars were secured, but of this Voltaire, strangely enough, took nothing.

That the bond between Émilie and Voltaire was very firm is shown by the fact that, after they had been together ten years, he declined to leave her to accept an invitation to visit Frederick the Great at Berlin. Frederick was a married man, but his was a strictly bachelor court—for prudential reasons. Frederick and Émilie had carried on a spirited correspondence, but this was as close as he cared for her to come to him. All of his communications with females were limited to letters, and Voltaire once said that that was the reason he was called Frederick the Great.

Madame du Chatelet died when she was forty-two; Voltaire was fifty-five. For fifteen years this strange and most romantic friendship had continued, and to a degree it had worn itself out. Toward the last the lady had been exacting and dictatorial, and thinking that Voltaire had slighted her by not taking her more into his confidence, she had accepted another lover, a man ten years her junior. If she had thought to make Voltaire jealous, she had reckoned without her host—he was relieved to find her fierce supervision relaxed.

When she passed away he worked his woe up into a pretty panegyric, closed up his affairs at Civey, and left there forever.

So far as the government was concerned, Voltaire seems to have passed his days in accepting rewards and receiving punishments. Interdict, exile, ostracism were followed by honors, pension and office.

His one lasting love was the drama. About every two years a swirl of excitement was caused at Paris by the announcement of a new play by Voltaire. These plays seemed to appeal mostly to the nobility, the clergy and those in public office. And the object in every instance was to get even with somebody, and place some one in a ridiculous light. Innocent historical dramas were passed by the censor, and afterward it was found that in them some local bigwig was flayed without mercy. Then the play had to be withdrawn, and all printed copies were burned in public, and Voltaire would flee to Brussels or Geneva to escape summary punishment.

However, he never fooled all of the people all of the time. There was always a goodly number of dignitaries who richly enjoyed the drubbing he gave the other fellow, and these would gloat in inward glee over the Voltaire ribaldry until it came their turn. Then the other side would laugh. The fact is, Voltaire always represented a constituency, otherwise his punishment might have been genuine, instead of forty lashes with a feather, well laid on.

About the time Madame du Chatelet passed away, Voltaire seemed to be enjoying a period of kingly favor. He had been made a Knight of the Bedchamber and also Historiographer of France. The chief duty of the first office consisted in signing the monthly voucher for salary, and the other was about the same as Poet Laureate—with salary in inverse ratio to responsibility. It was considered, however, that the holder of these offices was one of the King's family, and therefore was bound to indulge in no unseemly antics.

On June Twenty-sixth, Seventeen Hundred Fifty, Voltaire applied to the King in person for permission to visit Frederick of Prussia.

Tradition has it that the King replied promptly, "You may go—the sooner the better—and you may remain as long as you choose."

Voltaire pocketed the veiled acerbity without a word, and bowing himself out, made hot haste to pack up and be on his way before an order rescinding the permission was issued.

Frederick was a freethinker, a scientist, a poet, and a wit well worthy of the companionship of Voltaire. In fact, they were very much alike. Both had the dual qualities of being intensely practical and yet iconoclastic. Both were witty, affable, seemingly indifferent and careless, but yet always with an eye on the main chance. Each was small, thin and bony, but both had the intellect of the lean and hungry Cassius that looked quite through the deeds of man.

Frederick received Voltaire with royal honors. Princes, ministers of state, grandees and generals high in office, knelt on one knee as he passed. Frederick tried to make it appear that France had failed to appreciate her greatest philosopher, and so he had come to Prussia—the home of letters. His pension was fixed at twenty thousand francs a year, he was given the Golden Key of Chamberlain, and the Grand Cross of the Order of Merit. He was a member of the King's household, and was the nearest and dearest friend of the royal person.

Frederick thought he had bound the great man to him for life.

Personality repels as well as attracts. Voltaire's viper-like pen was never idle. He wrote little plays for the court, and these were presented with much eclat, the author superintending their presentation, and considerately taking minor parts himself, so as to divide the honors. But amateur theatricals stand for heart-burnings and jealousy. The German poets were scored, other writers ridiculed, and big scientists came in for their share of pen-pricking.

Voltaire corrected the King's manuscript and taught him the secret of literary style. Then they fell into a controversy, done in Caslon old-style, thundering against each other's theories in pamphlets across seas of misunderstandings. Neither side publicly avowed the authorship, but nobody was deceived. The King and Voltaire met daily at meals, and carefully avoided the topics they were fighting out in print.

Voltaire was rich and all of his wants were supplied, but he entered the financial lists, and taking advantage of his inside knowledge, speculated in scrip and got into a disgraceful lawsuit over the proceeds with a man he should never have known. Frederick was annoyed—then disturbed. He personally chided Voltaire for his folly in mixing with the King's enemies.

Voltaire had tired of the benevolent assimilation—he craved freedom. A friend who loves you, if he spies upon your every action, will become intolerable. Voltaire intimated to Frederick that he would like to go.

But Frederick had a great admiration for the man—he considered Voltaire the greatest living thinker, and to have such a one in the court would help give the place an atmosphere of learning. He recognized that there were two Voltaires—one covetous, quibbling, spiteful and greedy; and the other the peerless poet and philosopher—the man who hated shams and pretense, and had made a brave fight for liberty; the charming companion, the gracious friend. Frederick was philosopher enough to realize that he could not have the one without the other—if he had the angel he must also tolerate the demon. This he would do—he must have his Voltaire, and so he refused the passports asked for, and sought to interest his literary lion in new projects. Finally, court life became intolerable to Voltaire, as life is to anybody when he realizes that he is being detained against his will. Voltaire packed his effects, secured a four-horse carriage, and with his secretary, departed by night, without leaving orders where his mail should be forwarded.

When Frederick found that his singing bird had flown, he was furious. Fear had much to do with the matter, for Voltaire had taken various manuscripts written by the King, wherein potentates in high places were severely scored. The first thought of Frederick evidently was that Voltaire had really been a spy in the employ of the French government. He sent messengers after him in hot haste—the fugitive was overtaken, and arrested. His luggage was searched, and after being detained at Frankfort for three weeks he was allowed to depart for pastures new.

The news of his flight, arrest and disgrace became the gossip of every court of Christendom. Who was disgraced more by the arrest—Voltaire or Frederick—the world has not yet decided. Carlyle deals with the subject in detail in his "Life of Frederick," and exonerates the King. But Taine says Carlyle wrote neither history nor poetry, and certainly we do not consider the sage of Cheyne Row an impartial judge.

Voltaire took time to cool, and then wrote a history of the affair which is published in his "My Private Life," that is one of the most delicious pieces of humor ever written. That he should have looked forward to life at the Prussian Court as the ideal, and then after bravely enduring it for three years, make his escape by night, was only a huge joke. Nothing else could have been expected, he says. Men of fifty should know that environment does not make heaven, and people who expect other people to make paradise for them are forever doomed to wander without the walls.

Voltaire acknowledges that he got better treatment than he deserved, and makes no apology for working the whole affair up into good copy. The final proof that Voltaire was a true philosopher is that he was able to laugh at himself.

When Voltaire left Prussia, it was voluntary exile. Paris was forbidden—all of France was for him unsafe; England he had hopelessly offended. By slow stages he made his way to Switzerland. But on the way there his courage failed him and he wrote back to Frederick, suggesting reconciliation. But Frederick promptly reminded him that he had repeatedly broken promises by writing about Frederick's personal friends, and "Voltaire and Frederick had better keep apart, that their love for each other might not grow cold"—a subtle bit of sarcasm.

At Geneva, where Calvin had instituted a little tyranny of his own, Voltaire was made welcome. Nominally no Catholics were allowed in Geneva, and when Voltaire wrote to the authorities, explaining that he was a good Catholic, the matter was taken as a great joke. He bought a beautiful little farm a few miles away, on the banks of the river Rhone, overlooking the city of Geneva and the lake. It was an ideal spot, and rightly he called it "Delices." Here he was going to end his days amid flowers and birds and books and bees, an onlooker and possibly a commentator on the times, but not a doer. His days of work were over. Of the world of strife he had had enough—thus he wrote to Frederick.

Visitors of a literary turn of mind at Geneva began to come his way. He established an inn, and later built a theater out of the ruins of an old church that he had bought and dismantled. "This is what I am going to do with all the churches in France," he explained with a smile.

His pen was never idle. He wrote plays that were presented at his own little theater, and on such occasions he would send word to his Geneva friends not to come, as they could not be accommodated. Of course they came.

He wrote a history of Peter the Great, and this brought him into communication with Queen Catherine of Russia, with whom he carried on quite an animated correspondence. This worthy widow invited him to Saint Petersburg, and he slyly wrote to Frederick for advice as to whether he should go or not. It is said that Frederick advised him to go, pay court to the Queen, marry her, seize the throne, and get his head cut off for his pains, thus achieving immortality and benefiting the world at one stroke.

Voltaire had no intention of going to Saint Petersburg; he had created a little Court of Letters, of which he himself was the Czar, and for the first time in his life he was experiencing a degree of genuine content. His flowers, bees, manuscripts and theater filled every moment of the day from six in the morning until ten at night. He had arrived in Switzerland broken in health, with mind dazed, his frail body undone. There at the little farm at Delices, overlooking the lake, health came back and youth seemed to return to this man of three-score.

Some of the nobility in Paris, to whom he had loaned money, took advantage of his exile to withhold payments, but Voltaire secured an agent to look after his affairs, so his losses were not great.

He bought the tumbledown chateau of Tournay, near at hand, which carried with it the right to call himself Count Tournay. Frederick, with mock respect, so addressed his letters.

His next financial venture, begun when he was sixty-eight, might well have tested the strength of a much younger man. A few miles from Geneva, at Ferney, just over the border from Switzerland, Voltaire had bought a large tract of waste land, intending to use it for pasturage. Here he built a cottage and lived a part of the time when visitors were too persistent at Delices. Ferney was on French soil, Delices in Switzerland. Voltaire had criticized the Protestants of Geneva, and given it as his opinion that a Calvinistic tyranny was in no wise preferable to one built on Catholicism. Some then said, "This man is really what he professes—a Catholic." There had also been a demonstration to drive him out of Switzerland, since it was pretty well known that Voltaire's crowds of visitors were neither Catholic nor Protestant. "Delices is infidelic," was the cry, and this doubtless had something to do with Voltaire's establishing himself at Ferney. If Protestant Switzerland drove this Catholic over to France, why, Catholic France would not molest him.

Every country, no matter how tyrannical its government, prides itself on being the home of the exile, just as every man thinks of himself as being sincere and without prejudice.

It is now believed that Voltaire had much to do with inciting the civil riots in Geneva against the Catholics. He had circulated pamphlets purporting to be written by a Catholic, upholding the Pope, and ridiculing most unmercifully the pretenses of Protestantism, declaring it a compromise with the devil, made up of the scum of the Catholic Church. This pamphlet declared Calvin a monster, and arraigned him for burning Servetus, and hinted that all Calvinists would soon be paid back in their own coin. No one else could have penned this vitriolic pamphlet but Voltaire—he knew both sides. But since Geneva regarded Voltaire as an infidel, it never occurred to the authorities that he would take up the cudgel of the Catholic Church that had burned his books. The real fact was, the pamphlet wasn't a defense of Catholicism—it was only a drubbing of Calvinism, and the wit was too subtle for the Presbyterians to digest.

Very soon another pamphlet appeared, answering the first. It arraigned the Catholics in scathing phrase, suggested that they were getting ready to burn the city—hinted at a repetition of Saint Bartholomew, and declared the order had gone forth from Rome to scourge and kill. It was as choice an A.P.A. document as was ever issued by a relentless joker. The result was that the workers in the watch-factory and silk-mills who were Catholics found themselves ostracized by the Protestant workmen. I do not find that the authorities drove the Catholics out of Geneva, it was simply a species of labor trouble—Protestants would not work with Catholics.

At this juncture Voltaire comes in, and invites all persecuted Catholic watch-workers and silk-weavers to move to Ferney. Here Voltaire laid out a town—erected houses, factories, churches and schools. In two years he had built up a town of twelve hundred people, and had a watch-factory and silk-mill in full and paying operation.

The problem of every manufacturer is to sell his wares—Voltaire knew how to release purse-strings of friends and enemies alike. He sent watches to all of his enemies in Paris, bishops, priests and potentates, explaining that he had quit literature forever, and was now engaged in helping struggling, exiled Catholics to get an honest living—he was doing penance as foreman of a watch-factory—would the Most Reverend not help in this worthy work? Money flowed in on Ferney—Frederick ordered a consignment of watches, Queen Catherine did the same, and the Bishop of Paris sent his blessing and an order for enough silk to keep Voltaire's factory going for six months.

Voltaire really got the pick of the workmen of Geneva—the goods made were of the best, and while at first Catholics only were employed, yet in five years Ferney was quite as much Protestant as Catholic. Voltaire respected the religious beliefs of his workmen, and there was liberty for all. He paid better wages and treated his workers better than they had ever been treated in Geneva. Voltaire built houses for his people and allowed them to pay him in monthly instalments. And not only did he himself make much money out of his Ferney investment, but he established the town upon such a safe financial basis that its prosperity endures even unto this day.

It was at Ferney, in his old age, that Voltaire first made open war upon "revealed religion." All religions that professed a miraculous origin were to him baneful in the extreme, the foes of light and progress, the enemies of mankind. He did not perceive, as modern psychology does, that the period of supernaturalism is the childhood of the mind. Myths and fairy-tales are not of themselves base—the injury lies with the men who seek to profit by these things, and build up a tyranny founded on innocence and ignorance—seeking to perpetuate these things, issuing threats against growth, and offers of reward to all who stand still.

Voltaire called superstition "The Infamy," and he summoned the thinkers of the world to crush it beneath a heel of scorn. Letters, pamphlets, plays, essays, were sent out in various languages, by his own printing-presses. The wit of the man—his scathing mockery—were weapons no one could wield in reply. The priests and preachers did not answer him—they could not—they only grew purple with wrath and hissed.

Says Victor Hugo, "Jesus wept; Voltaire smiled." To which Bernard Shaw has recently rejoined, "Jesus wept; Voltaire smiled; William Morris worked."

From the prosperity, peace and security of Ferney, Voltaire pointed a bony finger at every hypocrite in Christendom, and laughed his mocking smile. The man expressed himself, and happiness lies in that and nothing else. Misery comes from lack of full, free self-expression, and from nothing else. The man who fights for freedom fights for the right of self-expression for himself and others—and immortality lies in nothing else.

There is no fight worth making—no struggle worth the while—save the struggle for freedom.

No name is honored among men—no name lives—save the name of the man who worked for liberty and light—who has fought freedom's fight.

Run the list in your mind of the names that are immortal, and you will recall only those of men who have widened the horizon for other men, and that select number who are remembered in infamy because they linked their names with greatness by doubting, denying, betraying and persecuting it—deathless through disgrace.

Voltaire sided with the weak, the defenseless, the fallen. He demanded that men should not be hounded for their belief, that they should not be arrested without cause and without knowing why, and without letting their friends know why. We realize his faults, we know his imperfections and limitations, yet, through his influence, life throughout the world became safer, liberty dearer, freedom a more sacred thing. His words were a battery that eventually razed the walls of the Bastile, and best of all, freed countless millions from theological superstition, that Bastile of the brain.

HERBERT SPENCER

What knowledge is of most worth? The uniform reply is: Science. This is the verdict on all counts. For direct self-preservation, or the maintenance of life and health, the all-important knowledge is—science. For that indirect self-preservation which we call gaining a livelihood, the knowledge of greatest value is—science. For the discharge of parental functions, the proper guidance is to be found only in science. For the interpretation of national life, past and present, without which the citizen can not rightly regulate his conduct, the indispensable key is—science. Alike for the most perfect production and present enjoyment of art in all its forms, the needful preparation is still—science. And for purposes of discipline—intellectual, moral, religious—the most efficient study is, once more—science.

—*Essay on Education*

HERBERT SPENCER

In Derby, England, April Twenty-seventh, Eighteen Hundred Twenty, Herbert Spencer, the only child of his parents, was born. His mother died in his childhood, so he really never had any vivid recollection of her, but hearsay, fused with memory and ideality, vitalized all. And thus to him, to the day of his death, his mother stood for gentleness, patience, tenderness, intuitive insight, and a love that never grew faint. Man makes his mother in his own image.

Herbert Spencer's father was a school-teacher, and in very moderate circumstances. Little Herbert could not remember when he did not go to school, and yet as a real scholar, he never went to school at all. The family lived over the schoolroom, and while the youngster yet wore dresses his father would hold him in his arms, and carry him around the room as he instructed his classes. William George Spencer was both father and mother to Herbert, and used to sing to him lullabies as the sun went down.

After school there were always walks afield, and in the evening the brother of the school-master would call, and then there was much argument as to Why and What, Whence and Whither.

People talk gossip, we are told, for lack of a worthy theme. These two Spencers—one a school-master and the other a clergyman—found the time too short for their discussions. In their walks and talks they were always examining, comparing, classifying, selecting, speculating. Flowers, plants, bugs, beetles, birds, trees, weeds, earth and rocks were scrutinized and analyzed.

Where did it come from? How did it get here?

I am told that lions never send their cubs away to be educated by a cubless lioness and an emasculated lion. The lion learns by first playing at the thing and then doing it.

A motherless boy, brought up by an indulgent father, one might prophesy, would be sure to rule the father and be spoiled himself through omission of the rod. But in the boy problem all signs fail. The father taught by exciting curiosity and animating his pupils to work out problems and make discoveries—keeping his discipline well out of sight. How well the plan worked is revealed in the life of Herbert Spencer himself; and his book, "Education," is based on the ideas evolved by his father, to whom he gives much credit. No man ever had so divine a right to compile a book on education as Herbert Spencer, for he proved in his own life every principle he laid down.

On all excursions Herbert was taken along—because he couldn't be left at home, you know. He listened to the conversations and learned by hearing the older pupils recite.

All out-of-doors was fairyland to him—a curiosity-shop filled with wonderful things—over your head, under your feet, all around was life—action, pulsing life, everything in motion—going somewhere, evolving into something else.

This habit of observation, adoration and wonder—filled with pleasurable emotions and recollections from the first—lasted the man through life, and allowed him, even with a frail constitution, to round out a long period of severe mental work, with never a tendency to die at the top.

Herbert Spencer never wrote a thing more true than this: "The man to whom in boyhood information came in dreary tasks, along with threats of punishment, is unlikely to be a student in after-years; while those to whom it came in natural forms, at the proper times, and who remember its facts as not only interesting in themselves, but as a long series of gratifying successes, are likely to continue through life that self-instruction begun in youth."

When thirteen years old Herbert went to live with his uncle, the Reverend Thomas Spencer, at Bath. Here the same methods of education were continued that had been begun at home—conversation, history in the form of story-telling, walks and talks, and mathematical calculations carried out as pleasing puzzles. In mathematics the boy made rapid progress, but the faculty of observation was the dominant one. Every phase of cloud and sky, of water and earth, rock and mountain, bird and bush, plant and tree, was curious to him. He kept a journal of his observations, which had the double advantage of deepening his impressions by recounting them, and second, it taught him the use of language.

The best way to learn to write is to write. Herbert Spencer never studied grammar until he had learned to write. He took his grammar at sixty, which is a good age to begin this interesting study, as by that time you have largely lost your capacity to sin. Men who swim exceedingly well are not those who have taken courses in the theory of swimming at natatoriums from professors of the amphibian art—they were boys who just jumped in. Correspondence-schools for the taming of broncos are as naught; and treatises on the gentle art of wooing are of no avail—follow Nature's lead. Grammar is the appendenda vermiformis of pedagogics: it is as useless as the letter q in the alphabet, or as the proverbial two tails to a cat, which no cat ever had, and the finest cat in the world, the Manx cat, has no tail at all.

"The literary style of most university men is commonplace, when not positively bad," wrote Herbert Spencer in his old age. "Educated Englishmen all write alike," said Taine. That is to say, they have no literary style, for style is character, individuality—the style is the man. And grammar tends to obliterate all individuality. No study is so irksome to everybody, except to the sciolists who teach it, as grammar. It remains forever a bad taste in the mouth of the man of ideas, and has weaned bright minds innumerable from all desire to express themselves through the written word. Grammar is the etiquette of words, and the man who does not know how to properly salute his grandmother on the street until he has consulted a book, is always so troubled about his tenses that his fancies break through language and escape.

Orators who keep their thoughts upon the proper way to gesticulate in curves impress nobody. If poor grammar were a sin against decency, or an attempt to poison the minds of the people, it might be wise enough to hire men to protect the well of English from defilement. But a stationary language is a dead one—moving water only is pure—and the well that is not fed by springs is a breeding-place for disease. Let men express themselves in their own way, and if they express themselves poorly, look you, their punishment shall be that no one will read them. Oblivion, with her smother-blanket, waits for the writer who has nothing to say and says it faultlessly. In the making of hare-soup, I am told the first requisite is to catch your hare. The literary scullion who has anything to offer a hungry world will doubtless find a way to fricassee it.

When seventeen, Herbert Spencer was apprenticed to a surveyor on the London and Birmingham Railway. The pay was meager—board and keep and five pounds for the first year, with ten pounds the second year "if he deserved it." However, school-teachers and clergymen are used to small reward, and to make a living for one's self was no small matter to the Spencers. The youth who has gotten his physical growth should earn his own living, this as a necessary factor in his further mental evolution.

Neither William George Spencer, Herbert's father, nor Thomas, his uncle, seemed ever to anticipate that they were helping to develop the greatest thinker of his time. They themselves were obscure men, and quite happy therein, and if young Herbert could attain to a fair degree of physical health, make his living as an honest surveyor or as a teacher of mathematics, it would be all one could reasonably hope for. And thus they lived out the measure of their days, and passed away unaware that this boy they claimed in partnership was to be the maker of an epoch.

Young Spencer began his surveying work by carrying a flag, and soon he was advanced to "chainman." His skill in mathematics made his services valuable, and his willingness to sit up nights and work out the measurements of the day, so pleased his employer that the letter of the contract was waived and he was paid ten pounds for his first year's work, instead of five. He invented shorter methods for bridges and culverts, and I believe was the first engineer to build a cantilever railroad-bridge in England.

When he was twenty-one he had so thoroughly mastered the work that his employers offered to place him in charge of a construction-gang at a salary of two hundred pounds a year, which was then considered high pay. He, however, loved liberty more than money, and his tastes were in the direction of invention and science, rather than in working out an immediate practical success for himself.

He returned home and invented a scheme for making type; and had another plan for watchmaking, which he illustrated with painstaking designs. Half of his time was spent in the fields, and he made a large botanical collection—indexing it carefully, with many notes and comments.

He also wrote articles for the "Civil Engineers' and Artisans' Journal." For these he received no pay, but the acceptance of manuscript gives a great glow to a writer's cosmos: young Spencer was encouraged in the belief that he had something to offer the public. But his father and kinsmen saw only failure in these days of dawdling; and the money being gone, Herbert Spencer, aged twenty-two, went up to London to try to get a renewal of the offer from his old employer.

But things had changed—chances gone are gone forever, and he was told that opportunity knocks but once at each man's door. Sadly he returned home—not disappointed in himself, but depressed that he should disappoint others. His inventions languished—nobody was interested in them.

To get a living was the problem, and writing seemed the only way. And so he prepared a series of articles for "The Non-Conformist," and there was enough non-conformity in them so he was paid a small sum for his work. It proved this, though—he could get a living by his pen.

In these "Non-Conformist" articles, Spencer put forth a daring statement concerning the evolution of the soldier, that straightway made him a few enemies, and gave his clerical uncle gooseflesh. His hypothesis was this: When man first evolved out of the Stone Age, and began to live in villages, the oldest and wisest individual was regarded as patriarch or chief. This chief appointed certain men to punish wrongdoers and keep order. But there were always a few who would not work and who, through their violence and contumacious spirit, were finally driven from the camp. Or more likely they fled to escape punishment—which is the same thing—for they were outcasts. These men found refuge in the mountain fastnesses and congregated for two reasons—one, so they could avoid capture, and the other so they could swoop down and "secure their own." Robbery and commerce came hand in hand, and piracy is almost as natural as production.

Finally, the robbers became such a problem to industry that terms were made with them. Their tribute took the form of a tax, and to make sure that this tax was paid, the robbers protected the people against other robbers. And then, for the first time, the world saw a standing army. An army has two purposes—to protect the people, and to collect the tax for protecting the people.

At the headquarters of this army grew up a court, and all the magnificent splendor of a capitol centered around the captains. In fact, the word "capitol" means the home of the captain.

Herbert Spencer did not say that a soldier was a respectable brigand, and that a lawyer is a man who protects us from lawyers, but he came so close to it that his immediate friends begged him to moderate his expressions for his own safety.

Spencer also at the same time traced the evolution of the priest. He showed how the "holy man" was one frenzied with religious ecstasy, who went away and lived in a cave. Occasionally this man came back to beg, to preach and to do good. In order to succeed in his begging, he revealed his peculiar psychic powers, and then reinforced these with claims of supernatural abilities. These claims were not exactly founded upon truth, but once put forth were in time believed by those who advanced them.

This priest, who claimed to have influence with the power of the Unseen, found early favor with the soldier—and the soldier and the priest naturally joined hands. The soldier protected the priest and the priest absolved the soldier. One dictated man's place in this world—the other in the next.

The calm way in which Herbert Spencer reasoned these things out, and his high literary style, which made him unintelligible to all those whose minds were not of scientific bent, and his emphatic statement that what is, is right, and all the steps in man's development mean a mounting to better things, saved him from the severe treatment that greeted, say, Charles Bradlaugh, who translated the higher criticisms for the hoi polloi.

Spencer's first essays on "The Proper Sphere of Government," done in his early twenties for "The Non-Conformist" and "The Economist," outlined his occupation for life—he was to be a writer. He became assistant editor of the "Westminster Review," and contributed to various literary and scientific journals.

These essays, enlarged, rewritten and revised, finally emerged in Eighteen Hundred Fifty-one in the form of "Social Statics, or the Conditions Essential to Human Happiness."

This book, so bold in its radical suggestions, now almost universally admitted, was printed at the author's expense—a fact that should put a quietus for all time upon all those indelicate and sarcastic allusions concerning "when the author prints." There was an edition of seven hundred fifty copies of the book, and it took every shilling the young man had saved, and a few borrowed pounds as well, to pay the bill.

The book made no splash in the literary sea—nobody read it except a dozen good people who did so as a matter of friendship.

After six years there were still five hundred copies left, and the author wrote this slightly ironical line: "I am glad the public is taking plenty of time to fully digest my work before passing judgment upon it. Of all things, hasty criticisms are to be regretted."

Yet there was one person who read Herbert Spencer's first book with close consideration and profound sympathy. This was a young woman, the same age as Spencer, who had come up to London from the country to make her fortune. Her name was Mary Ann Evans.

In "Notes and Comments," Spencer's last book, published two years before his death, are several quotations and allusions to George Eliot. No other woman is mentioned in the volume.

Herbert Spencer and Mary Ann Evans first met at the house of the editor of the "Westminster Review" about the year Eighteen Hundred Fifty-one. Their tastes, aptitudes and inclinations were much the same. They were born the same year; both were brought up in the country; both were naturalists by inclination, and scientists because they could not help it. "Social Statics" made a profound impression on George Eliot, and she protested to the last that it was the best book the author ever wrote. He had read her "Essay on Spinoza," and remembered it so well that he repeated a page of it the first time they met. They loved the same things, and united, too, in their dislikes. Both were democrats, and the cards, curds and custards of society were to them as naught. In a few months after the first meeting, George Eliot wrote to a friend in Warwickshire: "The bright side of my life, after the affection for my old friends, is the new and delightful friendship which I have found in Herbert Spencer. We see each other every day, and in everything we enjoy a delightful comradeship. If it were not for him my life would be singularly arid."

The Synthetic Philosophy was taking form in Spencer's mind, and together they threshed out the straw and garnered the grain. She was getting to be a necessity to Spencer—and he saw no reason why the beautiful friendship should not continue just this way for years and years. Both were literary grubbers and lived in boarding-houses of the Class B variety.

And here George Henry Lewes appeared upon the scene. Legend says that Spencer introduced Lewes to Miss Evans, and both Miss Evans and Mr. Spencer were a bit in awe of him, for he was a literary success, and they were willing to be. Lewes had written at this time sixteen books—novels, essays, scientific treatises, poems, and a drama. He spoke five languages, had studied medicine, theology, and had been a lecturer and actor. He was small, had red hair, combed his whiskers by the right oblique, and wore a yellow necktie. Thackeray says he was the most learned and versatile man he ever knew, "and if I should see him in Piccadilly, perched on a white elephant, I would not be in the least surprised."

None of the various ventures of Lewes had paid very well, but he had great hopes, and money enough to ride in a cab. He gave advice, and radiated good-cheer wherever he went.

In Eighteen Hundred Fifty-four Lewes and Miss Evans disappeared from London, having gone to Germany, leaving letters behind, stating that thenceforward they wished to be considered as man and wife. Lewes was in his fortieth year, and slightly bald; George Eliot was thirty-six, and there were silver threads among the gold.

They had taken the philosophy of "Social Statics" in dead earnest.

Herbert Spencer lost appetite, ceased work, roamed through the park aimlessly, and finally fell into a fit of sickness—"night air, and too close confinement to mental tasks," the doctor said.

Spencer was not a marrying man—he was wedded to science, yet he craved the companionship of the female mind. Had he and Miss Evans married, he would doubtless have continued his work just the same. He would have absorbed her into his being—they would have lived in a garret, and possibly we might have had a better Synthetic Philosophy, if that were possible.

But we would have had no "Adam Bede" nor "Mill on the Floss."

We often see mention, by the ready writers, of "mental equals" and "perfect mates," but in all business partnerships, one man is the court of last appeal by popular acclaim. If power is absolutely equal, the engine stops on the center. Twins may look exactly alike, but one is the spokesman. In all literary collaboration, one does the work and the other looks on.

When George Henry Lewes took Mary Ann Evans as his wife, that was the last of Lewes. He became her inspiration, secretary, protector, friend and slave. And this was all beautiful and right.

I believe it was Augustine Birrell who said, "George Henry Lewes was the busy drone to a queen bee." It probably is well that Mr. Spencer and Miss Evans did not marry—they were too much alike—they might have gotten into competition with each other.

George Eliot had a poise and dignity in her character that kept the versatile Lewes just where he belonged; and at the same time she lived her own life and preserved in ascending degree the strong and simple beauties of her character. Truly was George Eliot "a citizen of the sacred city of fine minds—the Jerusalem of Celestial Art." Lewes was the tug that puffed and steamed and brought the majestic steamship into port.

For one book George Eliot received a sum equal to forty thousand dollars, and her income after "Adam Bede" was published was never less than ten thousand dollars a year.

Spencer lived out his days in the boarding-house, and until after he was seventy, had not reached a point where absolute economy was not in order.

Spencer faced the Universe alone, and tried to solve its mysteries. Not only did he live alone, with no close confidants or friends, but when he died he left not a single living relative nearer than the fourth generation. With him died the name.

The leading note in "Social Statics" is a plea for the liberty of the individual. That government is best which governs least. The liberty of each, limited only by the liberty of all, is the rule to which society must conform in order to attain the highest development. Governments have no business to scrutinize the life and belief of the individual. Interference should only come where one man interferes with the liberties of another.

Liberty of action is the first requisite to progress, and the prime essential in human happiness. It is better that men have wrong opinions than no opinions—through our blunders we reach the light.

Government is for man, and not man for government. Men wish to do what is best for themselves, and eventually they will, if let alone, but they can only grow through constant practise and frequent mistakes. Plato's plan for an ideal republic provided rules and laws for the guidance of the individual. In the Mosaic Laws it is the same: every circumstance and complication of life is thought out, and the law tells the individual what he shall do, and what he shall not do. That is to say, a few men were to do the thinking for the many. And the argument that plain people should not be allowed to think for themselves, since the wise know better what is for their good, is exactly the argument used by slaveholders: that they can take better care of the man than the man can of himself.

There is a certain plausibility and truth in this proposition. It is all a point of view.

But to Herbert Spencer there was little difference between enslavement of the mind and enslavement of the body. Both were essentially wrong in this—they interfered with Nature's law of evolution, and anything contrary to Nature must pay the penalty of pain and death. All forms of enslavement react upon the slaveholder, and a society founded on force can not evolve—and not to evolve is to die. The wellsprings of Nature must not be dammed—and in fact can not be dammed but for a day. Overflow, revolution and violence are sure to follow. This is the general law; and so give the man liberty. One man's rights end only where another man's begin.

The idea of evolution, as opposed to a complete creation, was in the mind of Spencer as early as Eighteen Hundred Forty-eight. In that year he said, "Creation still goes forward, and to what supreme heights man may yet attain no one can say."

By a sort of general misapprehension, Darwin is usually given credit for the discovery and elucidation of the Law of Evolution, but the "Origin of Species" did not appear until Eighteen Hundred Fifty-nine, and both Spencer and Alfred Russel Wallace had stated, years before, that the theological dogma of a complete creation had not a scintilla of proof from the world of nature and science, while there was much general proof that the animal and vegetable kingdom had evolved from lower forms, and was still ascending.

The usual idea of the clergy of Christendom was that if the account of creation given by Moses were admitted to be untrue, then the Bible in all its parts would be declared untrue, and religion would go by the board. Now that the theory of evolution is everywhere accepted, even in the churches, we see how groundless were the fears. All that is beautiful and best we still have in religion in a degree never before known.

In an essay on "Manners and Fashion," published in the "Westminster Review" of Eighteen Hundred Fifty-four, Herbert Spencer says: "Forms, ceremonies and even beliefs are cast aside only when they become hindrances—only when some finer and better plan has been formed; and they bequeath to us all the good that was in them. The abolition of tyrannical laws has left the administration of justice not only unimpaired, but purified. Dead and buried creeds have not carried down with them the essential morality they contained, which still exists, uncontaminated by the sloughs of superstition. And all that there is of justice, kindness and beauty embodied in our cumbrous forms will live perennially, when the forms themselves have been repudiated and forgotten."

In the year Eighteen Hundred Fifty-five, Spencer issued his "Principles of Psychology," showing that the doctrine of evolution was then with him a fixed fact. The struggle was on, and from now forward his life was enlisted to viewing this theory from every side, anticipating every possible objection to it, and restating the case in its relation to every phase of life and nature.

Spencer's income was small, but his wants were few, and a single room in a boarding-house sufficed for both workshop and sleeping-room. To a degree, he now largely ceased original investigations and made use of the work of others. His intuitive mind, long trained in analytical research, was able to sift the false from the true, the trite from the peculiar, the exceptional from the normal.

The year Eighteen Hundred Sixty should be marked on history's page with a silver star, for it was in that year that Herbert Spencer issued his famous prospectus setting forth that he was engaged in formulating a system of philosophy which he proposed to issue in periodical parts to subscribers. He then followed with an outline of the ground he intended to cover. Ten volumes would be issued, and he proposed to take twenty years to complete the task.

The entire Synthetic Philosophy was then in his mind and he knew what he wanted to do. The courage and faith of the man were dauntless. Michael Rossetti once said, "Spencer, Darwin, Huxley, Tyndall and Wallace owe nothing to the universities of England, except for the scorn and opposition that have been offered them." But patriotic Americans and true are glad to remember that it was Professor E. L. Youmans of Yale who made it possible for Spencer to carry out his great plan. Five years after the prospectus was issued, Spencer was again penniless and was thinking seriously of abandoning the project. Youmans heard of this and reissued the prospectus, and sent it out among the thinking men of the world, asking them to subscribe. The announcement was then followed up by letters, and Youmans forced the issue until the sum of seven thousand dollars was raised. This he took over to Europe in person and presented to Spencer, with a gold watch and a box of cigars. Youmans found Spencer at his boarding-house, and together they wandered out in the park, where Youmans presented the philosopher the box of cigars. The great man took out one, cut it in three parts and proceeded to smoke one, then Youmans handed him the gold watch and the draft for the money. Spencer took the gifts of the watch and cigars and was much moved, but when it was followed by the draft for seven thousand dollars, he merely gasped and said: "Wonderful! Magnificent! Magnificent! Wonderful!" and smoked his third of a cigar in silence. And when he spoke, it was to say: "I think I will have to revise what I wrote in 'First Principles' on the matter of divine providence."

Those who have read Spencer's will must remember that this watch, presented to him by his American friends, is given a special paragraph.

Spencer once said to Huxley, "From the day I first carried that watch, every good thing I needed has been brought and laid at my feet."

"If I have succeeded in my art, it is simply because I have been well sustained," said Henry Irving in one of his modest, flattering, yet charming little speeches.

Sir Henry might have gone on and said that no man succeeds unless well sustained, and happy is that man who has radioactivity of spirit enough to attract to him loving and loyal helpers who scintillate his rays.

The average individual does not know very much about Edward L. Youmans, but no man ever did greater work in popularizing nature study in America. And if for nothing else, let his name be deathless for two things: he inspired John Burroughs with the thirst to see and know—and then to write—and he introduced Herbert Spencer to the world. It is easy to say that Burroughs was peeping his shell when Youmans discovered him, and that Spencer would have found a way in any event. We simply do not know what would have happened if something else occurred, or hadn't.

Youmans was born in a New York State country village, and very early discovered for himself that the world was full of curious and wonderful things, just as most children do. He became a district school-teacher, and so far as we know, was the very first man to publicly advocate nature study as a distinctive means of child-growth. He taught his children to observe; then he gave lectures on elementary botany; he studied and he wrote, and he worked at the microscope.

And he became blind.

Did the closest observer on the continent cease work and grow discouraged when sight failed? Not he.

He no more quit work than did Beethoven cease composing music when he no longer was able to hear it.

We hear with the imagination, and we see with the soul. Youmans' sister, Eliza Anne, became his guide and amanuensis; he saw the things through her eyes and inspected the wonders with his finger-tips.

He became professor of Physics and Natural History at Yale, and when the New England Lecture Lyceum was at its height, he rivaled Phillips, Emerson and Beecher as a popular attraction. He made science a pleasure to plain people, and started Starr King off on that tangent of putting knowledge in fairylike and acceptable form. Youmans' lecture on "The Chemistry of a Sunbeam" is one of the unforgettable things of a generation past, so full of animation and rare, radiant spirit of good-cheer was the man. He founded the "Popular Science Monthly," wrote a dozen books on science, and several of these are now used in most of the colleges and advanced schools of America and England.

The man had a head for business—he became rich.

It was about the year Eighteen Hundred Fifty-six that Youmans was in England on a business errand, introducing his books in the English schools, that he first met Herbert Spencer, having been attracted to him through a chance copy of "Social Statics" that his sister had read to him. Youmans saw that Spencer was going right to the heart of things in a way he himself could not. The men became friends, and of all Youmans' wonderful discoveries, he considered Herbert Spencer the greatest.

"Sir Humphry Davy discovered, and possibly evolved, Michael Faraday; but I didn't evolve Herbert Spencer, any more than Balboa evolved the Pacific Ocean," said Youmans at a dinner given to Herbert Spencer when he visited New York in Eighteen Hundred Eighty-one. The name of Youmans is not in the Hall of Fame as one of the world's great men, but as naturalist, teacher, writer, lecturer and practical man of affairs, he reflects credit on his Maker. The light went out of his eyes, but it never went out of his soul.

In making payment to a publishing-house for sixty volumes of an American historical work, Speaker Cannon recently made this endorsement on the back of the check:

"This check is in full payment, both legal and moral, for sixty volumes of books. The books are not worth a damn—and are dear at that. We are never too old to learn, but the way your gentlemanly agent came it over your Uncle Joseph, is worth the full amount."

When Speaker Cannon says the books are not worth a damn, he does not necessarily state a fact about the books: he merely states a fact about himself—that is, he gives his opinion. The value of the books is still undetermined.

The Speaker's discontent with the books seems to have arisen from the one fact that he had to pay for them.

This condition is a classic one, and the world long ago has conceded to the man who pays, the privilege of protest. When Herbert Spencer issued that world-famous prospectus, announcing his intention to publish ten volumes setting forth his Synthetic Philosophy, it was one of the most daring things ever done in the realm of thought. Spencer was forty, and he was penniless and obscure. He had issued two books at his own expense, and it had taken twelve years to dispose of seven hundred fifty copies of one, and most of the edition of the other was still on hand. Edward L. Youmans had such faith in Spencer that he sent out the prospectus, and followed it up with letters and personal solicitations, until seven thousand dollars was subscribed, and Herbert Spencer, relieved from the uncertainties of finance, was free to think and write.

Among other subscribers secured by Youmans, was the Reverend Doctor Jowett of Balliol. Spencer's books were issued in periodical parts. After paying for three years, Jowett sent a check to the publishers for the full amount of the subscription, saying, in an accompanying note: "To save myself the bother of periodical payments for Mr. Spencer's books, I herewith hand you check covering the full amount of my subscription. I feel that I have already had full returns, for, while the books are absolutely valueless, save as showing the industry of an uneducated and indiscreet person, yet the experience that has come to me in this transaction is not without its benefits."

This is the Oxford way of expressing the Illinois formula, "Your books are not worth a damn—and are dear at that."

But the curious part of this transaction is that, after the death of Doctor Jowett, his library was sold at auction, and his set of the Synthetic Philosophy brought an advance of eight times its original cost.

Truly my Lord Hamlet doth say:
Rashly,
And prais'd be rashness for it—let us know,
Our indiscretion sometimes serves us well,
When our deep plots do fail.

No one man's opinion concerning any book, or any man, is final. Speaker Cannon is admired by one set of men and detested by others—all of equal intelligence, although on this point the Speaker might possibly file an exception.

Books are condemned offhand, or regarded as Bibles—it all depends upon your point of view. Speaker Cannon may be right in his estimate of the newly annexed sixty volumes of history that now grace his library-shelves in Danville, proudly shown to constituents, or he may be wrong; but anyway, Cannon's judgment about books is probably worth no more than was the Reverend Doctor Jowett's. Gladstone spoke of Jowett as that "saintly character"; and Disraeli called him "the bear of Balliol—erratic, obtuse and perverse." But Jowett, Gladstone and Disraeli all united in this: they had supreme contempt for the work of Herbert Spencer; while the Honorable Joseph Cannon is neutral, but inclined to be generous, having recently in a speech quoted from the "Faerie Queene," which he declared was the best thing Herbert Spencer had written, even if it was not fully up to date.

All during his life, Spencer was subject to attacks of indigestion and insomnia. That these bad spells were "a disease of the imagination" made them no less real. His isolation and lack of social ties gave him time to feel his pulse and lie in wait for sleepless nights.

With the old ladies of his boarding-house, he was on friendly terms, and his commonplace talk with them never gave them a guess concerning the worldwide character of his work. Very seldom did he refer to what he was doing and thinking—and then only among his most intimate friends. Huxley was his nearest confidant; and a recent writer, who knew him closely in a business way for many years, says that only with Huxley did he throw off his reserve and enter the social lists with abandon.

No one could meet Spencer, even in the most casual way, without being impressed with the fact that he was in the presence of a most superior person. The man was tall and gaunt, self-contained—a little aloof—he asked for nothing, and realized his own worth. He commanded respect because he respected himself—there was neither abnegation, apology nor abasement in his manner. Once I saw him walking in the Strand, and I noticed that the pedestrians instinctively made way, although probably not one out of a thousand had any idea who he was. No one ever affronted him, nor spoke disrespectfully to his face; if unkind things were said of the man and his work, it was in print and at a distance.

His standard of life was high—his sense of justice firm; with pretense and hypocrisy he had little patience, while for the criminal he had a profound pity.

Music was to him a relaxation and a rest. He knew the science of composition, and was familiar in detail with the best work of the great composers.

In order to preserve the quiet of his thoughts in the boarding-house, he devised a pair of ear-muffs which fitted on his head with a spring.

If the conversation took a turn in which he had no interest, he would excuse himself to his nearest neighbor and put on his ear-muffs. The plan worked so well that he carried them with him wherever he went, and occasionally at lectures or concerts, when he would grow more interested in his thoughts than in the performance, he would adjust his patent.

So well pleased was he with his experiment that he had a dozen pairs of the ear-muffs made one Christmas and gave them to friends, but it is hardly probable they had the hardihood to carry them to a Four-o'Clock. Seldom, indeed, is there a man who prizes his thoughts more than a polite appearance.

In an address before the London Medical Society, in Eighteen Hundred Seventy-one, Spencer said, "The man who does not believe in devils during his life, will probably never be visited by devils on his deathbed." Herbert Spencer died December Eighth, Nineteen Hundred Three, in his eighty-fourth year. Up to within two days of his death, his mind was clear, active and alert, and he worked at his books with pleasure and animation—revising, correcting and amending. He never lost the calm serenity of life. He sank gradually into sleep and passed painlessly away. And thus was gracefully rounded out the greatest life of its age—The Age of Herbert Spencer.

He left no request as to where he should be buried, but the thinking people who recognized his genius considered Westminster Abbey the fitting place—an honor to England's Valhalla. The Church of England denied him a place there before it was asked, and the hallowed precincts which shelter the remains of Queen Anne's cook and John Broughton the pugilist are not for Herbert Spencer. His dust does not rest in consecrated ground.

Herbert Spencer had no titles nor degrees—he belonged to no sect, party, nor society. Practically, he had no recognition in England until after he was sixty years of age. America first saw his star in the east, and long before the first edition of "Social Statics" had been sold, we waived the matter of copyright and were issuing the book here. On receiving a volume of the pirated edition, the author paraphrased Byron's famous mot, and grimly said, "Now, Barabbas was an American."

However, Spencer was really pleased to think that America should steal his book; we wanted it—the English didn't. It took him twelve years to dispose of the seven hundred fifty volumes, and most of these were given away as inscribed copies. They lasted about as long as Walt Whitman's first edition of "Leaves of Grass," although Whitman had the assistance of the Attorney-General of Massachusetts in advertising his remarkable volume.

Henry Thoreau's first book fared better, for when the house burned where the remnant of four hundred copies lingered long, he wrote to a friend, "Thank God, the edition is exhausted."

England recognized the worth of Thoreau and Whitman long before America did; and so, perhaps, it was meet that we should do as much for Spencer, Ruskin and Carlyle.

One of the most valuable of the many great thoughts evolved by Spencer was on the "Art of Mentation," or brain-building. You can not afford to fix your mind on devils or hell, or on any other form of fear, hate and revenge. Of course, hell is for others, and the devils we believe in are not for ourselves. But the thoughts of these things are registered in the brain, and the hell we create for others, we ourselves eventually fall into; and the devils we conjure forth, return and become our inseparable companions. That is to say, all thought and all work—all effort—are for the doer primarily, and as a man thinketh in his heart, so is he. This sounds like the language of metaphysics, which Kant said was the science of disordered moonshine. But Herbert Spencer's work was all a matter of analytical demonstration. And while the word "materialist" was everywhere applied to him, and he did not resent it, yet he was one of the most spiritual of men. A meta-physician is one who proves ten times as much as he believes; a scientist is one who believes ten times as much as he can prove. Science speaks with lowered voice. Before Spencer's time, German scientists had discovered that the cell was the anatomical unit of life, but it was for Spencer to show that it was also the psychologic or spiritual unit. New thoughts mean new brain-cells, and every new experience or emotion is building and strengthening a certain area of brain-tissue. We grow only through exercise, and all expression is exercise. The faculties we use grow strong, and those not used, atrophy and wither away. This is no less true, said Spencer, in the material brain than in the material muscle. A new thought causes a new structural enregistration. If it is the repetition of thought, the cells holding that thought are exercised and trained, and finally they act automatically, and repeated thought becomes habit, and exercised habit becomes character—and character is the man. It thus is plain that no man can afford to entertain the thought of fear, hate and revenge—and their concomitants, devils and hell—because he is enregistering these things physically in his being. These physical cells, as science has shown, are transmitted to offspring; and thus through continued mind-activity and consequent brain-cell building, a race with fixed characteristics is evolved. Pleasant memories and good thoughts must be exercised, and these in time will replace evil memories, so that the cells containing negative characteristics will atrophy and die. And when Herbert Spencer says that the process of doing away with evil is not through punishment, threat or injunction, but simply through a change of activities—thus allowing the bad to die through disuse—he states a truth that is even now coloring our whole fabric of pedagogics and penology. I couple these two words advisedly, for fifty years ago, pedagogics was a form of penology—the boarding-school with its mentors, scheme of fines, repressions and disgrace! And now we have lifted penology into the realm of pedagogics. I doubt me much whether the present penitentiary is a more unhappy place than a boys' English boarding-school was in the time of Squeers.

All of our progress has come from replacing bad activities with the good. Bad people we now believe are good folks who have misdirected their energies; and we all believe a deal more in the goodness of the bad than the badness of the good, with the result that "total depravity" and "endless punishment" have been shamed out of every pulpit where sane men preach. No devils danced on the footboard of Herbert Spencer's bed, because there were no devil-cells in his brain.

Another great discovery of Herbert Spencer's was that the emotions control the secretions. And the quality of the secretions determines the chemical changes which constitute all cellular growth. Thus, cheerful, happy emotions are similar to sunshine—they stand for health and harmony, and as such, are constructive. Good-will is sanitary; kindness is hygienic; friendship works for health. These happy emotions secrete a quality in the blood called anabolism, which is essentially vitalizing and life-producing.

On the other hand, fear, hate, and all forms of unkindness evolve a toxin, katabolism, which tends to clog circulation, disturb digestion, congest the secretions and stupefy the senses; and it tends to the dissolution and destruction of life. All that saddens, embitters and disappoints produces this chemical change that makes for death. "A poison," said Spencer, "is only a concentrated form of hate."

Spencer's discoveries in electricity have been most valuable, and it was by building on his suggestions and seeing with his prophetic eye that the Crookes Tube, the Roentgen Ray, and the discovery of radium have become possible.

The distinguishing feature of radium is its radioactivity, brought about through its affinity for electricity. It absorbs electricity from the atmosphere and gives it off spontaneously in the form of light and heat without appreciable loss of form or substance. Every good thing in life is dual, and through this natural and spontaneous marriage of radium and electricity, we get very close to the secret of life. As the sun is the giver of life and death, so by the use of the salts of radium have scientists vitalized certain forms of cell-life into growth and activity, and by the same token, the use of the radium-ray, do they destroy the germs of disease.

By his prophetic vision, Spencer saw years ago that we would yet be able to eliminate and refine the substances of earth until we found the element that would combine spontaneously with electricity, and radiate life and heat. Among the very last letters dictated by Spencer, only a few days before his death, was one to Madame Curie congratulating her on her discovery of radium, and urging her not to relax in her further efforts to seek out the secret of life. "My only regret is," wrote the great man, "that I will not be here to rejoice with you in the fullness of your success." Thus to the last did he preserve the eager, curious and receptive heart of youth, and prove to the scientific world his theory that brain-cells, properly exercised, are the last organs of the body to lose their functions.

SCHOPENHAUER

Wherever one goes one immediately comes upon this incorrigible mob of humanity. It exists everywhere in legions; crowding, soiling everything, like flies in summer. Hence the numberless bad books, those rank weeds of literature which extract nourishment from the

corn and choke it. They monopolize the time, money and attention which really belong to good books and their noble aims; they are written merely with a view to making money or procuring places. They are not only useless, but they do positive harm. Nine-tenths of the whole of our present literature aims solely at taking a few shillings out of the public's pocket, and to accomplish this, author, publisher and reviewer have joined forces.
—*Schopenhauer*

SCHOPENHAUER

The philosophy we evolve is determined by what we are; just as a nation passes laws legalizing the things it wishes to do. "Where the artist is, there you will find art," said Whistler. We will not get the Ideal Commonwealth until we get Ideal People; and we will not get an ideal philosophy until we get an ideal philosopher. Place the mentally and morally slipshod in ideal surroundings and they will quickly evolve a slum, just as did John Shakespeare, when at Stratford he was fined two pounds ten for maintaining a sequinarium. All we can say for John is that he was the author of a fine boy, who resembled his mother much more than he did his father. This seems to prove Schopenhauer's remark concerning a divine sonship: "Paternity is a cheap office, anyway, accomplished without cost, care or risk, and of it no one should boast. A divine motherhood is the only thing that is really sacred."

It isn't his philosophy that makes a man—man makes his philosophy, and he makes it in his own image. Living in a world of strife, where the most savage beast that roams the earth is man, the Philosophy of Pessimism has its place.

Schopenhauer proved himself a true philosopher when he said: "All we see in the world is a projection from our own minds. I may see one thing, you another; and according to the test of a third party we are both wrong, for he sees something else. So we are all wrong, yet all are right."

He was quite willing to admit that he had a well-defined moral squint and a touch of mental strabismus; but he revealed his humanity by blaming his limitations on his parents, and charging up his faults and foibles to other people.

It is possible that Carlyle's famous remark about the people who daily cross London Bridge was inspired by Schopenhauer, who, when asked what kind of people the Berliners were, replied, "Mostly fools!"

"I believe," ventured the interrogator—"I believe, Herr Schopenhauer, that you yourself live at Berlin?"

"I do," was the response, "and I feel very much at home there."

Heinrich Schopenhauer, the father of Arthur Schopenhauer, was a banker and shipping merchant of the city of Danzig, Germany. He was a successful man, and, like all successful men, he was an egotist. Before the world will believe in you, you must believe in yourself. And another necessary element in success is that you must exaggerate your own importance, and the importance of your work. Self-esteem will not alone make you successful, but without a goodly jigger of self-esteem, success will forever dally and dance just beyond your reach. The humble men who have succeeded in impressing themselves upon the world have all taken much pride in their humility.

Heinrich Schopenhauer was a proud man—as proud as the Merchant of Venice—and in his veins there ran a strain of the blue blood of the Castilian Jew. Too much success is most unfortunate. Heinrich Schopenhauer was proud, unbending, harsh, arbitrary, wore a full beard and a withering smile, and looked upon musicians, painters, sculptors and writers as court clowns, to be trusted only as far as you could fling Taurus by the tail. All good bookkeepers have, even yet, this pitying contempt for those whose chief assets are ideas—the legal tender of the spirit. The Alameda smile is the smile of scorn worn by the bookkeepers who prepare the balance-sheets for the great merchants of San Francisco. Alameda is young, but the Alameda smile is classic.

When Heinrich Schopenhauer was forty he married a beautiful girl of twenty. She had ideas about art and poetry, and was passing through her Byronic stage, before Byron did, and taking it rather hard, when her parents gave her in troth to Heinrich Schopenhauer, the rich merchant. It was regarded as a great catch.

I wish that I could say that Heinrich and Johanna were happy ever after, but in view of the well-known facts put forth by their firstborn child, I can not do it.

Before marriage the woman has her way: let her make the most of her power—she'll not keep it long! Shortly after their marriage Heinrich saw symptoms of the art instinct creeping in, and players on sweet zither-strings, who occasionally called, compelled him to take measures. He bought a country seat, four miles from the city, on an inaccessible road, and sent his bride thither. Here he visited her only on Saturdays and Sundays, and her callers were the good folk he chose to bring with him.

Marital peace is only possible where women are properly suppressed—lumity dee!

It was under these conditions that Arthur Schopenhauer was born, on February Twenty-second—in deference to our George Washington—Seventeen Hundred Eighty-eight.

The chief quality that Schopenhauer inherited from his father was the Alameda smile—and this smile of contempt was for all those who did not think as he did. The mother never professed to have any love for her husband, or the child either, and the child never professed to have any love for his mother. He once wrote this: "I was an unwelcome child, born of a mother in rebellion—she never wanted me, and I reciprocate the sentiment."

In that troublous year of Seventeen Hundred Ninety-three, the Free City of Danzig fell under the sway of Prussia.

Heinrich Schopenhauer, who loved freedom, jealous of his privileges, fearful of his rights, immediately packed up his effects, sold out his property—at great loss—and moved to the Free City of Hamburg.

That his fears for the future were quite groundless, as most fears are, is a fact relevant but not consequent.

Johanna was vivacious and eminently social. She spoke French, German, English and Italian. She played the harp, sang, wrote poetry and acted in dramas of her own composition. Around her there always clustered a goodly group of men with long hair, dreamy eyes and pointed beards, who soared high, dived deep, but seldom paid cash. This is the paradise to which most women wish to attain: to be followed by a concourse of artistic archangels—what nobler ambition! And let the great biological and historical fact here be written down—that there are no female angels.

Heinrich did not settle down in Hamburg and go into business, as he expected. He and his wife and boy traveled much—through England, France, Germany and Switzerland.

This man and his wife were trying to get away from themselves. Long years after, their son wrote, "When people die and wake up in hell they will probably be surprised to find that they are just such beings as they were when they were on earth."

For a year the lad was left at school with a clergyman at Wimbledon, in England. The strict religious discipline to which he was there subjected seemed to have had much to do with forming in him a fierce hatred of English orthodoxy; but he learned the language and became familiar with the great names in English literature. The King Arthur stories pleased him, and he always took a peculiar satisfaction in the fact that the name Arthur was the same in English, German and French. He was a prenatal cosmopolitan.

Boarding-schools are a great scheme for getting the children out of the way—it throws the responsibility upon some one else. When nine years of age, Arthur was placed in a French boarding-school, remaining for two years. There he learned to speak French so fluently that when he returned to Hamburg and tried to talk to his mother in German, his broken speech threw that excellent woman into fits of laughter.

When the mature man of affairs takes a young girl to wife, he expects to mold her to his nature, but he reckons without his host. Heinrich Schopenhauer's opposition to his wife's wishes was not strong enough to crush her—it simply developed in her a deal of wilful, dogged strength.

One winter day in Eighteen Hundred Four the body of Heinrich Schopenhauer was found in the canal at Hamburg.

Arthur was then sixteen years of age—old for his years, traveled, clever—strong in body and robust in health.

In wandering with his parents, he had met Goethe, Wieland, Madame De Stael, Lord Nelson and Lady Hamilton, and many other distinguished people, for his mother was a famous lion-hunter, and wherever they went, the great ones were tracked to their lairs. But however much Madame Schopenhauer indulged in hero-worship, she had no expectations or ambitions for her son. She apprenticed him as a clerk and did her utmost to immerse him in commerce. What she desired was freedom for herself, and the popular plan to gain freedom is to enslave others. Madame Schopenhauer moved to Weimar and opened there a sort of literary salon. She wrote verses, novels, essays, and her home became the center of a certain artistic group. The fortune her husband had left was equal to about forty thousand dollars, one-third of which was to go to Arthur when he was twenty-one. The mother had the handling of it all until that time, and as the funds were well invested, her income was equal to about two thousand dollars a year.

A handsome widow, under forty, with no encumbrances to speak of, and a fair income, is very fortunately situated. Indeed, a great writer has recently written an essay showing that widows, discreetly bereaved, are the happiest creatures on earth.

Young Schopenhauer, at his desk in Hamburg, grieved over the death of his father. That which is lost becomes valuable—bereavement softens the heart. The only tenderness that is revealed in the writings of Schopenhauer refers to his father. He affirms the sterling honesty of the man, and lauds the merchant who boldly states that he is in business to make money, and compares him with the philosophers who clutch for power and fame and yet pretend they are working for humanity. When Schopenhauer was past sixty, he dedicated his complete works to the memory of his father. As nothing purifies like fire, so does nothing sanctify like death—the love we lose is the only love we keep.

Mathematics, bills and balance-sheets were odious to young Schopenhauer. He reverenced the memory of his father, but his mother had endowed him with a strong impulse for expression. He wrote little essays on the backs of envelopes, philosophized over his bills, sneaked out of the countingroom the back way to attend the afternoon lectures by the great Doctor Gall, and finally, boldly followed his mother to Weimar, that he might bask in the shadow of the mighty Goethe. It was shortly after this that he sat in a niche of Goethe's library, musing, sad and solitary, while a gay throng chattered by. Some young women, seeing him there, laughed, and one asked, "Is it alive?" And Goethe, overhearing the pleasantry, rebuked it by saying, "Do not smile at that youth—he will yet eclipse us all."

At Weimar there was no greeting for Schopenhauer from his mother—she welcomed all but her son. Unfortunately for her, she put herself on record by writing him letters. Scathing letters are all right, but they should be directed and stamped, then burned just before they are trusted to the mails. To record unkindness is tragedy, for the unkind word lives long after the event that caused it is forgotten. Here is one letter written by Madame Schopenhauer that this methodical son saved for posterity:

My Dear Son:

I have always told you it is difficult to live with you. The more I get to know you, the more I feel this difficulty increase. I will not hide it from you: as long as you are what you are, I would rather bring any sacrifice than consent to be near you. I do not undervalue your good points, and that which repels me does not lie in your heart; it is in your outer, not your inner being; in your ideas, your judgment, your habits; in a word, there is nothing concerning the outer world in which we agree. Your ill-humor, your complaints of things inevitable, your sullen looks, the extraordinary opinions you utter, like oracles, none may presume to contradict; all this depresses me and troubles me, without helping you. Your eternal quibbles, your laments over the stupid world and human misery, give me bad nights and unpleasant dreams....

Your Dear Mother, etc.,
Johanna Schopenhauer

The young man took lodgings at Weimar, at a goodly distance from his mother. Goethe held out a friendly hand, as he did to Mendelssohn, and all bright young men. They talked much, and Goethe read to Arthur his essay on the theory of colors (for Wolfgang Goethe was human and dearly loved the sound of his own voice). The reasoning so impressed the youth that he devised a chromatic theory of his own—almost as peculiar. Theories are for the theorizer, so all theories are useful.

At the earnest importunity of his mother, who starved him to it, Arthur went back to his clerkship, but soon returned and made terms, agreeing not to call on his mother, in consideration of a pound a week. He took lessons in Greek and Latin of a retired professor, attended lectures, fell in love with an actress—vowed he would marry her, but, luckily for her, he didn't.

When he was twenty-one, his mother turned over to him his patrimony, amounting to about fourteen thousand dollars; and suggested that he leave Weimar and make his fortune elsewhere—the world was wide.

His money was invested so it brought him an income of seven hundred dollars a year. And here seems a good place to say that Schopenhauer's income was never over a thousand dollars a year until after he was fifty-six years of age. Although he could not make money, yet he had inherited from his father an ability to care for it. Throughout his life he kept exact books of account, never ran in debt, and never allowed his expenditures to outrun his income, thus complying with Charles Dickens' recipe for happiness.

In still another way he revealed that he could apply philosophy to daily life: he exercised regularly in the open air, took long walks, was absurdly exact about his cold baths, and like Kant, served the neighbors as a chronometer, so they set their clocks at three when they saw him going forth for a walk. And in the interests of truth, we will have to make the embarrassing admission that the great Apostle of Pessimism was neither a dyspeptic nor an invalid—if he was ever aware that he had a stomach we do not hear of it.

The life of Schopenhauer is the life of a recluse—a visionary—a hermit who lost himself amid the maze of city streets, and moved solitary in the throng. Berlin, Dresden, Hamburg, Gottingen, Frankfort, engaged him, and from one to the other he turned, looking for the rest he never found, and which he knew he would never find, so in the vain search there was no disappointment. He was always happiest when most miserable, for then were his theories proved.

A single room in a lodging-house sufficed, and this room always had the appearance of being occupied by a transient. He had few books, accumulated no belongings in way of domestic ballast, persistently giving away things that were presented to him, satisfied if he had a chair, a bed, and a table upon which to write; getting his own breakfast, dining at the table d'hote of the nearest inn, with supper at a "Gast-Haus"—so passed his days. He had no intimate friends, and his chief dissipation was playing the flute. His black poodle, named "Homo" in a subtle mood of irony, accompanied him everywhere, and on this dog he lavished what he was pleased to call his love. He anticipated Rip Van Winkle concerning dogs and women, and when Homo died, he bought another dog that looked exactly like the first, and was just as good.

In a few instances Schopenhauer read his essays in public as lectures, but his ideas were keyed to concert pitch and were too pronounced for average audiences. He was offered a professorship at Gottingen and also at Heidelberg, if he would "tone things down," but he scornfully declined the proposition, and said, "The Universities must grow to my level before I can talk to them." By his caustic criticisms of contemporaries he became both feared and shunned, and no doubt he found a certain satisfaction in the fact that the so-called learned men of his time would neither listen to his lectures, read his books, nor abide his presence. He had made himself felt in any event. "Blessed are ye when men shall revile you," is the sweet consolation of all persecuted persons—and persecution is only the natural resentment towards those who have too much ego in their cosmos.

His opinions concerning love and marriage need not be taken too seriously. Ideas are the results of temperaments and moods. When a man amplifies on the woman question he describes the women he knows best, and more especially the particular She who is in his head. Literature is only autobiography, more or less discreetly veiled. Schopenhauer hated his mother to the day of her death, and although during the last twenty-four years of her life he never once saw her, her image could at any time be quickly and vividly thrown upon the screen. The women a strong man has known are never forgotten—here is where time does not tarnish, nor the days grow dim.

Between his twenty-eighth and fortieth years, Schopenhauer had wandered through Italy—spent months at Venice, and dawdled away the days at Rome and Florence. He had dipped deep into life—and the wrong kind of life. And his experiences had confirmed his suspicions—it was all bitter—he was not disappointed.

Until Schopenhauer was past thirty he was known as the son of Johanna Schopenhauer. And when he once told her that posterity would never remember her except as the mother of her son, she reciprocated by congratulating him that his books could always be had cheap in the first editions.

He retorted, "Mamma Dear, my books will be read when butchers are using yours for wrapping up meat." In some ways this precious pair were very much alike.

It is very probable that Schopenhauer's mother was not so base as he thought; and when he declared, "Woman's morality is only a kind of prudence," he might have said the same of his own. He stood aloof from life and said things about it. He had no wife, no child, no business, no home—he dared not venture boldly into the tide of existence—he stood forever on the bank, and watched the current carrying its flotsam and jetsam to the hungry sea.

In his love for the memory of his father, and in his tender care for his dog, we get a glimpse of depths that were never sounded. One side of his nature was never developed. And the words of the undeveloped man are worth what they are worth.

Schopenhauer once said to Wieland, "Life is a ticklish business—I propose to spend my time looking at it." This he did, viewing existence from every angle, and writing out his thoughts in terse, epigrammatic language.

Among all the German writers on philosophy, the only one who had a distinct literary style is Schopenhauer. Form was quite as much to him as matter—and in this he showed rare wisdom; although I am told that the writers who have no literary style are the only ones who despise it. Dishes to be palatable must be rightly served: appetite—literary, gastronomic or sexual—is largely a matter of imagination.

Schopenhauer need not be regarded as final. The chief virtue of the man lies in the fact that he makes us think, and thus are we his debtors.

In this summary of Schopenhauer's philosophy I have had the valuable assistance of my friend and fellow-worker in the Roycroft Shop, George Pannebakker, a kinsman and enthusiastic admirer of the great Prophet of Pessimism.

In talking to Mr. Pannebakker, I am inclined to exclaim, "Thou almost persuadest me to be a pessimist!" It is unfortunate that our English tongue contains no word that stands somewhere between pessimism and optimism—that symbols a judicial cast of mind which sees the Truth without blinking and accepts it without complaint. The word Pessimist was first flung in contempt at those who dared to express unpalatable truth. It is now accepted by a large number of intellectuals, and if to be a pessimist is to have insight, wit, calm courage, patience, persistency, and a disposition that accepts all Fate sends and makes the best of it, then pity 'tis we haven't more.

The root of existence, the inmost kernel of all being, the original vitalizing power, the fundamental reality of the universe, is, according to Schopenhauer, "WILL." What is Will? Will, in the usual sense, is the faculty of our mind by which we decide to do or not to do. Will is the power to choose. In Schopenhauer's philosophy, Will is something less as we know will, and something more than force. Will, connected with consciousness, as peculiar to man, is, in a less developed form, the real essence of all matter, of all things, organic or inorganic. Will is the blind, irresistible striving for existence; the unconscious organizing power, the omnipotent creative force of Nature, pervading the whole limitless universe; the endeavor to be, to evolve, to expand.

The whole world of phenomena is the objectivation or apparition of Will.

Will, the same force which slumbers in the stone as inert gravity, forms the crystals with such wonderful regularity.

Will impels a piece of iron to move with ardent desire toward the magnet. Will causes the magnet to point with unfailing constancy to the north. Will causes the embryo to cling as a parasite and feed on the body of the mother. Will causes the mother's breast to fill that her babe may be fed. Will fills the mother-heart with love that the young may be cared for.

The same force urges the tender germ of the plant to break through the hard crust of the earth and, stretching toward the light, to enfold itself in the proud crown of the palm-tree. Will sharpens the beak of the eagle and the tooth of the tiger and, finally, reaches its highest grade of objectivation in the human brain. Want, the struggle for existence, the necessity of procuring and selecting sufficient food for the preservation of the individual and the species, has at last developed a suitable tool, the brain, and its function, the intellect. With the intellect appear consciousness and a realm of rational life full of yearning and desires, pleasures and pain, hatred and love. Brothers slay their brothers, conquerors trample down the races of the earth, and tyrants are forging chains for the nations.

There is violence and fear, vexation and trouble. Unrest is the mark of existence, and onward we are swept in the hurrying whirlpool of change. This manifold restless motion is produced and kept up by the agency of two single impulses—hunger and the sexual instinct. These are the chief agents of the Lord of the Universe—the Will—and set in motion so strange and varied a scene.

The Will-to-Live is at the bottom of all love-affairs. Every kind of love springs entirely from the instinct of sex.

Love is under bonds to secure the existence of the human race in future times. The real aim of the whole of love's romance, although the persons concerned are unconscious of the fact, is that a particular being may come into the world.

It is the Will-to-Live, presenting itself in the whole species, which so forcibly and exclusively attracts two individuals of different sex towards each other.

This yearning and this pain do not arise from the needs of an ephemeral individual, but are, on the contrary, the sigh of the Spirit of the Species.

Since life is essentially suffering, the propagation of the species is an evil—the feeling of shame proves it.

In his "Metaphysics of Love," Schopenhauer says: "We see a pair of lovers exchanging longing glances—yet why so secretly, timidly and stealthily? Because these lovers are traitors secretly striving to perpetuate all the misery and turmoil that otherwise would come to a timely end."

Will, as the source of life, is the origin of all evil.

Having awakened to life from the night of unconsciousness, the individual finds itself in an endless and boundless world, striving, suffering, erring; and, as though passing through an ominous dream, it hurries back to the old unconsciousness. Until then, however, its desires are boundless, and every satisfied wish begets a new one. So-called pleasures are only a mode of temporary relief. Pain soon returns in the form of satiety. Life is a more or less violent oscillation between pain and ennui. The latter, like a bird of prey, hovers over us, ready to swoop down wherever it sees a life secure from need.

The enjoyment of art, as the disinterested cognition devoid of Will, can afford an interval of rest from the drudgery of Will service. But esthetic beatitude can be obtained only by a few; it is not for the hoi polloi. And then, art can give only a transient consolation.

Everything in life indicates that earthly happiness is destined to be frustrated or to be recognized as an illusion. Life proves a continuous deception, in great as well as in small matters. If it makes a promise, it does not keep it, unless to show that the coveted object was little desirable.

Life is a business that does not pay expenses.

Misery and pain form the essential feature of existence.

Life is hell, and happy is that man who is able to procure for himself an asbestos overcoat and a fire-proof room.

Looking at the turmoil of life, we find all occupied with its want and misery, exerting all their strength in order to satisfy its endless needs and avert manifold suffering, without daring to expect anything else in return than merely the preservation of this tormented individual existence, full of want and misery, toil and moil, strife and struggle, sorrow and trouble, anguish and fear—from the cradle to the grave.

Existence, when summed up, has an enormous surplus of pain over pleasure.

You complain that this philosophy is comfortless! But Schopenhauer sees life through Schopenhauer's eyes, and tells the truth about it as he sees it. He does not care for your likes and dislikes. If you want to hear soft platitudes, he advises you to go to a non-conformist church—read the newspapers, go somewhere else, but not to the philosopher who cares only for Truth.

Although Schopenhauer's picture of the world is gloomy and somber, there is nothing weak or cowardly in his writings, and the extent to which he is read, proves he is not depressing. Since a happy life is impossible, he says the highest that a man can attain to is the fate of a hero.

A man must take misfortune quietly, because he knows that very many dreadful things may happen in the course of life. He must look upon the trouble of the moment as only a very small part of that which will probably come.

We must not expect very much from life, but learn to accommodate ourselves to a world where all is relative and no perfect state exists.

Let us look misfortune in the face and meet it with courage and calmness!

Fate is cruel and men are miserable. Life is synonymous with suffering; positive happiness a fata morgana, an illusion.

Only negative happiness, the cessation of suffering, is possible, and can be obtained by the annihilation of the Will-to-Live.

But it is not suicide that can deliver us from the pains of existence.

Suicide, according to Schopenhauer, frustrates the attainment of the highest moral aim by the fact that, for a real release from this world of misery, it substitutes one that is merely apparent. For death merely destroys the phenomenon, that is, the body, and never my inmost being, or the universal Will.

Suicide can deliver me merely from my phenomenal existence, and not from my real self, which can not die.

How, then, can man be released from this life of misery and pain? Where is the road that leads to Salvation?

Slow and weary is the way of redemption.

The deliverance from life and its sufferings is the freedom of the intellect from its creator and despot, the Will.

The intellect, freed from the bondage of the Will, sees through the veil of selfhood into the unity of all being, and finds that he who has done wrong to another has done wrong to his own self. For selfhood—the asserting of the Ego—is the root of all evil.

Covetousness and sensuality are the causes of misery.

Sympathy is the basis of all true morality, and only through renunciation, through self-sacrifice, and universal benevolence, can salvation be obtained.

He who has recognized that existence is evil, that life is vanity, and self an illusion, has obtained true knowledge, which is the reflection of reality. He is in possession of the highest wisdom, which is not merely theoretical, but also practical perfection; it is the ultimate true cognition of all things in mass and in detail, which has so penetrated man's being that it appears as the guide of all his actions. It illumines his head, warms his heart, leads his hand. We take the sting out of life by accepting it as it is. "Drink ye all of it."

Arthur Schopenhauer very early in life contracted a bad habit of telling the truth. He stated the thing absolutely as he saw it. He spared no one's feelings, and conciliation was not in his bright lexicon of words. If any belief or any institution was in his way, the pilot in charge of the craft had better put his prow hard a' port—Schopenhauer swerved for nobody.

Should every one deal in plain speaking on all occasions, the philosophy of Ali Baba—that this earth is hell, and we are now suffering for sins committed in a former incarnation—would be fully proved. Our friends are the pleasant hypocrites who sustain our illusions. Society is made possible only through a vast web of delicate evasions, polite subterfuges, and agreeable falsehoods. The word person comes from "persona," which means a mask. The reference is to one who plays a part—assumes a role. The naked truth is not pleasant to look upon, and that is the reason it is so seldom put upon parade.

The man Schopenhauer would be intolerable, but the writer Schopenhauer is gaining ground in inverse ratio to the square of the distance we are from him. "Where shall we bury you?" a friend asked him a few days before his death.

"Oh, anywhere—posterity will find me!" was the answer. And so on the modest stone that marks his resting-place at Frankfort, are engraved the two words, ARTHUR SCHOPENHAUER, and nothing more. The world will not soon forget the pessimist who had such undying optimism—such unquenchable faith—that he knew the world would make a path to his tomb.

Schopenhauer was the only prominent writer that ever lived who persistently affirmed that life is an evil—existence a curse. Yet every man who has ever lived has at times thought so; but to proclaim the thought—or even entertain it long—would stagger sanity, befog the intellect and make mind lose its way.

And yet we prize Schopenhauer the more for having said the thing that we secretly thought; in some subtle way we get a satisfaction out of his statement, and at the same time, we perceive the man was wrong.

The man who can vivisect an emotion, and lay bare a heart-beat in print, knows a subtle joy. The misery that can explain itself is not all misery. Complete misery is dumb; and pain that is all pain is quickly transformed into insensibility. Schopenhauer's life was quite as happy as that of many men who persistently depress us by requesting us to "cheer up." Schopenhauer says, "Don't try to cheer up—the worst is yet to come." And we can not refrain a smile. A mother once called to her little boy to come into the house. And the boy answered, "I won't do it!" And the mother replied, "Stay out then!" And very soon the child came in.

Truth is only a point of view, and when a man tells us what he sees, we swiftly take into consideration who and what the man is. Everybody does this, unconsciously. It depends upon who says it! The garrulous man who habitually overstates—painting things large—does not deceive anybody, and is quite as good a companion as the painstaking, exact man who is always setting us straight on our statistics. One man we take gross and the other net. The liar gross is all right, but the liar net is very bad.

Schopenhauer was a talkative, whimsical and sensitive personality, with a fine assortment of harmless superstitions of his own manufacture. He was vain, frivolous, self-absorbed, but he had an eye for the subtleties of existence that quite escape the average individual. He lived in a world of mind—alert, active, receptive mind—with a rapid-fire gun in way of a caustic, biting, scathing vocabulary at his command.

The test of every literary work is time. The trite, the commonplace, and the irrelevant die and turn to dust. The vital lives. Schopenhauer began writing in his youth. Neglect, indifference and contempt were his portion until he was over fifty years of age. His passion for truth was so repelling that the Mutual Admiration Society refused to record his name even on its waiting-list. He was of that elect few who early in life succeed in ridding themselves of the friendship of the many. His enemies discovered him first, and gave him to the world, and after they had launched his fame with their charges of plagiarism, pretense, bombast, insincerity and fraud, he has never been out of the limelight, and in favor he has steadily grown.

No man was ever more thoroughly denounced than Schopenhauer, but even his most rabid foe never accused him of buying his way into popular favor, or bribing the judges who sit on the bookcase.

We admire the man because he is such a sublime egotist—he is so fearfully honest. We love him because he is so often wrong in his conclusions: he gives us the joy of putting him straight.

Schopenhauer's writing is never the product of a tired pen and ink unstirred by the spirit. With him we lose our self-consciousness.

And the man who can make other men forget themselves has conferred upon the world a priceless boon. Introspection is insanity—to open the windows and look out is health.

HENRY D. THOREAU

Seeing how all the world's ways came to nought,
And how Death's one decree merged all degrees,
He chose to pass his time with birds and trees,
Reduced his life to sane necessities:
Plain meat and drink and sleep and noble thought.
And the plump kine which waded to the knees
Through the lush grass, knowing the luxuries
Of succulent mouthfuls, had our gold-disease
As much as he, who only Nature sought.

Who gives up much the gods give more in turn:
The music of the spheres for dross of gold;
For o'er-officious cares, flame-songs that burn
Their pathway through the years and never old.
And he who shunned vain cares and vainer strife
Found an eternity in one short life.

HENRY THOREAU

As a rule, the man who can do all things equally well is a very mediocre individual. Those who stand out before a groping world as beacon-lights were men of great faults and unequal performances. It is quite needless to add that they do not live on account of their faults or imperfections, but in spite of them.

Henry David Thoreau's place in the common heart of humanity grows firmer and more secure as the seasons pass; his life proves for us again the paradoxical fact that the only men who really succeed are those who fail.

Thoreau's obscurity, his poverty, his lack of public recognition in life, either as a writer or lecturer, his rejection as a lover, his failure in business, and his early death, form a combination of calamities that make him as immortal as a martyr. Especially does an early death sanctify all and make the record complete, but the death of a naturalist while right at the height of his ability to see and enjoy—death from tuberculosis of a man who lived most of the time in the open air—these things array us on the side of the man 'gainst unkind Fate, and cement our sympathy and love.

Nature's care forever is for the species, and the individual is sacrificed without ruth that the race may live and progress. This dumb indifference of Nature to the individual—this apparent contempt for the man—seems to prove that the individual is only a phenomenon. Man is merely a manifestation, a symptom, a symbol, and his quick passing proves that he isn't the Thing. Nature does not care for him—she produces a million beings in order to get one who has thoughts—all are swept into the dustpan of oblivion but the one who thinks; he alone lives, embalmed in the memories of generations unborn.

One of the most insistent errors ever put out was that statement of Rousseau, paraphrased in part by T. Jefferson, that all men are born free and equal. No man was ever born free, and none are equal, and would not remain so an hour, even if Jove, through caprice, should make them so.

The Thoreau race is dead. In Sleepy Hollow Cemetery at Concord there is a monument marking a row of mounds where a half-dozen Thoreaus rest. The inscriptions are all of one size, but the name of one alone lives, and he lives because he had thoughts and expressed them. If any of the tribe of Thoreau gets into Elysium, it will be by tagging close to the only man among them who glorified his Maker by using his reason.

Nothing should be claimed as truth that can not be demonstrated, but as a hypothesis (borrowed from Henry Thoreau) I give you this: Man is only the tool or vehicle—Mind alone is immortal—Thought is the Thing.

Heredity does not account for the evolution of Henry Thoreau. His father was of French descent—a plain, stolid, little man who settled in Concord with his parents when a child; later he tried business in Boston, but the march of commerce resolved itself into a double-quick, and John Thoreau dropped out of line, and turned to the country village of Concord, where he hoped that between making lead-pencils and gardening he might secure a living.

He moved better than he knew.

John Thoreau's wife was Cynthia Dunbar, a tall and handsome woman, with a ready tongue and nimble wit. Her attentions were largely occupied in looking after the affairs of the neighbors, and as the years went by her voice took on the good old metallic twang of the person who discusses people, not principles.

Henry Thoreau was the third child in the family of seven. He was born in an old house on the Virginia Road, Concord, about a mile and a half from the village. This house was the home of Mrs. Thoreau's mother, but the Thoreaus had taken refuge there, temporarily, to escape a financial blizzard which seems to have hit no one else but themselves.

John Thoreau was assisted in the pencil-making by the whole family. The Thoreaus used to sell their pencils down at Cambridge, fifteen miles away, and Harvard professors, for the most part, used the Concord article in jotting down their sublime thoughts. At ten years of age, Thoreau had a furtive eye on Harvard, directed thither, they say, by his mother. All the best people in Concord, who had sons, sent them to Harvard—why shouldn't the Thoreaus? The spirit of emulation and family pride were at work.

Henry was educated principally because he wasn't very strong, nor was he on good terms with work, and these are classic reasons for imparting classical education to youth, aspiring or otherwise.

The Concord Academy prepared Henry for college, and when he was sixteen, he trudged off to Cambridge and was duly entered in the Harvard Class of Eighteen Hundred Thirty-seven. At Harvard, his cosmos seemed to be of such a slaty gray that no one said, "Go to—we will observe this youth and write anecdotes about him, for he is going to be a great man." The very few in his class who remembered him wrote their reminiscences long years afterward, with memories refreshed by magazine accounts written by pious pilgrims from Michigan.

In college pranks and popular amusements he took no part, neither was he a "grind," for he impressed himself on no teacher or professor so that they opened their mouths and made prophecies.

Once safely through college, and standing on the threshold (I trust I use the right expression), Henry Thoreau refused to accept his diploma and pay five dollars for it—he said it wasn't worth the money.

In his "Walden," Thoreau expresses his opinion of college training this way: "If I wished a boy to know something about the arts and sciences I would not pursue the common course, which is merely to send him into the neighborhood of some professor, where everything is professed and practised but the art of life. To my astonishment, I was informed when I left college that I had studied navigation! Why, if I had taken one turn down the harbor I would have known more about it."

It is well to remember, however, that Thoreau had no ambitions to become a navigator. His mission was simply to paddle his own canoe on Walden Pond and Concord

River. The men who really launched him on his voyage of discovery were Ellery Channing and Ralph Waldo Emerson—both Harvard men. Had he not been a college man, it is quite probable he would never have caught the speaker's eye. His efforts in working his way through college, assisted by his poverty-stricken parents, proved his quality. And as for his life in a shanty on the shores of Walden Pond, the occurrence is too commonplace to mention, were it not for the fact that the solitary occupant of the shanty was a Harvard graduate who used no tobacco.

Harvard prepares a youth for life—but here is a man who, having prepared for life, deliberately turns his back on life and lives in the woods.

A genuine woodsman is no curiosity, but a civilized woodsman is. The tendency of colleges is to turn men from Nature to books; from bonfires to stoves, steam-heat and cash-registers; but Thoreau, by reversing all rules, suddenly found himself, and others, explaining his position in print.

Harvard supplied him the alternating current; he influenced the people in his environment, and he was influenced by his environment.

But without Harvard there would have been no Thoreau. Having earned his diploma, he had the privilege of declining it; and having gone to college, it was his right to affirm the emptiness of the classics. Only the man with a goodly bank-balance can wear rags with impunity.

John Thoreau made his lead-pencils and peddled them out, and we hear of his saying, "Pencils, I fear, are going out of fashion—people are buying nothing but these miserable new-fangled steel pens." When called upon to surrender, Paul Jones replied, "We haven't yet begun to fight." The truth was, the people had not really begun to use pencils. Pencils weren't going out of fashion, but John Thoreau was. The poor man moved here and there, evicted by rapacious landlords and taken in by his relatives, who didn't care whether he was a stranger or not. If he owed them ten dollars, they took fifty dollars' worth of pencils and called it square.

Then they undersold John one-half, and he said times were scarce.

This, it need not be explained, was in Massachusetts.

A hundred years ago, these men who whittled useful things out of wood during the long winter days were everywhere in New England. The sons of these men invented machines to make the same things, and thus were started the New England manufactories. It was brains against hands, cleverness against skill, initiative against plodding industry. And the man who can tell of the sorrow and suffering of all those industrious sparrows that were caught and wound around flying shuttles, or stamped beneath the swift presses of invention, hadn't yet been born. God doesn't seem to care for sparrows—three-fourths of all that are hatched die in the nest or fall fluttering to the ground and perish, Grant Allen says.

Comparatively few persons can adjust themselves happily to new conditions: the rest are pushed and broken and bent—and die.

When Dixon and Faber invented machines that could be fed automatically, and turn out more pencils in a day than John Thoreau could in a year, John was out of the game.

John had brought up his children to work, and Henry became an expert pencil-maker. Henry, we say, should have found employment with Faber and Company, as foreman, or else evaded their patents and made a pencil-machine of his own. Instead, however, he settled down and made pencils just like his father used to make, and in the same way. He peddled out a few to his friends, but his business instinct was shown in that he himself tells how one year he made a thousand dollars' worth of pencils, but was obliged to sacrifice them all to cancel a debt of one hundred dollars.

And yet there are people who declare that genius is not transmissible.

John Thoreau failed at pencil-making, but Henry Thoreau failed because he played the flute morning, noon and night, and went singing the immunity of Pan. He fished, and tramped the woods and fields, looking, listening, dreaming and thinking.

At Keswick, where the water comes down at Lodore, there is a pencil-factory that has been there since the days of William the Conqueror. The wife of Coleridge used to work there and get money that supported her philosopher-husband and their children. Southey lived near, and became Poet Laureate of England through the right exercise of Keswick pencils; Wordsworth lived only a few miles away, and once he brought over Charles and Mary Lamb, and bought pencils for both, with their names stamped on them. The good old man who now keeps the pencil-factory explained these things to me, and also explained the direct relationship of good lead-pencils to literature, but I do not remember what it was.

If Henry Thoreau had held on a few years, until the pilgrims began to arrive at Concord, he could have gotten rich selling souvenir pencils. But he just dozed and dreamed and tramped and philosophized; and when he wrote he used an eagle's quill, with ink he himself distilled from elderberries, and at first, birch-bark sufficed for paper. "Wild men and wild things are the only ones that have life in abundance," he used to say.

Brook Farm was a serious, sober experiment inaugurated by the Reverend George Ripley with intent to live the ideal life—the life of useful effort, direct honesty, simplicity and high thinking.

But Thoreau could not be induced to join the community—he thought too much of his liberty to entrust it to a committee. He was interested in the experiment, but not enough to visit the experimenters. Emerson looked in on them, remained one night, and went back home to continue his essay on Idealism.

Hawthorne remained long enough to get material for his "Blithedale Romance." Margaret Fuller secured good copy and the cordial and lifelong dislike of Hawthorne, all through misprized love, alas! George William Curtis and Charles Dana graduated out of Brook Farm, and went down to New York to make goodly successes in the great game of life.

At Brook Farm they succeeded in the high thinking all right, but the entrepreneur is quite as necessary as the poet—and a little more so. Brook Farm had no business head, and things unfit fall into natural dissolution. But the enterprise did not fail, any more than a rotting log fails when it nourishes a bank of violets. The net results of Brook Farm's high thinking have passed into the world's treasury, smelted largely by Emerson and Thoreau, who were not there.

Immanuel Kant has been called the father of modern Transcendentalists: but Socrates and his pupil Plato, so far as we know, were the first of the race.

Neither buzzing bluebottles nor the fall of dynasties disturbed them. "The soul is everything," said Plato. "The soul knows all things," says Emerson.

In every century a few men have lived who knew the value of plain living and high thinking, and very often the men who reversed the maxim have passed them the hemlock.

All those sects known as Primitive Christians represent variations of the idea— Quakers, Mennonites, Communists, Shakers and Dunkards!

A Transcendentalist is a Dukhobortsi with a college education. A Quaker with an artistic bias becomes a Preraphaelite, and lo! we have News from Nowhere, a Dream of John Ball, Merton Abbey, Kelmscott, and half a world is touched and tinted by the simplicity, sterling honesty and genuineness of one man.

George Ripley, Bronson Alcott, and Ralph Waldo Emerson evolved New England Transcendentalism, and very early Henry Thoreau added a few bars of harmonious discords to the symphony. Horace Greeley once contended in a "Tribune" editorial that Sam Staples, the bum bailiff who locked Thoreau behind the bars, was an important factor in the New England renaissance, and as such should be immortalized by a statue made of punk, set up on Boston Common for the delectation of bean-eaters. I fear me Horace was a joker.

California quail are quite different from the quail of New York State, and naturalists tell us that this is caused by a difference in environment—quail being a product of soil and climate.

And man is a product of soil and climate—for only in a certain soil can you produce a certain type of man. As a whole, this world is better adapted for the production of fish than genius—most of the really good climate falls on the sea. Christian Scientists are

Transcendentalists whose distinguishing point is that they secrete millinery—California quail with rainbow tints and topknots, Balboaic instincts well defined.

Let this fact stand: it was Emerson who made Concord. He saw it first—he was on the ground, and the place was his by right of discovery, the title strengthened by the fact that four of his ancestors had been Concord clergymen, and the most excellent and venerable Doctor Ripley, a near kinsman.

Concord and Emerson, as early as Eighteen Hundred Forty, when Emerson was thirty-seven years old, were synonymous. He had defied the traditions of Harvard, been excommunicated by his Alma Mater, published his pantheistic Essay on Nature, and his thin little books and sermons had been placed on the Boston Theological Index Expurgatorius.

Through it all he had remained gentle, smiling, sympathetic, unresentful.

The world can never spare the man who does his work and holds his peace. Emerson was being lifted up, and souls were being drawn unto him.

In Eighteen Hundred Forty, Bronson Alcott, the American Socrates, with his interesting family, moved to Concord, drawn thither by the magnet of Emerson's personality. Louisa wore short dresses, and used to pick wild blackberries and sell them to the Emersons and get goodly reward in silver, and kindly smiles, and pats on her brown head by the hand that wrote "Compensation."

Alcott was a great, honest, sincere soul, and a true anarch, for he took his own wherever he saw it. He used to run his wheelbarrow into Emerson's garden and load it up with potatoes, cabbages or turnips, and once in response to a hint that the vegetables were private property, the old man somewhat petulantly exclaimed, "I need them!—I need them!"

And that was all: anything that any man needed was his by divine right. And the consistency of Alcott's philosophy was shown in that he never took anything or any more than he needed, and if he had something that you needed, you were certainly welcome to it. If Alcott helped himself to the thrifty Emerson's vegetables, both Emerson and Thoreau helped themselves to Alcott's ideas.

Once a wagonload of wood broke down in front of Alcott's house, and the farmer unhitched his horses and went on to the village to procure a new wheel. Before he got back, Alcott had carried every stick of the combustibles into his own wood-shed. "Providence remembers us!" he said. His faith was sublime.

When all the world reaches the Alcott stage, there will be no need of soldiers, policemen, night-watchmen, or bolts, bars and locks.

In Eighteen Hundred Forty, Nathaniel Hawthorne came to Concord from Salem, where he had resigned his clerkship in the custom-house, that he might devote all his time to literature. He moved into the Old Manse, which had just been vacated by Doctor Ripley, who had gone a-Brook-Farming—the Old Manse where Emerson himself once lived. Elizabeth Peabody, the talented sister of Hawthorne's wife, lived at a convenient distance, and to her Hawthorne read most of his manuscript, for I need not explain that literature is not literature until it is read aloud and reflected back by a sympathetic, discerning mind. Literature is a collaboration between the reader and the listener.

Margaret Fuller, with her tragic life-story still unwound, lived hard by, and Hawthorne had already worked her up into copy as "Zenobia." Margaret's sister Ellen had married Ellery Channing, the closest, warmest friend that Henry Thoreau ever knew. The gossips arranged a doublewedding, with Henry and Margaret as the other principals; but when interviewed on the theme, Henry had merely shaken his head and said, "In the first place, Margaret Fuller is not fool enough to marry me; and second, I am not fool enough to marry her."

An Irishman who saw Thoreau in the field making a minute in his notebook took it for granted that he was casting up his wages, and inquired what they came to. It was a peculiar farmhand who cared more for ideas than for wages.

George William Curtis was also a farmhand out on the Lowell Road, but came into town Saturday evenings—taking a swim in the river on the way—to attend the philosophical conferences at Emerson's house, and then went off and made gentle fun of them.

Little Doctor Holmes occasionally drove out from Boston to Concord in a one-horse chaise; James Russell Lowell had walked over from Cambridge; and Longfellow had invited all hands to a birthday fete on his lawn at Cambridge, but Thoreau had declined for himself, saying he had to look after his pond-lilies and the field-mice on Bedford flats.

Thoreau, at this time, was a member of Emerson's household, and in a letter Emerson says, "He has his board for what labor he chooses to do; he is a great benefactor and physician to me, for he is an indefatigable and skilful laborer, besides being a scholar and a poet, and as full of promise as a young apple-tree."

And again, in a letter to Carlyle: "One reader and friend of yours dwells in my household, Henry Thoreau, a poet whom you may one day be proud of—a noble, manly youth, full of melodies and invention. We work together day by day in my garden, and I grow well and strong."

To work and talk is the true way to acquire an education. All of our best things are done incidentally—not in cold blood. Hawthorne says in his Journal that most of Emerson's and Thoreau's farming was done leaning on the hoe-handles, while Alcott sat on the fence and explained the Whyness of the Wherefore.

But we must remember that in Hawthorne's ink-bottle there was a goodly dash of tincture of iron. In his Journal of September First, Eighteen Hundred Forty-two, he writes: "Mr. Thoreau dined with us yesterday. He is a singular character—a young man with much of wild, original nature still remaining in him; and so far as he is sophisticated, it is in a way and method of his own. He is as ugly as sin, long-nosed, queer-mouthed, and with uncouth and somewhat rustic ways, though his courteous manner corresponds very well with such an exterior. But his ugliness is of an honest character and really becomes him better than beauty." Little did Hawthorne's guests imagine they were being basted, roasted, or fricasseed for the edification of posterity.

Prosperity at this time had just begun to smile on Hawthorne, and among other extravagances in which he indulged was a boat, bought from Thoreau—made by the hands of this expert Yankee whittler. Hawthorne quotes a little transcendental advice given to him by the maker of the boat: "In paddling a canoe, all you have to do is to will that your boat shall go in any particular direction, and she will immediately take the course, as if imbued with the spirit of the steersman." Hawthorne then adds this sober postscript: "It may be so with you, but it is certainly not so with me."

Admiration for Thoreau gradually grew very strong with Hawthorne, and he quotes Emerson, who called Thoreau "the young god Pan." And this lends much semblance to the statement that Thoreau served Hawthorne as a model for Donatello, the mysterious wood-sprite in the "Marble Faun."

As to the transformation of Thoreau himself, one of his classmates records this:

Meeting Mr. Emerson one day, I inquired if he saw much of my classmate, Henry D. Thoreau, who was then living in Concord. "Of Thoreau?" replied Mr. Emerson, his face lighting up with a smile of enthusiasm. "Oh, yes, we could not do without him. When Carlyle comes to America, I expect to introduce Thoreau to him as the man of Concord," and I was greatly surprised at these words. They set an estimate on Thoreau which seemed to be extravagant.... Not long after I happened to meet Thoreau in Mr. Emerson's study at Concord—the first time we had come together after leaving college. I was quite startled by the transformation that had taken place in him. His short figure and general cast of countenance were, of course, unchanged; but in his manners, in the tones of his voice, in his modes of expression, even in the hesitations and pauses of his speech, he had become the counterpart of Mr. Emerson. Thoreau's college voice bore no resemblance to Mr. Emerson's, and was so familiar to my ear that I could have readily identified him by it in the dark. I was so much struck by the change that I took the opportunity, as they sat near together talking, of listening with closed eyes, and I was unable to determine with certainty which was speaking. I do not know to what subtle influences to ascribe it, but after conversing with Mr. Emerson for even a brief time, I always found myself able and inclined to adopt his voice and manner of speaking.

Thoreau had tried schoolteaching, but he had to give up his position because he would not exercise the birch and ferule. "If the scholars once find out the teacher is not goin' to sting 'em up when they need it, that is an end to the skule," said one of the directors, and he spat violently at a fly, ten feet away. The others agreeing with him, Thoreau was asked to resign.

William Emerson, a brother of Ralph Waldo's, a prosperous New York merchant, had lured Ralph Waldo's hired man away from him and taken him down to Staten Island, New York. Here Thoreau acted as private tutor, and imparted the mysteries of woodcraft to boys who cared more for marbles.

Staten Island was about two hundred miles too far from Concord to suit Thoreau.

His loneliness in New York City made Concord and the pine-trees of Walden woods seem paradise enow. There is no heart desolation equal to that which can come to one in a throng.

Margaret Fuller was now in New York City, working for Greeley on the editorial staff of the "Tribune." Greeley was so much pleased with Thoreau that he offered to set him to work as reporter, for Greeley had guessed the truth that the best city reporters are country boys. They observe and hear—all is curious and wonderful to them: by and by they will become blasé—sophisticated—that is, blind and deaf.

Greeley was a great talker, and he had a way of getting others to talk also. He got Thoreau to talking about communal life and life in the woods, and then Horace worked Henry's words up into copy—for that is the way all good newspaper-writers evolve their original ideas.

Thoreau was amazed to pick up a number of the daily "Tribune" and find his conversation of the day before, with Greeley, skilfully transformed into a leader.

Fourierism had been the theme—the Phalanstery versus Individual Housekeeping. Greeley had prophesied that the phalanstery, with one kitchen for forty families, instead of forty kitchens for forty families, would soon come about. Greeley's prophetic vision did not quite anticipate the modern apartment-house, which perhaps is a transitional expedient, moving toward the phalanstery, but he quoted Thoreau by saying, "A woman enslaved by her housekeeping is just as much a chattel as if owned by a man."

This was in Eighteen Hundred Forty-five, and Thoreau was now twenty-eight years of age. He was homesick for the dim pine-woods with their ceaseless lullaby, the winding and placid river, and the great, massive, sullen, self-sufficient boulders of Concord.

He was resolved to follow the example of Brook Farm, and start a community of his own in opposition. His community would be on the shores of Walden Pond, and the only member of the genus homo who would be eligible to membership would be himself; the other members would be the birds and squirrels and bees, and the trees would make up the rest. Brook Farm was a retreat for transcendentalists—a place to meditate, dream and work—a place where one could exist close to Nature, and live a simple, hardy and healthful life.

Thoreau's retreat would be the same, with the disadvantage of personal contact eliminated.

It was in March, Eighteen Hundred Forty-five, that Thoreau began building his shanty. The spot was in a dense woods, on a hillside that gently sloped down to the clear, cold, deep water of Walden Pond. The land belonged to Emerson, who obligingly gave Thoreau the use of it, rent free, with no conditions. Alcott helped in the carpenter work, and discussed betimes of the Wherefore, and when it came to the raising, a couple of neighboring farmers were hailed and pressed into service. The cabin was twelve by fifteen, and cost—furnished—the sum of twenty-eight dollars, good money, not counting labor, which Thoreau did not calculate as worth anything, since he had had the fun of the thing—something for which men often pay high.

The furniture consisted of a table, a chair, and a bed, all made by the owner. For bedclothes and dishes the Emerson household was put under contribution. On the door was a latch, but no lock.

And Thoreau looked upon his work and pronounced it good.

Stripped of the fact that a man of culture and education built the shanty and lived in it, the incident is scarcely worth noting. Boys passing through the shanty stage, all build shanties, and forage through their mothers' pantries for provender, which they carry off to their robbers' roost. Thoreau was an example of shanty-arrested development.

But as the import of every sentence depends upon who wrote it, and the worth of advice hinges upon who gave it, so does the value of every act depend upon who did it. Thus when a man, who was in degree an inspiration of Emerson, takes to the woods, it is worth our while to follow him afield and see what he does.

Thoreau set to work to clean up two acres of blackberry brambles for a garden-patch. He did not work except when he felt like it. His plan was to go to bed at dusk, with window and door open, and get up at five o'clock in the morning. After a plunge in the lake he would dress and prepare his simple breakfast. Then he would work in his garden, or if the mood struck him, he would sit in the door of his shanty and meditate, or else write. In the arrangement of his home he followed no system or rule, merely allowing the passing inclination to lead.

His provisions were gotten of friends in the village, and were paid for in labor. It was part of Thoreau's philosophy that to accept something for nothing was theft, and that the giving or acceptance of presents was immoral. For all he received he conscientiously gave an equivalent in labor; and as for ideas, he always considered himself a learner; if he had thoughts they belonged to anybody who could annex them. And that Emerson and Horace Greeley were alike in their capacity to absorb, digest and regurgitate, is everywhere acknowledged. To paraphrase Emerson's famous remark concerning Plato: Say what you will, you will find everything mentioned by Emerson hinted at somewhere in Thoreau. The younger man had as much mind as the elder, but he lacked the capacity for patient effort that works steadily, persistently, and weighs, sifts, decides, classifies and arranges. The voice was the voice of Jacob, but the hand was the hand of Esau. That is to say, Thoreau lacked business instinct. During the Winter at Walden Pond, all the work Thoreau had to do was to gather firewood. There was plenty of time to think and write, and here the better part of "Walden" and "A Week on the Concord and Merrimac Rivers" were written. He had no neighbors, no pets, no domesticated animals—only the squirrels on the roof, a woodchuck under the floor, the scolding blue jays in the pines overhead, the wild ducks on the pond, and the hooting owls that sat on the ridgepole at night.

Thoreau loved solitude more because he prized society—the society of simple men who could talk and tell things. Thoreau was no hermit—at least twice a week he would go to the village and meander along the street, gossiping with all or any. Often he would accept invitations to supper, but on principle refused all invitations to remain overnight, no matter what the weather. Indeed, as Hawthorne hints, there is a trace of the theatrical in the man who leaves a warm fireside at nine or ten o'clock at night and trudges off through the darkness, storm and sleet, feeling his way through the blackness of the woods to a cold and cheerless shanty which he with unconscious humor calls home. Hawthorne hints that Thoreau was a delightful poseur—he posed so naturally that he deceived even himself. On one particular visit to the village, however, he did not go back home for the night. It seems that he had been called upon by the local taxgatherer for his poll-tax, a matter of a dollar and a quarter. Thoreau argued the question at length, and among other things, said, "I will not give money to buy a musket, and hire a man to use this musket to shoot another." And also, "The best government is not that which governs least, but that which governs not at all."

"But what shall I do?" said the patient publican.

"Resign," said the philosopher.

Thoreau seemed to forget that officeholders seldom die and never resign. In the argument the publican was worsted, but he was not without resource. He went back to town and told the other officials what had happened. Their dignity was at stake. Alcott had been guilty of a like defiance some time before, and now it was the belief that he was putting the younger man up to insurrection.

The next time Thoreau came over to the village for his mail he was arrested and lodged in the local bastile.

Emerson, hearing of the trouble, hastened to the jail, and reaching the presence of the prisoner asked sternly, "Henry, why are you here?"

And the answer was, "Waldo, why are you not here?" Emerson had no use for such finespun theories of duty, and the matter was too near home for a joke, so he turned away and let the culprit spend the night in limbo. The next morning Thoreau was released, the tax having been paid by some unknown person—Emerson, undoubtedly. This was a tame enough ending to what was rather an interesting affair—the hope of the best citizens being that Thoreau would get a goodly sentence for vagrancy. The townfolk looked upon Thoreau and Alcott with suspicious eyes. They both came in for much well-deserved censure, and Emerson did not go unsmirched, since he was guilty of harboring and encouraging these ne'er-do-wells.

Thoreau's cabin-life continued for two Summers and Winters. He had proved that two hours' manual work each day was sufficient to keep a man—twenty cents a day would suffice.

The last year in the woods he had many callers: Agassiz had been to see him, Emerson had often called, Ellery Channing was a frequent visitor, and picnickers were constant. Lowell had made a few cutting remarks to the effect that "as compared with shanty-life, the tub of Diogenes was preferable, as it had a much sounder bottom," and Hawthorne had written of "the beauties of conspicuous solitude."

Thoreau felt that he was attracting too much attention, and that perhaps Hawthorne was right: a recluse who holds receptions is becoming the thing he pretends to despise. Besides that, there was plenty of precedent for quitting—Brook Farm had gone by the board, and was but a memory.

Thoreau's shanty was turned over to a utilitarian Scotchman with red hair. Later the immortal shanty was a useful granary. Thoreau went back to the village to live in a garret and work at odd jobs of boat-building and gardening.

Now only a pile of boulders marks the place where the cabin stood. For some years, each visitor to the spot threw a stone upon the heap, but recently the proposition has been reversed, and each visitor takes a stone away, which reveals not a reversal in the sentiment toward the memory of Thoreau, but a change in the quality of the Concord pilgrim.

Thoreau's early death was the direct result of his reckless lack of common prudence. That which made him live, in a literary way, curtailed his years. The man was improperly and imperfectly nourished, physically. Men who live alone do not cook any more than they have to: men and women, both, cook for emulation. That is to say, we work for each other, and we succeed only as we help each other.

Thoreau was such a pronounced individualist that he cared for no one but himself, and he cared for himself not at all. It is wife, children and home that teach a man prudence, and make him bank against the storm. "At Walden no one bothered me but the State," said Thoreau. If Thoreau had had a family and treated his household as he treated himself, that scorned thing, the State, would have stepped in and sent him to the workhouse, and his children to the Home for the Friendless.

If he had treated dumb animals as he treated himself, the Society for the Prevention of Cruelty to Animals would have interfered. The absence of social ties and of all responsibilities fixed in his peculiar temperament an indifference to hunger, heat, cold, wet, damp, and all bodily discomfort that classes the man with the flagellants. He tells of whole days when he ate nothing but berries and drank only cold water; and at other times of how he walked all day in a soaking rain and went to bed at night, supperless, under a pine-tree. Emerson records the fact that on long tramps Thoreau would carry only a chunk of plum-cake for food, because it was rich and contained condensed nutriment.

The question is sometimes asked, "How can one eat his cake and keep it too?" but this does not refer to plum-cake.

A few years of plum-cake, cold mince-pie and continual wet feet will put the petard under even the stoutest constitution.

During his shanty-life Thoreau was imperfectly nourished, and for the victim of malassimilation, tuberculosis hunts and needs no spyglass.

It is absurd for a man to make a god of his digestive apparatus, but it is just as bad to forget that the belly is as much the gift of God as the brain.

In childhood, Thoreau was frail and weak. Outdoor life gradually developed on his slight frame a splendid strength and a power to do and endure. He could outrun, outrow, outwalk any of his townsmen. In him developed the confidence of the athlete—the confidence of the athlete who dies young. Thoreau was an athlete, and he died as the athlete dieth. Irregular diet and continued exposure did their work—the vital powers became reduced, the man "caught cold," bronchitis followed, and the tuberculæ laughed.

During Thoreau's life he published but two volumes, and these met with scanty sale. Since his death ten volumes have been issued from his manuscripts and letters, and his fame has steadily increased.

Boston had no recognition for Thoreau as long as he was alive. Among the most popular writers of the time, feted and feasted, invited and exalted, were George S. Hillard, N. P. Willis, Caroline Kirkland, George W. Green, Parke Godwin and Charles F. Briggs. These writers, who had the run of the magazines, would have smiled in derision if told that the name and fame of uncouth Thoreau would outlive them all. They wrote for the people who bought their books, but Thoreau dedicated his work to time. He wrote what he thought, but they wrote what they thought other people thought.

In the publication of "The Dial," Thoreau took a hearty interest, and was a frequent contributor. The official organ of the transcendentalists, however, paid no honorariums—it was both sincere and serious, and died in due time of too much dignity. The "Atlantic Monthly" accepted one article by Thoreau, and paid for it, but as James Russell Lowell, the editor, used his blue pencil a trifle, without first consulting the author, he never got an opportunity to do so again.

Horace Greeley had interested himself in Thoreau's writings and gotten several articles accepted by Graham's and also Putnam's Magazine. "The Week" had been published on the author's guaranty that enough copies would be sold the first year to cover the cost. After four years, of the edition of one thousand copies only three hundred were disposed of, and these were mostly given away. To pay the publisher for the expense incurred, Thoreau buckled down and worked hard at surveying for a year.

The only man he ever knew, of whom he stood a little in awe, was Walt Whitman. In a letter to Blake he says:

Nineteenth November, Eighteen Hundred Fifty-six.—Alcott has been here, and last Sunday I went with him to Greeley's farm, thirty-six miles north of New York. The next day Alcott and I heard Beecher preach; and what was more, we visited Whitman the next morning, and we were much interested and provoked. He is apparently the greatest democrat the world has seen, kings and aristocracy go by the board at once, as they have long deserved to. A remarkably strong though coarse nature, of a sweet disposition, and much prized by his friends. Though peculiar and rough in his exterior, he is essentially a gentleman. I am still somewhat in a quandary about him—feel that he is essentially strange to me, at any rate; but I am surprised by the sight of him. He is very broad, but, as I have said, not fine.

Seventh December, Eighteen Hundred Fifty-six.—That Walt Whitman, of whom I wrote you, is the most interesting fact to me at present. I have just read his second edition (which he gave me), and it has done me more good than any reading for a long time. Perhaps I remember best the poem of "Walt Whitman an American" and the "Sundown" poem. There are two or three pieces in the book which are disagreeable, to say the least, simply sensual.... As for its sensuality—and it may turn out to be less sensual than it appears—I do not so much wish that those parts were not written, as that men and women were so pure that they could read them without harm.

On the whole, it sounds to me very brave and American, after whatever deductions. I do not believe that all the sermons, so called, that have been preached in this land, put together, are equal to it for preaching. We ought greatly to rejoice in him. He occasionally suggests something a little more than human. You can't confound him with the other inhabitants of Brooklyn. How they must shudder when they read him!

To be sure, I sometimes feel a little imposed on. By his heartiness and broad generalities he puts me into a liberal frame of mind, prepared to see wonders—as it were, sets me upon a hill or in the midst of a plain—stirs me well up, and then—throws in a thousand of brick. Though rude and sometimes ineffectual, it is a great primitive poem, an alarum or trumpet-note ringing through the American camp. Wonderfully like the Orientals, too, considering that, when I asked him if he had read them, he answered, "No; tell me about them."

Since I have seen him, I find that I am not disturbed by any brag or egoism in his book. He may turn out the least of a braggart of all, having a better right to be confident. Walt is a great fellow.

A lady once asked John Burroughs this question: "What would become of this world if everybody in it patterned after Henry Thoreau?" And Ol' John replied, "It would be much improved."

But your Uncle John is a humorist—he knows that Henry Ward Beecher was right when he said, "God never made but one Thoreau—that was enough, but we are grateful for the one."

Thoreau was a poet-naturalist, and the lesson he taught us is that this is the most beautiful world to know anything about, and there are enough curious and wonderful things right under our feet, and over our heads, and all around us, to amuse, divert, interest and instruct us for a lifetime. We need only a little.

Use your eyes!

"How do you manage to find so many Indian relics?" a friend asked Thoreau. "Just like this," he replied, and stooping over, he picked up an arrowhead under the friend's foot. At dinner once at a neighbor's he was asked what dish he preferred, and his answer was, "The nearest." To him, everything was good—he uttered no complaints and made no demands.

When asked by a clergyman why he did not go to church, he said, "It is the rafters—I can't stand them—when I look up, I want to gaze straight into the blue sky." Then he turned the tables and asked the interrogator a question: "Did you ever happen, accidentally, to say anything while you were preaching?" Yet preachers of brains were always attracted to him: Harrison Blake, to whom he wrote more letters than to any one else, was a Congregational preacher. And when Horace Greeley took Thoreau to Plymouth Church, Beecher invited him to sit on the platform and quoted him as one who saw God in autumn's every burning bush.

The wit of the man—his direct speech, and all of his beautiful indifference for the good opinion of those whom others follow after and lie in wait for—was sublime. Meanness, hypocrisy, secrecy and subterfuge had no place in Thoreau's nature.

He wanted nothing—nothing but liberty—he did not even ask for your applause or approval. When walking on country roads, laborers would hail him and ask for tobacco—seeing in him only one of their own kind. Farmers would stop and gossip with him about the weather. Children ran to him on the village streets and would cling to his hands and clutch his coat, and ask where the berries grew, or the first spring flowers were to be found. With children he was particularly patient and kind. With them he would converse as freely as did George Francis Train with the children in Madison Square. The children recognized in him something very much akin to themselves—he would play upon his flute for them and whittle out toy boats, regardless of the flight of time.

Imbeciles and mental defectives from the almshouse used occasionally to wander over to his cabin in the woods, and he would treat them with gentle consideration, and accompany them back home.

His lack of worldly prudence, Blake thought, tokened a courage which under certain conditions would have made him as formidable as John Brown. Blake tells this: Once on a lonely road, two miles from Concord, two loafers stopped a girl who was picking berries, and began to bother her. Thoreau just then happened along, and seeing the young woman's distress, he collared the rogues and marched them into the village, turning them over to that redoubtable transcendentalist, Sam Staples, who locked them up. Thoreau's hook nose and features could be transformed in rare instances into a look of command that no man dare question—it was the look of the fatalist—the benign fanatic—the look of Marat—the look of a man who has nothing but his life to lose, and places small store on that. "A little more ambition, and a trifle less sympathy, and the world would have had a Cæsar to deal with," says Blake.

Cowardice is only caution carried to an extreme. Thoreau exercised no prudence in making money, securing fame, preserving his health, holding his friends or making new ones. This Spartan-like quality, that counts not the cost, is essentially heroic.

But Thoreau was not given to strife; for the most part, he was non-resistant. The chief thing he prized was equanimity, and this you can not secure through struggle and strife. His game was all captured with the spyglass, or carried home in his botanists' drum. For worldly wealth and what we call progress, he had small appreciation—this marks his limitations. But his reasons are surely good literature:

They make a great ado nowadays about hard times; but I think that the community generally, ministers and all, take a wrong view of the matter. This general failure, both private and public, is rather occasion for rejoicing, as reminding us whom we have at the helm—that justice is always done. If our merchants did not most of them fail, and the banks too, my faith in the old laws of the world would be staggered. The statement that ninety-six in a hundred doing such business surely break down, is perhaps the sweetest fact that statistics have revealed—exhilarating as the fragrance of the flowers in the Spring. Does it not say somewhere, "The Lord reigneth, let the earth rejoice"? If thousands are thrown out of employment, it suggests that they were not well employed. Why don't they take the hint? It is not enough to be industrious; so are the ants. What are you industrious about?

The merchants and company have long laughed at transcendentalism, higher law, etc., crying, "None of your moonshine," as if they were anchored to something not only definite, but sure and permanent. If there were any institution which was presumed to rest on a solid and secure basis, and more than any other, represented this boasted commonsense, prudence, and practical talent, it was the bank; and now these very banks are found to be mere reeds shaken by the wind.

Scarcely one in the land has kept its promise. Not merely the Brook Farm and Fourierite communities, but now the community generally has failed. But there is the moonshine still, serene, beneficent and unchanged.

Thoreau was no pessimist. He complained neither of men nor of destiny—he felt that he was getting out of life all that was his due. His remarks might be sharp and his words sarcastic, but in them there was no bitterness. He made life for none more difficult—he added to no one's burdens. Sympathy with Nature, pride, buoyancy, self-sufficiency, were his prevailing traits. The habit of his mind was hopeful.

His wit and good-nature were his to the last, and when asked if he had made his peace with God, he replied, "I have never quarreled with Him."

He died, aged forty-four, in the modest home of his mother. The village school was dismissed that the scholars might attend the funeral, and three hundred children walked in the procession to Sleepy Hollow. Emerson made an address at the grave; Alcott read selections from Thoreau's own writings; and Louisa Alcott read this poem, composed for the occasion:

We sighing said, "Our Pan is dead;
His pipe hangs mute beside the river,
Around it wistful sunbeams quiver,
But Music's airy voice is fled.
Spring mourns as for untimely frost:
The bluebird chants a requiem;
The willow-blossom waits for him;—
The Genius of the wood is lost."

Then from the flute, untouched by hands,

There	came	a	low,	harmonious		breath:
"For	such	as	he	there	is no	death;
His	life	the		eternal	life	commands;
Above	man's		aims	his	nature	rose.
The	wisdom		of	a	just	content
Made	one		small	spot	a	continent,
And	turned		to	poetry		life's	prose.

"To	him	no	vain	regrets		belong,
Whose	soul,		that		finer	instrument,
Gave	to	the	world	no	poor	lament,
But	wood-notes		ever	sweet	and	strong.
O	lonely	friend!		he	still will	be
A	potent		presence,		though	unseen—
Steadfast,		sagacious,			and	serene;

Seek not for him—he is with thee."

SO HERE ENDETH "LITTLE JOURNEYS TO THE HOMES OF GREAT PHILOSOPHERS, BEING VOLUME EIGHT OF THE SERIES, AS WRITTEN BY ELBERT HUBBARD; EDITED AND ARRANGED BY FRED BANN; BORDERS AND INITIALS BY ROYCROFT ARTISTS, AND PRODUCED BY THE ROYCROFTERS, AT THEIR SHOPS, WHICH ARE IN EAST AURORA, ERIE COUNTY, NEW YORK, MCMXXII.

Made in the USA
Columbia, SC
21 January 2025